An
Occupation
for Gentlemen

FREDRIC
WARBURG

An

Occupation

for Gentlemen

"It is writers who are the kings
and queens of the publishing
trade." — page 152

WITH ILLUSTRATIONS

HOUGHTON MIFFLIN COMPANY BOSTON

THE RIVERSIDE PRESS CAMBRIDGE

1960

To
my wife
PAMELA DE BAYOU
who speaks for
herself

Acknowledgements

MANY PEOPLE have given me information which has proved useful in the writing of this book. I wish particularly to thank *The New Yorker* for allowing me to make use in Chapter 1 of material that appeared in their columns in a slightly different form and *The Bookseller* for permission to use in Chapters 6 and 7, also in somewhat different form, material originally printed by them.

F. W.

Contents

Illustrations

George Orwell, John McNair and others, in 1938

Lewis Mumford

Pamela de Bayou in 1959 — photograph by Angus McBean

The author in 1959 — photograph by Angus McBean

H. G. Wells — from an unfinished oil by Pamela de Bayou, 1943-4

Note on Title

SOME YEARS AGO, at a cocktail party given by my firm to launch the new novel of a promising young author, I fell into animated conversation on the subject of publishing with a middle-aged man of distinguished appearance. I didn't know him from Adam, nor he me, and he didn't seem to fit into any of the usual literary categories. A lawyer perhaps or some kind of public servant, I supposed, wondering vaguely why he had been invited. Suddenly I woke up to realize that he was asking me a question to which no simple answer was available. 'Tell me,' he inquired, 'since you seem to know something about it, is publishing an occupation for gentlemen or is it a real business?' We discussed the matter for a quarter of an hour, at the end of which he thanked me for the light I had thrown on his question.

'By the way,' he added, 'whom have I the honour of addressing?'

'I'm Fredric Warburg,' I said, 'the managing director of this firm. Who are you?'

'Israel Sieff of Marks & Spencer,' he replied, 'and if ever I have a publishing problem, I'll call you up about it.'

It is from I. M. Sieff's question that I have drawn the title of my book, which in a way is an attempt to answer it more fully than I was able to when first he asked me.

11

Foreword

HAROLD MACMILLAN remarked in a speech not long ago that he suffered under a severe handicap as prime minister, since he was both a publisher and a politician, two professions which were highly unpopular. Politicians may be disliked, though I notice they get cheered a good deal from time to time, but publishers seem to me more sympathetically regarded nowadays than in the past. Lord Byron's famous phrase, 'Barabbas was a publisher,' has naturally done us no good, but that was a long time ago. Since then we've abandoned the more disreputable practices which brought us into odium, helped by the kind attention to detail of the literary agents, who scrutinize with an experienced eye every phrase which we write into our contracts and tell us (to put it crudely) where we get off.

The mutual relationship of publisher and author is a complex one. Here I would only say that some degree of mutual admiration between them is at the very least as common as its opposite. But in the eyes of the public generally, I suggest that the publisher cuts rather a romantic figure. In the gossip columns of our newspapers, which mirror the *mores* of our time much more accurately than the leading articles and the news pages, publishers feature with ever increasing frequency. They do not appear, of course, as often as models, minor film stars, or the children of the aristocracy when gainfully employed, but their standing in this respect is tolerably high.

The glamour of a publisher is partly secondhand and derived from his association, real or alleged, with great authors, or, more precisely, with 'genius'. He is pictured as the friend of geniuses, partaking maybe in those orgies to which geniuses are notoriously addicted, sharing their inmost thoughts and present at their recurring moments of crisis. My own life would undoubtedly have been far more interesting, had this been true. In fact, one of the greatest writers I have ever known, George Orwell, when I asked him the plot of his next book, far from favouring me with his confidence, fobbed me off with the remark 'it's all about animals and very anti-Russian! I'm afraid you're not going to like it.' He was wrong, for *Animal Farm* is my favourite Orwell volume.

The confusion in the public mind about what a publisher is and what he does is extraordinary. Some think, for instance, that we are printers; others believe that we review the books we publish; not a few are convinced that we actually write them. But most people have what is basically the correct idea, that we get hold from somewhere of an author's book, manufacture it, and sell it in thousands to an eager public. This is certainly what we aim at doing, though often the public is less than eager. This is what I have attempted to describe in the following pages.

More than once I've been asked to write a book about publishing, usually under the title, *How to Succeed.* I've always refused, because I don't know the secret of success, and can't therefore convey it to others. A publisher, if he is not to be a wholly commercial operator, must put a lot

14

of his own personality into his firm. It must reflect him directly or indirectly, and if it does it will have a recognizable character. Many English publishing houses do have such a character, unlike their American counterparts most of which, for various reasons, are a medley of differing and often conflicting tendencies. No doubt my view of a publishing house as having a personality can be regarded as highbrow. It will be said that a publisher is a tradesman who is not in business for his health; his job is to take a book that in his view has a sales potential and boost it to the skies, regardless of its merits or lack of them. This view I understand, respect, and profoundly disagree with. Pushed to its logical conclusion, it produces trash, corrupts the public's taste, and allows the pornographer an unrestricted run for his, or the reader's, money.

The wise man, it has been said, seeks health and happiness by indirect means, by following a bent, by sticking to a set of principles in which he believes, or by taking his wife's advice. It is the same with publishing. Look after the books . . . and the pounds will look after themselves, *if* you're a good publisher. And if you're not? Why the hell are you wasting your time in an overcrowded profession, one whose rewards are poor in comparison with others involving an equal skill? Publish what you fancy and hope for the best; you may be lucky.

Few books about publishing by publishers exist. Of these few only a handful are readable. The standard work is Sir Stanley Unwin's well-known textbook, *The Truth About Publishing*, which describes its techniques with a lucidity and an occasional acidity that is a joy to all who are sincerely interested in the job. My only criticism of this excellent book is that it tends to assume that publishing is a rational process. If it were, the earnest student would

15

merely have to follow the wise precepts of Sir Stanley, and success could be almost guaranteed.

But publishing is not, in fact, a purely rational occupation. It requires energy, enthusiasm, optimism and pessimism, the ability to make decisions, a willingness to guess, and all manner of unconscious processes. A cross between power politics and scholasticism, with more than a hint of the circus barker is not too fanciful a description. So I have tried to recreate the atmosphere of my career, rather than give a comprehensive and perhaps prosaic account of the facts, figures and events. I have been concerned on the whole with the whirligig variations in mood of a publisher, the early agonies, the provisional satisfactions at partial successes, the excitements and disappointments, even at times the triumphs. But my own publishing career is, thank God, not yet ended; there is more to happen yet; and no publisher should be called happy till he is dead, and buried in the presence of at least some of his weeping authors.

The task I have set myself is an ambitious one, and I am conscious of having fallen far short of my intention. Since publishers are not expected to write, and many believe that they are unable to read, I am hopeful that the book's faults will be looked on forgivingly. Some of these faults can be attributed to the fact that many of the *dramatis personae* are still alive, and the law of libel is strict. To my own authors who may dutifully read it, I say: 'Don't worry. As a writer I'm an amateur, and have no thought of turning professional. I have no intention of neglecting my duties and your sales by immersion in the sea of creation.' To my colleagues, the last word of all: 'My firm represents my own way of publishing, modified by your untiring help and constant hindrance. I am as grateful to you for the one as for the other.'

16

1   No. 21
and No. 8

PADDINGTON FIVE THREE, Paddington 53—it was
before the days when we had to call it double 0 five three—
that was the number my parents asked for every day, the
phone number of my grandmother's house, 8 Porchester
Terrace, Hyde Park. For No. 8 was the tribal centre, the
headquarters from which my paternal grandmother issued
her frequent fiats and to which her children and grand-
children repaired for Sunday lunch, week in, week out.

Her husband, Fredric Elias Warburg, had come to
England from Sweden around 1860, and died in 1899, just
after I was born. He must have been a second cousin once
removed to the two Warburg brothers who settled in New
York—Felix, the first Kuhn Loeb partner, and Paul,
co-father (if the phrase is permissible) of the Federal
Reserve System. These two great men, as is well known
across the Atlantic, made huge fortunes, and in the process
assisted the development of the banking and industrial
structure of the United States. Without question, they were
tycoons; they founded dynasties and families; the dynasties
waxed and the families expanded and grew richer; today
in the United States the Warburg name stands for wealth,

17

banking, industrial efficiency, philanthropy, and the most generous patronage of the arts. If only it had been likewise in England!

At first, it might have appeared to an imaginary and objective observer that all was well, that the unusual genes that made the American Warburgs so successful in the accumulation of wealth were present also in the English branch. Certainly Fredric Elias made a magnificent start. At one time associated with the financier, Sir Ernest Cassel, he took a hand in building the first of London's underground railways, the Central London or Twopenny Tube, as it was called, because you could go from one end of the line to the other for twopence. The project must have netted him a pretty penny, and doubtless there were other operations of which I was not informed.

Fredric Elias seems to have been a stern father, feared rather than loved by his children, for whom perhaps he had too little time as he busied himself with the creation of the family fortune. But on this hard-earned foundation, no great superstructure was to be raised by any of his three sons. Believe it or not, he was the only English Warburg with a genuine talent for money-making.[1] It was with money ultimately inherited from him that I started as a publisher on my own in 1936.

His widow, my grandmother, a matriarch of great beauty, lived on till 1925. It was perhaps her iron will, coupled with the deeply rooted conviction that her three sons, and my father in particular, were too fragile in health to pursue active careers, that crushed any latent aptitude for money-making the three young men possessed. The road of financial gigantism was open, but none of them walked along it. The oldest brother, my father John

---

[1] My second son, Hew Warburg, has made a remarkable start in the last ten years towards the amassing of wealth. But it would be premature to say with real certainty that he has inherited the gold-bearing genes of his great-grandfather.

Cimon, had the best excuse of the three, for it was upon him that the full force of my grandmother's adoration was directed. But the other two did but little better.

Frederic Samuel, the second brother and indisputably my favourite uncle on either side, did indeed carry on business operations of some kind in his early manhood, but they came to nothing. I heard it said that Uncle Fred could not get on with his partners, surely no excuse for a Warburg to relinquish his efforts. He was a man of unusual charm, a good mixer, and a first-class lawn-tennis player in the days of the great champion, Anthony Wilding, with whom I once saw him compete. He married a charming red-headed girl from Edgbaston, Warwickshire, without any great financial resources of her own, a grave error in a man who intends to make money. By her he had four daughters, an expensive hobby this, and a son who was to become the business manager of a radio firm. But there's no real solid cash in this kind of thing.

The third brother, Oscar Emmanuel, was a man of intellect. A senior wrangler at Cambridge, he put his great mathematical abilities at the disposal of the nation during World War I, thus enabling the Admiralty to chart the route of the Zeppelins approaching London with hostile intent. Uncle Oscar was unquestionably knowledgeable about the Stock Exchange, and looked after what family fortunes there were in a thoroughly competent way. I have always thought that he made money, but never on the grand scale. In the long run he was far more interested in horticulture—his monograph on rock roses is a model— his family of four sons and a career in London's local politics that led him to the chairmanship of the London County Council and a knighthood. His sons include a distinguished lecturer in Botany at Oxford University, co-author of a standard work on British wildflowers,

19

a chemical engineer, a civil service geologist, and a lieutenant-colonel in the Regular Army. It is notorious that there's no money in being a Regular.

It is idle perhaps to deal in this analytical manner with the daughters, my Aunt Lily and my Aunt Agnes. Aunt Lily married a Swedish paper-maker and went to live in Gothenburg. But though her husband was well-off, he was not a Warburg, and her two sons became professional men. As for Aunt Agnes, she stayed at home at No. 8, sacrificing herself, as girls did in those days, to my widowed grandmother. Aunt Agnes was a woman of considerable personality, and had a great effect on my own fortunes in the years to come. But she was, of course, no money-maker. Indeed, she *gave* her money away in her early middle-age, presenting to the nation a part of Box Hill where George Meredith lived, now become a place of pilgrimage for Meredithians, if any yet remain, and a beauty spot with a view for the others.

But, of all the five children of Fredric Elias, none was so remiss, none so disinterested in the art of accumulation as my father, John Cimon Warburg. Convinced by my grandmother in his teens that even a few months hard work in an office would cause him to collapse, he spent the sixty-five years of his life as a man of leisure. He was a gifted photographer, amateur of course, who dabbled in science and regarded the policy of the pre-1914 Liberal government as recklessly spendthrift.

We lived at No. 21 Pembridge Gardens, Bayswater, a four-storied double-fronted house with an extensive basement in a street of similar houses occupied by families of similar standing in the community. At the back, the garden stretched away to a distance of some 150 feet with a breadth of 50 feet. A rectangular lawn occupied most of the space, surrounded by a gravel path, bordered by flowerbeds. At the far end stood a group of lilac and other bushes, known as 'the shrubbery', an almost indispensable element in Victorian gardens. My father took a great interest in this estate, aided by a jobbing gardener, and grew a wide range of flowers, including roses, on the beds facing south, though the northern exposure presented him with horticultural problems beyond his ability to solve.

The house was large, and it exhausts me today even to recall the hundred or so stairs that had to be surmounted from the ground to the attic floors. On the left of the hall as you entered the front door lay the drawing-room, stretching from front to back and ending in a conservatory, full of potted palms and greenery of many kinds. All the furniture in this room was uncomfortable and expensive; it included a grand piano and a large book-case cupboard, filled rather sparsely with books including complete well-bound editions of Dickens and Thackeray. This room was used only for large parties and my mother's at-home days, Wednesday afternoon, 3.30 to 6. On the right of the hall was the dining-room, its floor covered by a hideous Turkish carpet; a potted palm in the window obscured most of the light; the walls, papered in dark brown, were crammed with huge pictures, mostly of my forefathers, men and women whose features (with one exception) I hoped would not reproduce themselves too accurately in my own face. This room, as you may suppose, was always shadowy and smelt of stale sherry, but it was a popular room with me, owing to its association with the joys of eating.

At the back of it lay the schoolroom, so-called, a room as devoid of furniture, other than a table and chairs, as the dining-room was crammed. A peculiarly horrible mantelpiece surmounted the fireplace, on which were displayed red cups with white spots, a relic perhaps of some ghastly prize won in a raffle years before. In the

21

schoolroom, which was chilly, with an enormous expanse of window overlooking the garden, my sisters and I learned our first lessons from Miss Coolie, our governess. Mild as a rule, but at times driven to a frenzy by some unusual display of bad manners from her three little charges, she taught us reading, writing, elementary arithmetic, and a little history. She did me no harm in the years between six and nine, when I was sent to a preparatory school.

An imposing flight of stairs led to the first floor, which contained four rooms and a bathroom. The two front rooms, exposed to the not inconsiderable noises of the street, were naturally bedrooms, since our fathers and mothers were sounder sleepers than us, guilty accessories to the murder of civilization as we know ourselves to be. Cupboards, chests of drawers, beds, bed-tables, sofas and dressing-tables crowded these chambers, so that it was only with difficulty that even a small child could thread his way from one side to the other. My mother's bedroom smelt of face powder, my father's of medicine, which I hated. The rooms were divided by a bathroom, featuring an enormous bath with a brown wooden side. It was here that I was often expected in the morning to talk to my father while he bathed. My father was a hairy man, which I disliked, and these conversations have probably left indelible traumas in my memory.

One of the first-floor back rooms was my father's dark-room, used for the development, printing and enlargement of photographic plates and other mysteries of his art. From this room at all times emanated a powerful smell of chemicals. The other room was the sitting-room and here at least it might be thought that my mother would get a chance of relaxation and privacy denied her elsewhere. In fact, it was quite otherwise. There was a huge bookcase full of unreadable volumes, with storage space below; a vast cupboard containing heaven-knows-what often wrapped up in brown paper; a big armchair for my father and a much smaller one for my mother; an upright piano, a huge table covered by a woollen table-cloth, a bookcase that revolved noisily, topped by a small potted palm; a gigantic desk for my father and a small desk for my mother; a sofa and small chairs in profusion. These bulky objects cluttered up the room beyond all reasonable bounds. But for my father they were not enough. An ardent collector of butterflies and moths as a young man, he had housed his undeniably attractive collection of specimens in two great mahogany cabinets of drawers, each about six feet long and five feet high. These were placed in a solid block along more than half one of the two longer walls of the room. Try as she would, my mother could never induce my father to remove these wholly useless cabinets from the house's principal living-room. It may well have been this failure that broke her spirit.

On the floor above that were the day and night nurseries, and the second bathroom of the house, with a tiny window about two foot square and a gas ring. It was on this that, as children, we were taught by our nurse the art of making toffee on rainy days too wet for walks in Kensington Gardens. The smell of melting butter remains with me as one of the pervasive smells of childhood. Above this floor were the servants' rooms, into which we were never allowed to penetrate.

In this hideous and uncomfortable house my mother lived quietly in those few square feet of space unoccupied by my father's egoism. She was a beautiful girl, as shown by the portrait of her at the age of sixteen by Solomon J. Solomon which hangs in my bedroom to this day. Her photographs prove it too. At the age of twenty-nine she had met my father, aged thirty, at a kind of pageant in Cannes. The play, which included singing, was concerned with Isaac meeting Rebecca at the well and falling in love with her. So had my father fallen in love with my mother, as the two of them played the leading roles. On his return to London, my father had persuaded, or perhaps bullied, his mother into agreeing to the marriage. It has never been revealed to me how he accomplished this difficult feat. My grandmother must inevitably have taken the view that to entrust a young man of thirty, standing well over six feet high in his stockinged feet, broad-shouldered, bearded and muscular, to the care of an untried and strange young woman of twenty-nine who lacked a nursing diploma, was a perilous risk not to be taken lightly. But that she took this risk is a matter of history. Within five years there were three children, myself and my two sisters. With the aid of a nanny and a nursery maid, my mother brought us up in the respectable traditions of the Edwardian *bourgeoisie*.

She had, I am certain, many difficulties to contend with. There were, for a start, my father's continuous attacks of asthma and bronchitis, which we should today describe as psycho-somatic in origin. There must have been frequent advice and interference from my grandmother in the workings of my mother's household. There was the perpetual irritation of having him at home all day, so that she could never chat to the cook or talk with her women friends without interruption from my father. Every day, as lunch-time drew near, he would announce that he was going out for his 'constitutional'. Every day she would say to him, 'don't be late for lunch, John, it's at half past one.' Every day John returned home at quarter to two, to find my mother in a frenzy that luncheon was spoilt. At an early age I wondered why the hour for lunch could not be postponed or the length of my father's walk abbreviated. But it never was.

Even I, a far from perceptive child, could sense that my father was a selfish man. It simply did not occur to him that his ways and habits could be other than right, however much annoyance or trouble they caused my mother. In the cluttered, boring, rigid and slightly laboratory atmosphere that my father created around him, she existed rather than lived. Trained from infancy to accept man in general and a husband in particular as the master half of the race, she never rebelled, never (so far as my knowledge goes) cast her eyes on another man, rarely lost her temper. Perhaps she wept in private. Possibly she took her hair down with her two close woman friends, each of whom regarded my father as unworthy of her. But in public she remained a loyal consort, taking his side against mine in the arguments which increasingly embittered my relations with him. To me her 'father knows best' attitude was the one flaw in her character. She never succeeded in convincing me that my father was right and that I was wrong. Indeed, she stimulated, without meaning to, a permanent attitude of hostility to my father's authority, and so produced in me the heterodoxy of my adult years. It never came naturally to me to assume without investigation that the powers that be necessarily had right on their side.

Yet I must admit that my childhood years were happy. Adored by my mother, spoilt by my grandmother, with two sisters to play with, living in a large house, with plenty of money, waited upon by four servants, and cared for by a nurse and a nursemaid, the occasional dust-up with my father did little to disturb my basic equanimity. I collected shells, as my father had collected butterflies before me, and spent many long hours in the evenings arranging and identifying them. I played chess up to the age of fourteen, when I found it took too much time from my homework, and croquet in the summer months. I read books. I learned my lessons from the sweet and colourless Miss Coolie. Year by year I became more priggish. Fortunately, at the age of nine, I went to a preparatory school, and in its wholly masculine atmosphere began to shed some of the unhealthy innocence acquired by overmuch immersion in the atmosphere of women.

Like Galsworthy's Forsytes, the Warburgs lived in Bayswater, as a matter of fact all of them within a stone's throw of that Central London Railway which was the foundation of the family fortunes. Of all four mansions, the largest and the most impressive was naturally my grandmother's, No. 8 Porchester Terrace. This was the Mecca to which all were summoned by my grandmother's muezzin once a week for Sunday lunch. The occasion had all the marks of a ritual, as uncles and aunts with their children, friends and acquaintances, and distinguished visitors from abroad, gathered at the appointed time.

For this feast my sisters and I were prepared with a lunatic routine. Since it was assumed by my mother that we should over-eat on Sunday, a forecast which was basically correct, and develop what was known in those days as 'a liver attack', we were dosed on Saturday evening at bed-time with a powerful purge. Reluctantly swallowing the loathsome brown liquid, we lay down to sleep, to be woken early the next morning by the sharp internal pains which were its inevitable consequence. After some hours of agony, comparable to that felt twenty years later by the enemies of Mussolini, we were clothed in our Sunday best and led out for a walk in Kensington Gardens with our parents. Up and down the Broad Walk we stumbled, breathing in the fresh air which was to stimulate our appetites for the gargantuan feast to come, obtaining that exercise which my mother deemed essential for the healthy mind in the healthy body, admiring and being admired by the other families who were engaged in similar activities, as the great church at Lancaster Gate expelled its congregation after the morning service. This purgatory—and no other word could be more appropriate—often ended in disaster, if the hasty dash to No. 8, some ten minutes walk away, were left even one minute too late.

Once washed, tidied, brushed, and allowed to relax in my grandmother's drawing-room, the day took a turn for the better. We could then play and quarrel with a growing number of male and female cousins, and listen surreptitiously to the exciting, if incomprehensible, talk of our elders. Above all, we could anticipate the delights of luncheon, and these were certainly worth waiting for.

Around the enormous table sat down about twenty persons. As the eldest son of the eldest son, I sat on my grandmother's right hand and surveyed the groaning board. The gleam of silver, the winking of cut glass, flowers, salted almonds, sweets of half a dozen different kinds, stretched agreeably before me. Here was a solid Edwardian comfort that has vanished for ever. The food had a taste and a quality hard to rediscover in these degenerate days. Plovers' eggs, caviare, or *pâte de foie gras* would start the meal. To follow, as often as not, a sirloin of beef roasted in the great kitchen below on a spit, accompanied by Yorkshire pudding and a plethora of vegetables. The dessert course was usually a strawberry ice, built up on a broad foundation into a huge pyramid and of an indescribably exquisite flavour. Cheese of many kinds, and fruit concluded the meal, which ended at about 3 p.m.

The rest of the day remained for me, and I imagine for my sisters and cousins, a blank. Our energies thereafter were wholly employed in the labour of digestion. On Monday morning, surprisingly recovered from Sunday's joys, I would return to school.

Wilkinson's preparatory school for boys was a good one. It was situated in St. Petersburg Place, just off the Bayswater Road, about fifteen minutes walk from No. 21. My mother, fearful that I should be run down by a horse-drawn vehicle, or even by the new motor-cars and electric broughams that were fast coming into vogue, insisted at first that I should be accompanied by my nurse to within a hundred yards of the school entrance. Until this shameful shepherding was withdrawn, my life at the age of nine was a misery.

At Wilkinson's I received an excellent educational grounding in the classics. I learned to fight, to bully and be bullied, to play cricket moderately well and football moderately badly. I learned to despise girls. During our studies of the contemporary world, I was made aware that large sections of the maps in our geography books were red, because they were British, which meant that they were happy, prosperous and well governed, unlike nearly every other region of the world which languished under foreign dominion. While the British were practically perfect, other nations suffered from a variety of unfortunate characteristics. The French were amorous and unreliable; the Germans hard-working and uppish; the Italians idle macaroni-eaters; the Dutch clean, living exclusively on canals. The Americans were second-rate Britishers, too far behind the times to bother with, but good at mechanical inventions. The Russians were mysterious, bearded, and untrustworthy; it was never clear to me whether they had to be welcomed as allies or hated for their evil designs on India. The Chinese were the yellow peril, and much to be

28

feared as such. The Japanese, despite their similar pigmentation, were oddly enough good chaps, the British of the East and our friends.

Both at school and with the help of my father, I pursued the study of sociology. I had no difficulty in discovering that this was the century of progress, that scientific knowledge was leading the world by steady degrees towards a materialist utopia, wherein pain and poverty would be abolished, probably under a conservative government with liberal leanings. I learned that the working classes were poor, either because they were bone idle or because they had gravely defective heredities. Strikes were due to their failure to understand the problems of industry or the benevolence of employers. Unemployment was caused by the will of God, in whom my father did not believe, and should therefore be accepted humbly as part of the divine process.

The history of England, often described as Our Island Story, was another subject in which I received instruction. It was taught as a kind of national pilgrim's progress or obstacle race, in which the mother country, by her courage and ingenuity, defeated all the knavish tricks of foreigners, especially the French. Scarred but fundamentally sound, a matronly Britannia emerged, holding a sceptre with which to prod in the backside any new upstarts who were unaware that Britain ruled the waves. As for warfare on land, it was well known that one British Tommy was the equal of any three foreign soldiers, that the battle of Waterloo was won on the playing fields of Eton, to which I regretted I was not to be sent, and that the charge of the Light Brigade at Balaclava proved the importance of cavalry in modern war, despite the fact disclosed by Tennyson that few of those who charged returned alive.

Nevertheless, Latin and Greek were taught well,

and so was mathematics. I won a scholarship to Westminster School at the age of thirteen, and started there in
company with my friend, Edwin, son of Mr. Herbert
Samuel.

My five years at Westminster, or least the first two of
them, were among the most hateful in my life. Not for
£10,000 would I consent to go through with them again.
The hurly-burly of a public school can be, and perhaps is
intended to be, a cruel experience, designed to make men
out of milksops. Certainly I was a milksop when I started;
my mother had seen to that. And my father had done
nothing to prepare me for the horrors to come, since
naturally my grandmother had ensured that he himself
had not been exposed to so barbaric an institution, but
had provided private tutors for him at home. I therefore
went like a lamb to the slaughter, and survived, scarred
but still fortunately sane, into my senior years.

Like most little boys I had a deep longing to be orthodox, to be so like my schoolmates that I was indistinguishable from them. Unfortunately I was then what has now
come to be called an 'outsider', introverted, repressed, bad
at games, but clever. This would clearly have been a fatal
mixture under any circumstance. But circumstances were
against me as well. I was a Jew, and the anti-semitism
of the British upper classes was then substantial if superficial.
The only way in which, as a Jew, I differed from the rest
was in my non-attendance at a ten-minute service in the
Abbey before school started. I had no objection myself
to attendance, quite the contrary, but my mother was
adamant. It wouldn't be right, she said.

The Judaism of the English Warburgs remains a
difficult matter for me to interpret. Neither my grandfather nor my grandmother, though undeniably born Jews—

whatever that may mean—ever practised the Jewish
religion by attending synagogue or following the dietary
laws or fastening over their lintels the Tables of the Law,
as they should have done, had they been orthodox. My
father married a Jewish girl, and my grandmother disliked
her as a daughter-in-law. Both my uncles married non-
Jewish girls, and my grandmother disliked them as strongly
as she disliked my mother or even more so. In fact, what
she disliked was daughters-in-law as such, whether Jewish
or non-Jewish. On marriage my uncles ceased to be Jews,
or so I must assume, since their children were brought up
in the Church of England. But my father, who married
'inside the faith', as the saying goes, remained a Jew.
He was married in a synagogue, and, when he died, he
was buried in a Jewish cemetery, though this may have
been because, an ardent genealogist himself, he felt that
future genealogists would know better where to find him,
if he followed the family tradition.

The position of my mother, on the other hand, was
somewhat different. She was of course not a Warburg,
but a Sichel, Violet Amalia Sichel, and she had undoubted
need of the consolations of religion. Lonely and taken for
granted by my father as a fairly important piece of his
property, meek and mild despite her beauty, bullied by
her in-laws for her lack of conversation and assumed
absence of intelligence, she must often have felt unhappy.
In consequence, she went to synagogue on the Sabbath
day, Saturday morning, to commune with her personal god.
What resemblance this god bore to Jehovah, mighty in
battle, I am unable to say. But my belief is that the Jewish
deity worshipped by my mother was indistinguishable in
all fundamentals from the divinity of the New Testament.

Nevertheless, my mother took her religion seriously,
and she considered that her three children should receive

31

religious, that is Jewish, instruction. For a few months, therefore, a special tutor came to the house to teach us Judaism, though what he taught I can no longer clearly remember, except that it was a simple gloss on the books of the Old Testament in which the order of succession of the kings of Israel, alleged to be of importance, was learnt by heart. There were periods when my mother took us to synagogue with a certain amount of regularity on the Sabbath day, and I certainly attended many times on one or other of the five great Jewish holy days. But on the most holy of all Jewish celebrations, the Day of Atonement, when fasting is obligatory, and some devout Jews do not even clean their teeth for fear that they may swallow some drops of water off the toothbrush, we ate substantial meals without a qualm. My mother's fondness for her children did not permit the smallest degree of religious fanaticism.

The fact was, I suppose, that the Warburgs were Jews because they were born of Jewish parents and believed themselves to be Jews. But their religious feeling was slight and their racial exclusiveness negligible. Too proud or too lethargic to lay aside their Jewishness by conversion or otherwise, they stayed 'Jews' until something happened to make them change. They then changed with as little fuss as a man changing from one lounge suit to another of a slightly different colour. So they remained basically the same, substituting for the practice of not going to synagogue the rather similar practice of not going to church.

So it was that I was not allowed to attend divine service in Westminster Abbey before the first class of the day. This had one great advantage; I had ten minutes longer in the morning before being forced to go to school. But the disadvantages were greater by far, since my non-attendance marked me, and a few others, as different from our fellow schoolmates, a crime in their eyes comparable with sneaking. To the horrors of being a new boy at a public school was added the horror of being known as a Jew, and I suffered profoundly. Time, the great healer, as a leading English writer has phrased it, has obliterated the fearful emotions of those years, and I now attempt to look back upon them as a season of mellow fruitfulness before the world sank deliriously into barbarism. But in my heart I know that it was not so. At the time it was tough.

I had been at Westminster about two years when World War I broke out in August 1914. We were at Trefriw near Bettws-y-coed in North Wales, and I was playing in my first croquet tournament. Since my father constantly believed himself to be in delicate health, he had indulged throughout his life in no more violent sport than croquet, which he played well and enjoyed. Ever since I was old enough to hold a croquet mallet, round about the age of four, I had played the game with him, and by 1914 was quite a good performer with an official handicap. Croquet is a game wrongfully despised, for it is in fact one that demands skill, courage, concentration, and forethought to a very high degree, and may be considered as akin to billiards played outdoors. I was at least as fond of it as my father was, and it formed a much needed bond between us. After the war was over, I was to become highly skilled, and played once in the championships at Roehampton Club, where I was beaten in the third round, a fate liable to overtake even better performers than myself. But in my first tournament at Trefriw I was nervous, and was defeated in round one.

Among the Welsh hills, on the smooth green lawns, with the pleasant sound of croquet mallet hitting croquet ball, the war seemed far away. I did not guess that it was to engulf me. I took it for granted, as my father did and all the generals except Kitchener, that it would be 'over by Christmas', a view for which I could have given no valid reason except that 'obviously' the British could beat the Germans in the long run without an ally, but that with the French and the Russians to help them, it would only be a matter of a few months to victory. These four weeks in Wales were probably the last in which I enjoyed without anxiety the full and fine aroma of the world that was being shot to pieces across the English Channel. Thereafter there was always a worm, however insignificant, in the apple. The Pax Britannica was shattered. The age without pity had begun.

None of this was in my mind, as I returned to school that September. I was about to begin my third year. The horrors of fagging were over. I was quite a big boy now, and for me to be bullied was becoming rarer. Naturally there was much talk at school about the war, and many regretted that it would inevitably be over before they could 'get into it'. I was secretly delighted that I would be too young to fight, not so much because I feared being wounded or killed, but because I had grave doubts about my ability to handle even the simpler weapons of war, such as a rifle and a bayonet, and anticipated sarcastic comments on my clumsiness and lack of manual skill. In any case, I was convinced that my health would never stand the hardships of campaigning, since regularly every winter, following in my father's footsteps, I developed severe attacks of asthma and bronchitis, which made it difficult for me to attain the scholastic standards expected.

Through the next three years I continued at Westminster in a life affected by the war, but not noticeably so. Food got rather scarce, as the U-boat campaign grew fiercer, but there was always enough to eat, and no one worried except my mother who vainly tried to maintain a pre-war standard which had become unattainable. Boys I had known, distinguished seniors, heroes of the cricket and football teams, left school and joined one of the services. Some of them were killed, and their deaths were duly recorded in the school magazine, *The Elizabethan*. With the horrifying insensitiveness of the young, I took their deaths for granted. I had not known them intimately enough to be concerned. My imagination could not encompass the long-continued horrors of the French battlefields. I continued my studies, entered the Sixth Form for a year under the great John Sargeant, then the Seventh and highest form under Mr. Smedley, known as Snogger. I became a prefect. I drilled diligently, but not very smartly, in the Officers Training Corps.

It was a peaceful life, with the occasional bout of excitement when the Germans raided London with a handful of planes, scattering 25 pound bombs, or when the silhouette of a Zeppelin, cruising high over London at night, sent shivers down the backs of the womenfolk. Standing at the top of the stone steps which led down to the kitchen and basement of No. 21, peering out over the garden at the back, I was privileged to observe with several million others the destruction of a Zeppelin over Cuffley by British planes. The war was only a couple of hundred miles away across the Straits of Dover, no farther than York is from London. But though you could often hear the noise of the barrage borne on a favouring wind, it was in another world that hostilities took place. In England it was business as usual, and the profits of business were high.

It was a peaceful life, and most peaceful of all on a Saturday morning, when I used to walk to Queen's Road, Bayswater, about a mile from home, and spend a happy hour or so in Brown's, the second-hand bookshop, browsing along the endless shelves. Here I became familiar with books and authors not dreamed of in the school curriculum, old border ballads, gallant memoirs of the French *grand' epoque*, eighteenth-century English poets, nineteenth-century sermons, Daniel Defoe's *Moll Flanders*, narratives of the early travellers. Every Saturday I brought home with me a few volumes and added them proudly to 'my library'. The world of books, that spacious universe where a multitude can dwell in harmony, took form in my mind. It acquired a solid reality more pleasing than the trivial discontents of family life, more encouraging than the boredom of Latin composition or the artificiality of arithmetic, more peaceful by far than a world which had clearly become, even to my barely opening eyes, dangerous and destructive. The smell of old books slowly decaying became as familiar and delightful to me as that of perfume to the young girl dressing for an evening party. Though I could not realize it, I was preparing for a life of whose existence I had no knowledge, the life of a publisher.

At school I was working for a prize, the translation of a passage from Quintilian's *Institutio Oratoria*. The polished sentences of this first-century educator and teacher of rhetoric contrasted strangely with the real-life performances of that greatest of all English orators, David Lloyd George, then prime minister. One day in Brown's bookshop I found an old Bohn library edition of Quintilian, and bought it. In due course, I discovered the passage set for the translation prize, and corrected my own version with its aid, removing a few howlers I had perpetrated. I also modernized and, so I believed, improved the rather stilted style of the Bohn version. On the appointed day, I delivered my work to the master in charge, and waited. A week later, the master beckoned to me across the school courtyard, and told me that I had won the prize.

'An excellent version, Warburg,' he said, 'easily the best submitted. I must congratulate you.'

'I based it, sir, on the old translation in Bohn's library,' I replied, 'modernized and made as fluent as possible.'

The master's expression changed. 'Oh, so you had a crib,' he said, nastily, 'we had hoped that candidates would use their own brains for the task.'

I won the prize, for there was nothing to be found in the regulations that forbade a crib. But the incident shows my profound lack of sense at this period of my life, for it had never for a moment entered my head that I might be accused of cheating. I had simply done the best I could, using all the means at my disposal. It was perhaps my first lesson in diplomacy, in the art of saying no more than is necessary. I doubt whether I have learned the lesson fully to this day.

By now I was nearly eighteen, and the war went on and on. It would last into 1919 and beyond, some people said. By degrees it became clear to me that I was to become a warrior after all. I was called up for interview by the commanding officer of the Training Corps to discover what service I wished to enter. The machine-gun corps, I told him solemnly. Why I had chosen it, I cannot today do more than guess. Certainly I did not realize it was the most dangerous of all the services. Perhaps I imagined myself invulnerable, lying behind this powerful weapon spraying death upon my field-grey enemies. Fortunately I was pronounced unfit to procure for myself the probability of an early death. I was posted instead to the Royal Garrison Artillery.

At this period of the war, mid-1917, there was a grave

shortage of officers, and all public schoolboys were regarded as potential officer material. The possession of fairly well-off parents, of a 'good' accent, of a slight knowledge of Greek and Latin (or on the modern side, a smattering of science)— these together with skill however partial at cricket and football and a sense of responsibility towards the lower orders engendered by the relationship of prefect to fag— were humorously regarded as sufficient to transform an eighteen-year-old boy into an officer and a gentleman. It is remarkable how frequently the trick was performed successfully, for the conjurors who trained us—the old sweats, the sergeant-majors, the aging or crippled officers, rarely concealed anything up their sleeves save brawn.

That summer of 1917 I learned that I had won a scholarship to the University, either a scholarship proper to Trinity College, Cambridge, or an exhibition to Christ Church, Oxford. I chose the latter. My Uncle Oscar had been to Cambridge. I had no intention of following in his footsteps.

That summer of 1917 I learned that Falkner and Abrahams, the two most brilliant men of the year senior to me had been killed in battle. They would never take up the scholarships they had won, and English life in the years to come would be impoverished by their eternal absence.

That summer of 1917 saw the beginnings of what was to become the battle and blood-bath of Passchendaele, in whose aftermath I was to play an active if insignificant role. Meanwhile, I said good-bye to my headmaster, my form master, my house master, my school friends, and handed over my locker key to the matron. I said good-bye to my family, and embraced my mother, who wept. She did not understand the war or why men should continue fighting so fiercely in a world full of good things.

Nor, as a matter of fact, did I. It seemed to me to be due to the inconceivable stupidity of the Germans, who should have known from the beginning that they hadn't a chance, and to the wicked ambitions of the Kaiser and Generals Ludendorff and Hindenburg. Over forty years later, in my heart of hearts, I don't think very differently.

That summer of 1917, naively clad in the traditional dress of the Westminster schoolboy, Eton jacket and a top hat, and carrying an umbrella, I took the train from Paddington to Bournemouth, where my training as an officer-cadet was to begin. My attire created much ribaldry on arrival, but the top hat was useful. I dug it into the earth outside my tent, and employed it as a wash-basin until it fell to pieces. The umbrella was lost. I could have wished that Neville Chamberlain had not found it twenty years later.

2 A Man Called Hetherington

MY MILITARY TRAINING was pursued at the pleasant south coast resorts of Bournemouth and Bexhill, and occupied four months. If it is objected that the time is short in which to learn the noble art of war, the reply must be that the need was great . . . for cannon-fodder. At school I had penetrated a short distance into the life of the mind; in the army the manual skills, and the build-up of character and self-reliance were of more importance. By degrees the sickly schoolboy with his ailments, induced by the fondness of a doting mother and a hypochondriac father, made way for a reasonably muscular and tough young man. The attacks of asthma vanished, not to be revived even by the stinking mud and vaporous air of the icy Flanders winter of 1917. War, that age-old human condition, had vanquished Home, that yet more aged human institution, to my lasting benefit. By degrees, the silly simpleton of Bayswater began to learn a little about the realities so carefully hidden from him by school and family. I learned to smoke, to swear and to assert myself. I learned the power of sex over men. Imperceptibly I was growing up.

In Bournemouth we drilled all day long and did physical exercises. The P.T. developed many unnecessary muscles of which previously I had had no knowledge, and produced such rigidity of pose when standing, sitting or walking that I developed shocking lumbago in early middle-age. Flexibility was not a quality favoured by the army authorities of World War I. But the drill was a different matter. Of course, it had no value whatever in or near the front-line, but it is just conceivable that it inculcated in us a self-discipline unusual in civilian life.

In Bexhill we abandoned parade-ground exercises for gun drill. I cannot recall whether the guns were actually real six-inch howitzers, for which we were destined, or merely colourable imitations, but we learned how to lift 100 lb. shells and place them on a two-handled tray, how to carry the tray to the breech of the gun, how to push the shell into the mouth of the breech by hand, how to ram the shell firmly home by means of a wooden ramrod, how to pack in the propellant contained in white cotton-bags, how to swing shut the heavy breech block, and how finally to take up our firing positions and pull the lanyard attached to the firing-pin which activated the whole mechanism. When we had reached a reasonable stage of proficiency in these intricate manoeuvres, we were taken to Lydd and fired real shells out of real howitzers at unreal targets.

None of this proved difficult for me to learn, despite my fundamental lack of mechanical understanding. To this day, I feel sure I could, on the command 'Ram!', shove a ramrod against a shell with the requisite amount of strength, neither too much nor too little. As for the pull on the lanyard which activated the firing mechanism, no words can convey the exquisite sense of power experienced by the performer of this simple action. A little tug on a string, followed by a click, and suddenly an ear-splitting explosion, a great belch of flame and smoke from the squat ugly muzzle, a furious recoil driving the trail of the howitzer back against its support, and the shell itself whirring invisibly out of sight to an unseen destination up to 10,000 yards away. Perhaps the golfer who has just hit a perfect tee-shot can appreciate the juicy thrill of firing this kind of weapon.

I received my commission as a second-lieutenant in the Royal Garrison Artillery in October. The course had lasted three months. I passed the theoretical and practical examinations, and there I was, an officer. Now I had an income of sorts, and a special allowance with which I bought my uniforms at Hawkes in Old Burlington Street, as so many thousands of others. I walked around, upright and intolerably stiff like one of the ramrods I had been trained to handle, proud to be serving H.M. George V, admired by the girls, diligently returning the salutes of all non-commissioned men within miles. I was sent to the vicinity of Aldershot early in November, and settled down comfortably to military life. I hardly expected to go overseas until far into the New Year; it did not seem to me that I was yet fully mature as an officer or as an artillery man. The War Office, however, thought otherwise. It may have been that they would have agreed with me on reflection that I had not yet fully developed the power of commanding men liable to be from five to twenty-five years my seniors, but they had no time and perhaps no inclination to reflect on my deficiencies, or perhaps, having reflected, decided to give me the benefit of the doubt. At any rate, they posted me to the 184th Siege Battery within a few days of my nineteenth birthday. The battle of Passchendaele had been fought, and not won, at the expense of 400,000 casualties. I was to be sent out to endeavour to turn the tide.

Even today I feel a slight resentment. At that period the regulations did not permit a man or an officer to be sent on active service until he had reached the age of nineteen. The War Office might, I felt, have allowed a greater fraction of my twentieth year to elapse before sending me to whatever unknown destination lay ahead. Of this naturally I said nothing to anybody. I bought the equipment expected of one in my position—camp-bed, sleeping-bag, blankets, revolver, whistle and lanyard, field-glasses—and embarked, loaded down like a Christmas tree, for the front.

We spent a few days at the great port of Le Havre, going through forms of processing, like sausage meat in a sausage machine, and then entrained for the forward areas. It was bitterly cold. The poor old train creaked its way at a funereal pace through an icy countryside to Rouen, where it paused for an hour or two to regain its energy. Here I had a hot drink of cocoa, and for a few minutes stopped shivering. But soon enough we went on hour after hour, with the wind blowing freely through the windows of the compartment, every pane of whose glass was missing. We passed through Abbeville, St. Pol, Bailleul to Poperinghe, if I remember correctly, and at Poperinghe a car from the battery picked me up, me and Hetherington. For somewhere on this dismal journey between Le Havre and Poperinghe I had met him.

Who was Hetherington, what was his Christian name, where was he born and bred, how old was he? I cannot remember, perhaps I never knew. But through the eleven months to the Armistice of 11 November, 1918, and the three months beyond that till I was demobilized, he was my twin, my *alter ego*, my brother-in-arms, whom I loved with a sexless devotion.

Peering back through the mists of time, I discern a young man, three or four years older than myself, below the average in height, swarthy in colour, with a small toothbrush moustache. His eyes are alive and shrewd and full of that knowledge of men and women which I was not to possess till many years later; his mouth is set in a quizzical expression which seems to say—struggle if you must, but you'll have to accept the inevitable at last.

Hetherington was not a public school boy; a scholarship and a grammar school education had made him a teacher; he had come up through the ranks to achieve a commission; he lacked an Oxford accent; he was no Londoner; he was a man of and from the people, the very first I had met in the cloistered nineteen years of my life. What he saw in me, I cannot imagine. My face was empty, slightly sullen, a trifle intolerant, cold though not calculating, with a flicker of intelligence about the eyes. Perhaps the attraction was one of opposites; or he wished fraternally to protect me against the follies to which my ignorance was likely to propel me; or again he may have sensed below my frigid exterior a warm heart struggling to break through the icy surface of a public school discipline. But that he liked me, I put down unhesitatingly on the credit side of my account, far above the rather second-rate exploits of a short and undistinguished career as a warrior. He would not have liked me, had I been the kind of young man I seem to myself now to have been then. Somewhere inside me he must have found a spark, and fanned it to fitful warmth. Without him I might have emerged from the war a man cased in his own egotism, conventional, self-righteous, and unimaginative.

It was a few days before Christmas when Hetherington and I arrived at the battery's rear billets, a group of Nissen huts in a smashed-up countryside. As an officer I had one to myself, and a batman. This devoted individual served me throughout the war as valet, cook, doctor, and teacher of etiquette. I was grateful to him, and he to me because, as batman, he was excused the more dangerous duty of serving the guns. He set up my camp-bed and arranged my clothes and belongings with Jeevesian precision. Here was my home, as magnificent as the Savoy Hotel, compared to the hovels in which the poor bloody infantry of the line passed the interminable months of their service. Yet to me it seemed a hardship to reach the battlefield at so inauspicious a time of year, and I said as much to Hetherington, who shrugged. He could think of many worse things happening than that.

The battery was commanded by Major Church, a tall handsome man with a big black moustache and a pleasant smile. At the age of twenty-eight he seemed to me on the elderly side, and I observed with some surprise that he was able to walk, run and even jump with at least as much agility as myself. His second-in-command was a year or two younger, a graduate of Trinity College, Dublin. There were some six other officers, including Hetherington and myself.

The N.C.O.s were good. The sergeant-major, with a face like an undercooked steak, stood six foot six inches in his socks. His energy and efficiency were amazing. He treated me with an exquisite courtesy, which concealed the contempt he felt for such riff-raff as myself who bore the insignia of officer rank without the training and character which alone could make it valid. The first time I gave him an order, I felt as if I had put my tongue out at a prince of the royal blood. I was astounded when he obeyed it without comment.

The men (about 250 all told) were mostly northerners from Hartlepool and West Hartlepool, some of them miners, a majority married and in their thirties or even forties. They could not have been called warlike by the greatest stretch of the imagination. Kindly, conscientious and puzzled at a fate which had dragged them from the hills and dales of the finest county in England to fight a war, they seemed to me more like sheep on the way to a slaughter-house than soldiers. Their patience, as I gave them their orders, and at times exhorted them to special efforts, was incredible. Often I felt that they ought to answer back or refuse to obey, a situation with which I knew I could not have coped. But they never did. In those days it was accepted without question by the majority that any young idiot who had been to the right school had the ability to command implanted in him. Indeed, ranker officers, with years in the regular army behind them and a distinguished record with medals in the war itself, were still regarded with suspicion, as if somewhere below the ribbons a yellow streak might be concealed. It was preposterous. The class snobbery of Victorian England took a long time to die, if indeed it is dead yet.

Morale was low. Even I could observe this elementary fact. Too many men had been wounded or died during the previous autumn. The 184th Siege Battery was itself a living reminder of the fact. It had been formed by the amalgamation of two four-gun batteries, whose casualties had been so great that between them they could barely produce a full battery complement. Each contributed one gun, so that on my arrival we had two guns in action.

The battery position lay to the north of Ypres and the north-west of Passchendaele near the village of Dixmude, about fifteen miles from the coast between Calais and Ostend. It was on a slight eminence, looking out over a Flanders landscape of mud, tree stumps and duckboards described lovingly or otherwise in a thousand books. I was to go up with a senior officer the day before Christmas for my first tour of duty. The previous evening a stray shell fragment had put one of our two howitzers out of action.

Before dawn I set out on the three-mile walk over the duckboards and through the mud, a dreary plod which I came to know only too well in the coming months. At every unfamiliar sound I started nervously. I was raw. I could not yet interpret the danger of an approaching projectile from the kind of noise it made. We reached the battery about dawn. The two howitzers reared their ugly noses to the skies under tattered wisps of camouflage canvas. The gun platforms were built on planks. The mud was everywhere. The smell of a dead horse buried at the battery entrance nauseated me. The air was cold and damp. A weary officer who had been on duty for three days saluted the senior officer and me, and welcomed us in.

I was shown round the battery position, which occupied only a few score square yards; I was taken into the dug-outs with the wire-netting beds; I was presented to the sergeant and the men, about ten in number; the landmarks were explained to me on the map; all that I needed to know to command a one-gun battery in this god-forsaken place was conveyed to me. A few minutes later I was left alone. I was in command. They must be mad, I thought, to put me in charge. What shall I do if anything happens? Wildly I looked toward the enemy lines, expecting at any moment to see a horde of field-grey figures stealing towards me. Nothing moved. The drizzle continued. I went into the dug-out and began talking to the sergeant. I felt fine.

Before midnight we received by phone orders to fire

a few rounds. Probably the major thought it would be a good idea to get me up and out on my first tour of duty. Shuffling around in my gumboots, with the sergeant at my side to prevent disaster, I supervised the sighting, ranging and loading of our solitary weapon, fussing round like an old hen with her chicks, though each and every man on the gun-site had forgotten more about gunnery than I had yet learned. However, the men, and even the sergeant, treated me with tolerance. There were many worse things in life to them than an ignorant and stuck-up junior officer. When all was ready I stood back, put my hands to my ears, and gave the command, 'Fire!' A startling noise rent the silence of the night. Reload! Fire! A second 100 lb. shell whirred its way to the enemy lines. Reload! Fire! A third shell left the muzzle, the howitzer appeared to recoil in the accustomed manner, but it did not slide back into the firing position as it should have done. Sergeant and I approached and examined the huge mechanism. It was jammed. We pulled, shoved, twisted and banged at it, in vain. I rang up the C.O. to report the battery out of action. In the event of an enemy attack that night, we had nothing but my revolver and one rifle with which to resist. The major seemed reassuringly calm. 'I'll send up the artificers at dawn,' he told me. At dawn they duly arrived. They pulled, shoved, twisted and banged at my howitzer for some time. 'Nothing to be done, sir,' they told me, 'ordnance will have to fetch it away for repair at base.' I reported to the C.O. who ordered me to bring the men back to rear billets immediately. Cheerfully, we collected our belongings and plodded back over the duckboards I had so recently traversed in the opposite direction. I got back at noon, and went to bed, exhausted. My batman roused me at 7 p.m. for Christmas dinner. We had a wonderful meal. Whoever had dropped a spanner in the howitzer's slide, as ordnance reported later as the cause of the catastrophe, had secured for me, as for himself, Christmas in rear billets. We might be far from home, but, comfortable and well-filled with food, we celebrated the traditional feast in high spirits. It was perhaps magnificent, but it certainly was not war. Morale, as I have said, was low, and a make-shift battery of elderly married Yorkshire miners is not the stuff of which heroes are made, at least not rapidly. It was two weeks before we got our howitzers back into action. By then I thought myself a seasoned campaigner.

Life in the Ypres salient during that winter was an unmitigated bore. Every evening after dinner the officers played bridge in the Mess. We got to know each other's game so well that the cards might almost have been down on the table face upwards. The gramophone ground out the same old tunes night after night, though occasionally we added new records from a shop at Bailleul. During January I developed a raging fever while on duty at the battery position, and was ordered to return at once to rear billets. Slowly and painfully, with a temperature that turned out to be a 104° F. I marched back alone over the duck-boards. Shelling was brisk. Small 25-and 60-pound shells were exploding near me, or near enough. The steel fragments whistled nastily past my head, my feet, my midriff. I regarded them calmly. Sickness is an excellent remedy for fear. But on the whole dangerous days were few. What put the wind-up me was an altogether different matter.

One day in February the major paraded all officers, N.C.O.s, and men who were not on duty at the guns, and read out to us a communication he had received from G.H.Q. The collapse of Russia, it said, following the

Bolshevik Revolution, had released 120 divisions for service on the Western Front. The allied armies should prepare to resist a strong German offensive in the spring. The Commander-in-Chief expected all ranks to give a good account of themselves. 'Battery, dis-miss!' The news made a strong impression on me. I felt that we had already enough Germans in front of us to keep us busy for a long time ahead. The Russian Revolution, with which I vaguely sympathized, as did Hetherington, should not, I thought, have abandoned the armies on the Western Front in the middle of a war against a ruthless enemy who was their enemy also. Capitalist exploiters we might be at heart, but in the army a primitive communism prevails, and the only opportunity for making money was the age-old practice of scrounging. It may well be that this announcement played its part in forming the ambivalent attitude to Communism, and even to Trotskyism, which stood me years later in such good stead. The Marxist revolutionaries were giving me a longer war to fight than I had bargained for, and doubling the possibility of my being wounded, captured or killed. It was altogether too much of a good thing.

On 14 March, after three months in the line, I was granted fourteen days leave. With five pounds of butter and a store of petrol coupons, I returned to London and the family circle. Since my adventures had on the whole been insignificant, I prepared a few lively stories to retail to the good folks at home. I need not have bothered. To them, as to me nine months before, the war was unimaginable. The adventures I had had, or claimed to have had, were like dreams to them. My mother, dear soul, was concerned lest I went out after dark without a muffler. My father's interest seemed concentrated in aerial photography, a subject of which I had no knowledge. My sisters made a fuss of me, but clearly their interests lay in young men who were not their brother, rather than aiming posts, tri-nitro-toluene, and lifting barrages. Once or twice foolishly I tried to tell them the truth, but I soon abandoned the attempt. All front-line soldiers experienced the same blank wall; we could only talk to each other.

Men on leave in London went to the theatre. I was no exception. I saw seventeen 'shows' in fourteen days. We wanted to look at women, young, beautiful, attractive girls. We wanted colour and music and bright lights. We hungered for rich foods. We basked in warmth, hot rooms and hot baths. We required sleep. At the end of my leave I had stored up enough glamour to see me through the months ahead, like a camel who stores up water for a prolonged trek through the desert. Tired but also refreshed, I returned to France in expectation of another leave three months later. It was to be eleven months before I saw England again, when I came back to be demobilized. For now at last the slow-moving, murderous, ill-conducted war was moving to a climax. The Yanks were coming a trifle late to support the cause of freedom. To forestall them on 21 March, 1918, the Germans delivered a tremendous blow, from which the allied armies reeled back in disorder. I was, fortunately, in bed at No. 21 Pembridge Gardens at the time. When I heard the news a day later, I was worried. What had become of my friends? I wanted to return to the front. The battery had become my life. The shows of London were a temporary distraction, my family amiable ghosts living in a meaningless past.

It was in an apple orchard in the suburbs of Arras that I found the battery on my return. It had been pulled out of Flanders a few days after the German attack, but not

51

without casualties. An officer had been killed and several men wounded by a stray shell falling among the rear billets 7,000 yards behind the front line. But Hetherington was all right, and he too had had leave. 'We're going to have a sticky time now,' he told me, 'the Jerries will try and break us before we get too strong for them.' Everywhere there was a sense of menace in the air. When I went up to the forward observation post 500 yards from the front line on Telegraph Hill, I felt tense and patted my revolver in its holster, while praying that its use, in which I was pitifully unskilled, would not be required of me. Though I rarely saw a German, I constantly imagined feverish activity behind the enemy lines. Once we fired for three days and nights at two-minute intervals on a certain cross-roads to repel a powerful attack. The breech-blocks of the guns became so hot that we had to keep throwing pails of water over them. Blossom came out on the apple trees. Spring had arrived. It quite surprised me. One morning at the O.P. I observed movement behind the enemy lines, and frantic with excitement rang up the battery and requested permission to fire. It was granted. I gave the estimated range and angle of fire. I heard the shell pass over my head, and saw it explode about half a mile from the target. I corrected the range and fired again. The shell-burst seemed little nearer than before. The tiny figures of my enemies continued calmly with their sinister activities (probably the carrying of food supplies into a company H.Q.). Again and again I fired, twenty or thirty rounds, none of them near the target, before I abandoned the foolish enterprise. Each shell cost the exchequer £100. Never since then have I been in a position to waste the national substance on so lavish a scale.

At the end of July we pulled out of the line and drove south to an unknown destination. About 5 August, at dead of night, we passed through Amiens to the north-east and took up our position in a small wood about a mile behind the front. The wood was packed with batteries of many different calibres. All activity by day was forbidden. The great counter-attack of 8 August was being prepared, the onslaught which was the beginning of the end for the Germans.

The battery was rested and well-equipped. In a small clearing at the edge of the wood, the four howitzers were emplaced little more than five yards apart in a straight line. We had not yet fired from this position and were not to do so until zero hour. Direction was established by means of aiming posts. Huge stocks of ammunition were placed conveniently to the rear of the guns. Work was continuous throughout the day of 7 August, but always under cover of the trees. That evening I went to bed early. I had to be up at 3 a.m. At 4 a.m. the battle was to begin, though we hoped the enemy did not know it. Hetherington commanded one two-gun section, I commanded the other. We stood about twenty yards behind our own howitzers. We had the ranges and the times written on a sheet of paper; it was in fact to be a lifting barrage. We were to fire continuously and as fast as possible. It was estimated that each howitzer could probably manage thirty rounds an hour. Immaculately shaved with my steel helmet at a rakish angle, in full fig, the lanyard of my whistle white in the first light of morning, I emerged from my hutment soon after 3.30 a.m. It was going to be a beautiful day. To my left stood Hetherington, an untidy dresser on this as on all other occasions. He winked at me. 'This is it,' he said. For the third time I ran through the programme for the shoot with my sergeant, who knew it no doubt at least as well as I did. There was hardly a sound, except the gentle rustle of the leaves on the trees and bushes, the song of birds, the occasional crump of a shell exploding in the distance, and the clank of metal on metal as our preparations went forward. By now it was 3.55 a.m. I kept staring at my watch, which of course had been synchronized with tens of thousand of other watches the previous evening. For a moment only, my mind flashed to the infantry men in front, in their trenches. I thought of their tension, as they waited to clamber out into the open and advance towards the enemy lines. Thank God I'm a gunner, I thought. I murmured to myself: it's going to be all right, this time we shall break through. My watch registered three-fifty-nine. I looked towards Hetherington. His eyes were on his watch. My mouth felt slightly dry. The seconds ticked on. The four howitzers, their muzzles pointing not very high, stood there like primitive mastodons, loaded. To the right of each one stood No. 2 of the gun crew, in his hands one end of the firing cord attached to the T-pin of the firing mechanism. The second hand of my watch clicked round for the last time. No. 1 and No. 2 guns, Fire! I shouted in a voice hoarse with excitement. No. 3 and 4 guns, Fire! shouted Hetherington within a split second of me. The four guns belched their flames and recoiled. The gun crews ran to reload. No. 1 and 2 guns ready, reported my sergeant. No. 3 and 4 guns ready, reported Hetherington's. Fire! Fire! All around me the air pulsated with a noise greater than any I had ever heard before or have ever heard since, even at the height of the London blitz. Thousands of guns packed into a few square miles were in continuous action. It was impossible to make my orders heard. I walked up to my section and stood between the guns shouting the orders into the ears of my gun commanders a foot or two away. Hetherington was doing the same. It was, to use the traditional phrase, an inferno. For the enemy at the receiving end it must have been

54

terrible. No hostile shells came back at us. The batteries had been smashed to pieces, as I saw for myself the next day. Around 11 a.m. we had lifted to 10,000 yards and were ordered to cease fire. The enemy was out of range. Our troops were five miles through and advancing rapidly. At last, I thought, we shall get into the open. Hetherington and I walked back together to the mess, utterly exhausted by the noise and our own efforts. The C.O. was cheerful. 'Any minute now I expect orders to pull out of here and advance,' he told us.

So began for me the surge forward of the allied armies which continued until the Armistice. We moved, of course, over ground recently occupied by the enemy. For the first time I saw dead Germans, lying in the awkward postures of the dead, not yet buried. I saw German guns, shells, rifles, grenades, all the paraphernalia abandoned by an army in retreat strewn over a countryside that looked untouched by the smear of war. I inspected dug-outs, filled with the private property of men like ourselves. I saw on their walls the crude sex drawings of men who had not been near a woman for many months. I secured a German revolver handier and more effective than my own. Victory seemed in the air; Hetherington and I had sniffed the heady smell of it as early as 9 August. Already, and at first imperceptibly, our thoughts began to turn to England, to a civilian life and the beginnings of a career. Hetherington was a vastly better soldier than I was, but like me he was only an amateur.

For us in the gunners, at least in my battery, danger now seemed far away. But this illusion did not last long. One afternoon a German plane flew over the battery position and dropped a few bombs. There were several casualties, one in my own gun crew. The wound was caused by a steel fragment which penetrated not very deeply into the flesh on the left side of the man's back. It was the first time in nine months of war that I had seen one of my own men wounded. To this day I can imagine him lying on his side on the grass, groaning, with blood seeping from his back. The incident left an impression, stronger perhaps than if a hundred men had been killed or wounded around me. It brought home the simple vulnerability of human flesh. During the blitzes of World War II in London, I used sometimes to visualize beneath the business suit of the ordinary English citizen, the white body exposed day after day to the terror that came from the skies.

One day in September, or perhaps October, still advancing, we were ordered to a position which, as it turned out, was less than eight hundred yards from the recently established front line. Heavy firing could be seen ahead of us in a wood across the fields. We emplaced the guns and waited for our orders. None came. 'If the Jerries counter-attack,' Hetherington said, 'we shall have to fire over open sights.' Suddenly, to the rear, I heard an unfamiliar noise, the clip-clop of horses' hooves, and a minute later there rode past us about five hundred mounted men, with rifles slung over their shoulders. 'It can't really be true,' I said to Hetherington. 'Poor devils,' Hetherington said sadly as he watched them go by, 'Those bloody brasshats believe we can fight the Crimean War all over again.'

The men on their heavy mounts rode steadily away from us and were lost to sight. Ten minutes passed. Suddenly the firing flared up ahead with renewed violence. We waited. As usual in war, there was nothing to be seen, though plenty to be heard. Half an hour later the horsemen returned, riding slowly through and around our position. There were fewer of them, and many were wounded.

Riderless horses came too. Had there really been a cavalry charge, I wondered? Was it possible that, in this technological age these noble animals and their riders had been thrown against a hail of steel? I never found out. In a battle the man who fights never knows what is happening except for a few yards to his right and left, to his front and rear. But to the best of my belief, here about midway between Amiens and Mons—for I forget the name of the place—in September or October 1918, there took place the last cavalry charge of military history, conducted by rather fewer men than at Balaclava with approximately the same percentage of casualties.

On 10 November we were over the Belgian border within twenty miles of Mons. We knew that at 11 a.m. on the 11th, the Armistice would be declared. The major decided to motor into Mons the next day, starting about 9 a.m. and told me to be ready to accompany him. We got into the battery car and drove off. There was little or no firing. A few miles from our destination we passed a small trench system. One or two English infantrymen, covered with sheets, lay there dead. We stopped to inquire. Yes, there had been a small engagement at 6 a.m. that morning. A few casualties had been sustained. It seemed to me heart-breaking to die so near the end. So, as I learned later, died the English poet, Wilfred Owen. So died, no doubt, many others. It was too much. I said so to the major, who smiled sadly at my vehemence. 'Warburg,' he said 'you've been out here for nearly a year, but you have seen nothing. You have been lucky. Those of us who were at the Somme, at Passchendaele, at all the big killing-grounds, have seen enough to last us our lifetime. There must never again be a war like this. The Boche must be kept down for good.' A moment later we were in Mons. It was not much of a place, this little town where the war had started in a famous battle at which, for reasons never clear to me, angels had appeared.

The morning was a grey one. As eleven o'clock drew near, men and women began coming out of their houses, walking through the streets, lining the pavements, welcoming with moderate exhilaration the British troops advancing through the town to the Armistice line. Soon it was eleven o'clock. The war was over. A ragged cheer went up. Then there was silence, not as later for the appointed two minutes, but for a long, long time. The guns had stopped firing. It was a silence that I believed I would never want interrupted. But I was mistaken. In September 1938, and indeed years earlier, I longed, prayed and worked for war. Pacifism is not enough. A man must fight when there is no other way—or he ceases to be a man. Even in the age of the H Bomb, a man must stand up.

The rest was anti-climax. Life was cushy again. Creature comforts returned. We were instructed to teach our men what we knew. There were courses in strange subjects. Did I lecture on Roman prosody? I cannot remember. I had a week's leave in Paris. There, as in London, it seemed as if the war had never happened. I stayed with an aged French female relative in a sumptuous house. I wore her late husband's flannel nightgown. Rummaging round my room I discovered a cache of pornographic literature in French, and read the lot. I have never been able to read pornography since then. I dined with my wealthy young French cousin, who talked sex to me. He knew a great deal more about it than I did. He was too young to have fought in the war and I regarded him with contempt. He discussed money and banking, and how to start a career. 'What will you do when you get back to England?' he asked.

'Go up to Oxford and take my degree,' I said.

'It's a waste of time,' he told me, 'you must get yourself ranged. Things will be hard now that the war is over. Good jobs will be difficult to get.'

I looked at him in amazement. This was no way to talk to an officer, who had fought in a great war, which we had won. When I was back again I would go to the university. War had been an interruption, no more, to the advance of civilization. Life could be resumed as if nothing much had happened. We parted without great cordiality. Soldier and civilian in those days had a hard time understanding each other.

In February 1919 the hour came for my demobilization. Students destined for universities were being demobbed early. I surveyed my companions of the officers' mess. They had been good to me, tolerant of my youth, my inexperience, my narrowness. They had been with me, and I had been with them. But now they were figures belonging to my past. I could not care less whether I ever saw them again. But Second-Lieutenant Hetherington, that was a different matter altogether. He had been my friend for fourteen months; he was, I hoped, to be my friend through the peaceful years to come. The time came to leave, and I walked into his room to say good-bye. His demobilization too was imminent.

'What will your address be when you're out of the army?' I asked him.

'I'm not sure yet.'

'Well, where can I write you?'

'I'll have to let you know.'

It seemed a satisfactory answer, but something in

the way he spoke the words roused my suspicions. 'Hetherington,' I said suddenly, 'don't you want to see me again?'

He looked embarrassed. 'It's not that,' he said at last, 'we've been good friends in the army. But in civvy life everything will be different. You have your place and I have mine. They lie a long way apart.'

I stared at him in horror. 'What do you mean?' I asked.

'You're a gentleman,' he said quietly, 'and I'm not, thank God. It wouldn't suit me. Too much bloody fuss, too much hypocrisy and dressing up. But you've been brought up to it. You'll go to Oxford and live in London, and have a fine career. Your social life won't be at all like mine. I shall be a teacher in a secondary school in the Midlands. We shouldn't have anything in common after three months. A few letters, interesting at first and then a bore to write them. A meeting now and then, only to discover that there's nothing left. I prefer to end it now, and the hell with it. We've had some fine times together. Let's keep it that way.'

'Don't be ridiculous,' I said indignantly, though I knew already that the battle was lost. 'Why should I let my best friend go for no good reason whatever?'

'Because,' he said, 'the war created our friendship, and the peace will destroy it.'

'Damn the peace,' I said.

'Damn the war,' said Hetherington.

For a long time I argued, implored, stormed at him. At that time he was nearer to me than anyone else had ever been, except my mother when I was a child. But Hetherington had made up his mind. We shook hands for the last time. I gave him my address, and told him that I knew he would alter his mind when he was back in blighty. He took the paper from me and put it in his pocket. Without looking back I left the room. A few minutes later I was on my way home.

I was demobbed on Wimbledon Common. It was a bitterly cold day. When I got back in my civvies to No. 21 I felt ill. Next day the family doctor diagnosed bronchial pneumonia. I was in bed for three weeks. As soon as I was recovered, I started preparing for my first term at Christ Church.

I never saw Hetherington again, or heard from him or about him. I don't think of him often, but sometimes his workmanlike figure and pleasant ugly face comes into my mind. Not brave and not cowardly, far above the average in intelligence, competent and good with his hands, sensitive and capable of love, he was not a gentleman. He was, of course, far more than that. He was a man, a better man than I, more patient, more tolerant, more understanding. If I am a better man today than I was at nineteen, I owe a lot of it to him. If he is still alive, and happens to read these words, I hope he will write and tell me how things are with him. If he leaves his address off the notepaper, I shall understand. One cannot go back into the past, except in memory. That is why, no doubt, I never revisited the Flanders battlefields when the war was over, despite an almost irresistible longing at times to do so. The past is dead, but the memory lingers on. The mud flats of Passchendaele, the orchards round Arras, the rolling country to the north-east of Amiens to the Belgian border, these were the scenes of my youth, where I learned how to be cold and hungry, to be afraid and to conquer fear, to go on living since life was meant to be lived, to make a friend and do without him, to rely on myself in the last resort. I learned the lesson of the Stoics, how to face the intolerable and surmount it. I learned the lesson of Epicurus, to have a good time when the going was good. Flanders provided me with better education than Westminster School. And there it was that I met and loved and parted with my first true teacher, one whose Christian name I cannot remember, a man called Hetherington.

3   A Place
for Talking

AT TWENTY a man is resilient. In a matter of weeks
I had recovered from the pneumonia, and the enigmatic
figure of Hetherington began to recede into memory. I was,
of course, overjoyed at being out of the army and out of
the war. I was smugly satisfied that I had 'done my bit'
and served my country in a righteous cause, but now the
time had come for the cultivation of the mind and the
sensibility. Active service might have firmed up my
character, but inevitably it had left my brain to rust.
To burnish it for its life-work, whatever that might be,
was the task that faced me next. But here a certain difficulty
arose, which was to recur from time to time in the years
ahead. I had no glimmering of what my life-work was to be,
an impenetrable vagueness lay over my future.

It was my father who undertook to dispel my
uncertainty. With the dogmatic superiority of a man who
had never done a stroke of work for his living, he argued
that it would be an error to revert to the Greek and Latin
exercises of my Westminster days. Imbued since his
formative years with the Darwinian doctrine in its most
mechanistic form, he was convinced that the fittest survive,

ignoring (as I realized later) that, if fitness was the criterion, he would barely have survived himself unaided for a twelvemonth. To him science was a beacon, though he could not himself drive, let alone repair, the Rolls-Royce my grandmother had presented to him. Science, he thought, should be a beacon for me as well. His son should practise the great profession from which only his own ill-health had kept him. 'At Oxford,' he said emphatically, 'you must take physics or chemistry.'

What induced me to agree with him? I cannot remember. My vagueness perhaps, that drifting quality of some members of the Warburg family which I have already referred to. Perhaps a distaste for returning to a study of the dead languages which I had largely forgotten in the twenty months of my military career. Perhaps I had become used to obeying orders from above. But agree with him I did. When I set out for the university, it was to take a degree in chemistry.

Oxford Station was unimpressive, but I was excited as the train rolled slowly in past the reservoir. The road uphill from the station to Carfax was something of a slum, with the mouldering stones of the prison on the right hand for full measure. At Carfax, with the station behind you, there is the choice of three ways. To the left or north lie the intricacies of Cornmarket, bustling traffic and lively shops. Ahead, winding down to Magdalen Bridge and the Isis, is the exquisitely curved sweep of the High, a prospect of cathedral, colleges and large buildings generally. To the right or south, stretching down in a straight line to Folly Bridge and the boats, lay St. Aldates. This was my road. Half-way down on the left rose Tom Tower, surmounting the great gateway into Christ Church and the world of learning. It was a view I shall never forget. When last I saw it a year or so ago, it seemed to me as lovely as ever.

Christ Church, originally Cardinal College after Wolsey who founded it in 1535, is spacious. It contains three quadrangles, each of differing architectural accomplishment, and a line of hideous buildings, known as Meadows, facing south over great fields, cut by a magnificent avenue of elms through which a broad path leads down to the river. Here in Meadows V.3, that is, in the third room on the fifth staircase, I was to pass the next two years of my life. The war to end all wars was over. The world had learned its lesson for ever. Nations, enjoying the right of self-determination guaranteed them by the wisdom of President Wilson, would lie down with nations. The League of Nations would exert from Geneva a sedative influence on the fractious. England, securely in control of a vast empire, would increase her wealth by the work of her citizens and the ingenuity of her business men and inventors. A wonderful time lay ahead for all of us. As for myself, I had good health and brains and enough money from my exhibition and my father to live with moderate ostentation. I was free from the odious tutelage of schoolmasters. I had escaped the dangers of war and the discipline of an army in battle. I had eluded my family. The future was rosy, it stretched ahead for a lifetime. There was no hurry. There was no limit. In the spring of 1919 all was for the best in the best of all possible worlds.

Without undue delay I went to see my tutor and started work in the laboratory. Science till then had been a closed book to me. Now I read the texts—heat, light, and sound; inorganic and organic chemistry; analytical chemistry. Test-tubes, Bunsen burners, crystals, the nauseating smell of sulphuretted hydrogen, glass-blowing, litmus paper, these became my toys and they fascinated me. My tutor

65

was pleased. 'Remarkable progress,' he told me after a few months, 'considering that you never worked at science before coming here.' In that year the whisper ran from mouth to mouth that the great Rutherford had smashed the atom, that tiny particle which my books informed me was indivisible. In the Clarendon Laboratory, only a mile or so away from where I worked, great events were taking place in the science I was making my own. Man would be set free from Adam's curse to cultivate the garden of the self. Freud and his disciples would remove, at a price, any weeds that remained to be plucked.

Soon I began to feel a trifle lonely. I missed the warm and intimate comradeship of an officers' mess. Acquaintances I had in plenty, but no friends, unless perhaps Philip Usher with whom I played tennis once or twice a week. Himself an old Westminster from the same house as mine, he had virtually missed the war by being a year too young. He was taking history and had a great interest in the church which he proposed to enter. Soon he introduced me to others, a group of young men whom I knew only slightly, Ralph Owen, Basil Herbert, Philip Rea, all of Westminster and Christ Church, and Roy Harrod, who had a scholarship to New College. We six formed a band of intimates, which was not to be entirely disrupted till we went down. Evening after evening we met in the rooms of one or other, smoking, drinking, joking, laughing and talking till we were exhausted.

Our characters contrasted nicely. Herbert had had a tough war in the infantry and won a Military Cross. He was the man of the world, with a deeper knowledge of women than the rest of us. He had a gift for rhetoric and a quick temper, which dominated the group when he lost it. Rea was the exquisite, whose taste in clothes was individual and good. His rooms were decorated in recognizable style. He played the piano well and sang. For him it was enough to be himself, rather than bother to work hard for a degree. Owen was an ambivalent character, part clergyman, part business man in the making. He had a strong core of common sense, which rivalled that of Herbert. Usher was quiet, subtle, learned, hiding ambition beneath a suave exterior. Last came Harrod, with the massive head and lofty brow and russet cheeks, a Forbes-Robertson on his mother's side. His was one of the most brilliant intellects of his day and he seemed to us all destined to become at least Prime Minister.

As for myself, I shared something in common with all of them, unconsciously taking from each what was open to me to receive, and so slowly building up a character which was something of a blank in those days, forming it in argument, in clash of wills, in concession here, in resistance there, groping to discover what I was, what I wanted, where I was going, what role in life was mine to play.

What is Oxford? A duality, of course, city and university, town and gown. And what is the university of Oxford? Stone and brick and mortar, composing some thirty-six colleges and halls which house the young men, a pleasant place for tourists to stroll through. And Oxford is also the dons, the fellows and students who teach and lecture and do research on almost every worthwhile subject under the sun. Then too it is the young men themselves (and the young women) who pass through it into the greater world outside, not without being changed. But above all, Oxford is a spirit, an atmosphere, an idea, a tradition stretching back four hundred years into the past, reaching forward into the future. It is a spirit that changes while remaining unchanged, a theme with variations. Subtle, pervasive, and at times searching, it is not altogether indefinable. Max Beerbohm has perhaps caught it best in the mannered pages of *Zuleika Dobson*, mannered because Oxford is mannered.

It is John Tankerton (pronounced Tacton), the fourteenth Duke of Dorset, who enshrines the Oxford manner in his elegant person. He is, of course, a dandy and an aristocrat, without a trace of the common touch. His powers of persuasion are negligible and he is wholly unable to induce one other undergraduate to refrain from suicide in their hopeless love for the beautiful Zuleika. He lives by *noblesse oblige* and would no more break a social engagement to which he had pledged himself than cheat at cards. He has no belief in the sound instincts of the common herd; 'never had he given an ear to that cackle called Public Opinion.' His attitude to Americans is one that seems to spring eternal in the English breast; he held 'in his enlightened way that Americans have a right to exist'. Dorset, like a majority of undergraduates, has little knowledge of the world. When he asks the adored one, in a discussion of 'the love that corrodes, the love that ruins', whether she has ever 'dipped into the Greek pastoral poets or sampled the Elizabethan sonneteers', she replies, with crushing effect, 'No, never. You will think me lamentably crude: my experience of life has been drawn from life itself.'

But, as the story tells, love in the end has its way with Dorset. Love and Zuleika are fatal to him, to dandyism, and to the whole rarefied atmosphere of Oxford. Clad in his garter robes, he throws himself into the reedy waters of the Isis and drowns. It is the fate that awaits so many of Oxford's sons, who forsake the lovely backwaters and gardens of earth's most beautiful city. We fall in love, and drown the restless, undemocratic and exquisite spirit of Oxford manhood in the waters of matrimony.

But, before we do so, like Dorset, we talk. We cannot hope to rival the Duke in his marriage proposal, which runs a full eight pages in the 1912 edition, almost without interruption from the lady, ending with the never-to-be-forgotten words 'In fine, Miss Dobson, I am a most desirable *parti*'. But we do our best. We talk. At least the under-graduates talked in my day. And so did the Six three nights out of five, without any apparent signs of flagging.

I wish I had a tape-recording of some of those evenings at the House or at New College. But the conversations of nearly forty years ago are beyond recall. The intricate jousting of half a dozen sharp minds cannot be remembered beyond the next day or two. Yet one sentence from those talks is alive in my memory as if it was yesterday, a sentence which (so it seems to me now) was the one which changed the course of my life. We were in Rea's room that night, all six of us. It must have been the late autumn of 1919, near midnight. The talk had been, as it often was, rather on the philosophical side. Herbert had the floor, and was holding forth, perhaps on the usefulness of lawyers to a political party. His argument annoyed me. Suddenly, out of the hidden depths of my mind, unbidden, emerged the question: 'But what's the use of use?' I said it out loud. Herbert lost his temper; to him the remark seemed trivial, and besides it had spoilt the splendid flow of his words. Rea smiled, as if he knew just what I meant. Owen was nearly asleep. But Harrod pounced on it. He silenced Herbert's guns, and held forth at length on the significance of my remark and its implications. I listened in awe as he developed his attack on utilitarian doctrine, on the importance of standards in a world which seemed to have lost them. It was a dazzling performance, and left us all speechless. Soon after we broke up and went to our own rooms. But Harrod had planted a seed in my mind, which was to flower a few months later.

It happened suddenly in the spring of 1920. One morning, as I woke up, I realized that chemistry was not to be my life-work. Science would perhaps change the face of the world, but it would have to do it without my assistance. Words for me, as for the Duke of Dorset, before he sank under the Isis, were the stuff out of which I had to manufacture the fabric of my life. There are no words in chemistry, only symbols and experiments. There are no words in physics, only mathematics and more experiments. But I could not express myself without the use of words, and it was words, my own words, 'what's the use of use?' that had jolted me back into my proper path. It was the words of Harrod, that lucid exponent of doctrine, that had confirmed the significance of what had seemed at the time a chance remark. Chemistry for me, like pacifism, was not enough. It was useful, but what's the use of that? It was respectable. But this bourgeois virtue made small appeal to me. It would provide me with a living. How utterly disgusting! The influence of Oxford had won; it had defeated my dawning common sense and my father's rationalism. Within weeks I was composing indifferent short stories and sketches, two of which appeared in the *Oxford Outlook*. There could be no looking back.

When I looked forward, however, there were frightful problems to solve. My father would have to be informed of my decision, and so would the Dean of Christ Church. I consulted my friends. Delighted that I was to forsake the false gods of science to return to the pursuit of humane studies, they made light of my difficulties. Tell the Dean first, they advised sagely, he's bound to be sympathetic.

When you have his consent, what can your father possibly say? I did as they suggested. The Dean was kindness itself. With an equal interest, in his official capacity, in all the schools which undergraduates are heir to, he was partial to history, theology and Greats. He sanctioned my *volte-face* after a mere half-an-hour's conversation to make sure I knew what I was up to. The talk with my father in London was stormy at times, but its outcome was inevitable. You can take a young man to the laboratory, but you can't make him experiment. In the spring term of 1920 I was studying for a degree in Greats.

Greats, the school of *literae humaniores*, is a course in classics, ancient history and philosophy, the most difficult and the most unworldly that Oxford presents. Now the smells and sounds of a lab., with other students working to left and right of me, gave place to the ivory tower. Alone in my rooms I struggled to read the two dead languages, familiarity with which was obligatory. I spent two months of the Long Vacation of 1920 studying the sentences of the *Odyssey*, rolling tumultuously and inexorably forward like the wine-dark sea that figures so frequently in the narrative. I listened to a course of lectures on *The Republic* of Plato, a set book. I had resembled, so it seemed to me, the unfortunate persons chained immovably in the famous simile of the Cave, staring at the blank wall on which was reflected, in the light of a fire, men and objects passing behind them. I had been observing appearances, mere shadows, not reality. The sun of reality was blazing outside, up the rough path which led out of the cavern, and now at last my feet were on its slippery surface. But I must admit I found the going hard. Plato's views, as expressed in *The Republic*, were beautifully arranged, but what on earth had they to do with the reality which I had experienced in Flanders? The discrepancy seemed to me too great.

On the whole, I much preferred *The Politics of Aristotle*, by a man who had some feeling for empiricism. My study of chemistry had not been altogether in vain; I had at least grasped that truth cannot be discovered by sitting in a chair and contemplating dispassionately the abstractions of philosophy and politics. It is necessary to go out and look for the data, to experience for oneself the rigours and adventures of life in society. I could well understand the sentence of *The Politics*, 'Man is by nature one who lives in cities.' Modern man also lived in cities, bigger if not better than Athens and Sparta and Corinth, from which he had so recently marched out, like the Greeks, to battle. In Thucydides' *History of the Peloponnesian War*, the consequences of war were set out with a clarity that left nothing to be desired. It was easy to see Germany in the role of Sparta, as the wicked nation in this deadly clash, and France and England as Athens, with whom my sympathies emphatically lay. My mind, in those days, loved to see the world in terms of good or evil, and the clash between them. It led me into inconceivable stupidities later on, but at least it inoculated me against the deadly virus of indifferentism. To me there was not right on both sides; to me it was not six of the one and half a dozen of the other. I did not believe that there were mysterious and inexorable forces in the world which forced whole peoples to behave badly, and that one should try sympathetically to understand what made such people so nasty. In fact, then as now, I was a partisan, and if the causes which I supported were often lost ones (as in a son of Oxford is only fitting), at least I never became a neutral, that despicable being whose tendency must always be to side with the big battalions.

With such an attitude of mind, I found my work on the philosophical side doubly difficult. Once a week I had to take to my tutor an essay on some philosophical subject, read it to him, and discuss it. Hour after hour between lectures, tennis in the afternoon with Usher, attendance at the Union where Herbert spoke with effect, evenings with the Six, the theatre, the clubs, the breakfast and lunch parties, I wrestled with the age-old problems of metaphysics, the freedom of the will, the nature of causation, universal and particular, the limits of moral feeling. As I sat in my armchair, staring out at the green beauty of Meadows in summer, or in winter at the dancing flames in the fireplace, my eyes would close, my mouth drop open, my head fall forward on my chest. Half an hour later I would wake up with a start, my mind blank, my essay unwritten.

The fact was that philosophy, at least as it was taught at Oxford, was incomprehensible to me. The subject matter of metaphysics, the abstractions of moral and political philosophy, were, so it seemed to me, unreal. The course in Greats was like a race-course. I was riding a horse over hurdles, but it was not a flesh-and-blood horse, though at first sight it looked like one, nor were the hurdles real brushwood obstacles, though they often tripped me up all the same. I could not believe in the concepts presented to me. I kept turning them this way and that, to discover where their counterparts could be found in the living world of which I had some knowledge. But, since they were not present in that world, I had to attribute to them a reality they did not really enjoy, to take them *as if* they were true, important and universal. Somehow I never quite succeeded. I got a good second, instead of the first my tutor anticipated for me. For months after I came down, my failure depressed me. I would wake up at night, dreaming that I was idling away the hours meant for philosophical exercises. I should have known better. I should have known that you cannot see the universal except in the particular, that there is no justice without a good man doing a righteous deed, that there is no perfect society, with or without the help of Plato and Aristotle, in a world inhabited by imperfect, untidy, miserable and passionate individuals. Greats is (or was) for abstract philosophers. I struggled helplessly to fill out the abstractions, but I had neither the intellectual power nor the extensive experience to bring so prodigious a feat within my feeble grasp.

After two years in my rooms, the time had come to leave college and lodge outside. With Herbert and Harrod to share them, I found rooms in the High over a saddler's shop, almost opposite the dread Examination Schools. In those days there was not much traffic in the High. Much of the Duke of Dorset's Oxford survived for a few years after 1918, as long perhaps as the memories of pre-1914 England lived on in the minds of the undergraduates. But as the great Edwardian leisure and peace was shattered by war and the rise of the Labour Party, so the tranquillity of Oxford was destroyed by the internal combustion engine. When the products of Lord Nuffield's great factory began to pass in ever increasing numbers up the High, the past was dead. Within a year of my graduation, my quiet rooms in the High became intolerable to those whose hearing was normal.

My last year at Oxford was not as enjoyable as the first or the second. It was not only the growing din of motor-cars outside my rooms; there was also the sound of all the chickens coming home to roost. The week of the final examinations was drawing near with its awful test.

Women and the probability of marriage slowly loosened the artificial brotherhood of the Six. It was, I think, Rea who started the rot by falling in love with a lively Scottish girl. Now he had dreams to dream which had little to do with academic work and his masculine friends of yesterday. Herbert next, with his thoughts energetically turning towards a career at the Bar, had become engaged to Rea's beautiful sister, Isabella. He too had less time to spare for the graceful exercise of polite conversation. As for myself, I became engaged to a friend of my sister's, and found it hard to combine the urgencies of courtship with the Greco-Roman complexity of my studies. Only Owen and Usher remained heart-free, but leaning more heavily to the theological preoccupations on which they were to build their lives. And, of course, Harrod, who stayed on one year later. With ease his powerful mind was to add a first in Greats to his first in History. To him, then, the academic world, it seemed, was the world that mattered. He alone among us adorned it, and it in return took him to its bosom. He was to become a student at Christ Church, and a lecturer in economics. He is there still, though he has been married for many years, an active embodiment of the strength, and the weakness, of the spirit of Oxford.

What does Oxford mean to me looking back over this great stretch of time? First, the talk, the million million words of which I have remembered only a simple sentence— what's the use of use? Second, the 101 strokes of Great Tom tolling at five past nine every evening, a mournful reminder of the eternity that we mortals do not enjoy. Third, the white mists of winter rising ghostlike from the Meadows outside my window, lulling the active mind of youth into a temporary tranquillity. It is the Oxford climate which veils the gleaming temptations of the outer world from the little world of Oxford, so that they may be analysed with amusement and rejected without contempt.

But above all Oxford for me is the great Hall of Christ Church at dinner time. Up the stone staircase from Tom Quad under the loveliest fan-vaulting in England into the huge rectangular chamber I walked at seven-thirty every evening. Ahead the High Table at which the Dean and the students dine, and a little below it the three long tables stretching down, was it 100 feet, to the door. Here on most nights with hundreds of my fellow undergraduates I would sit down to the evening meal. The benches were hard and the food of merely average quality. From the walls the portraits of scores of distinguished men stared gravely down at the newest generation of their successors. Henry VIII, by an unknown painter in the tradition of Holbein, had naturally pride of place over the centre of the High Table. Here also were the features of John Locke by Kneller, John Wesley by Romney, Archbishops Reynolds and Markham by Sir Joshua, Thomas Lawrence's Canning, Millais's Gladstone, Herkomer's Lewis Carroll, and the rest, a goodly company, statesman and priest, soldier and merchant adventurer, judge and scholar. On each side of me sat my contemporaries, a friend, an acquaintance, perhaps, a man I barely knew. We talked of sport and politics, schools and the future, the fabric of our world. Talked, as they were talking in nearly two score halls in various parts of Oxford, joking, laughing, talking ourselves into manhood, into the future, into the unknowable world that confronted us outside.

4 Blundering into Publishing

WHEN I CAME DOWN from Oxford I was fit for practically nothing or, perhaps more accurately, for nothing practical. The war had toughened my body and given me self-assurance. I knew how to order subordinates around, but now it seemed inevitable that I was to be the subordinate. The revolver I had taken from a dead German and kept hidden under my shirts—since I had no licence for it—appeared to me a symbol of my manhood. But it takes more than a pistol to make a man of a man. Oxford had certainly developed my mind, which was now polished and sceptical, at least on the surface. It had taught me how to pass examinations with honours, but an ability rather different from this is a prerequisite for a worldly career. 'That College aroma which the most heroic efforts of a lifetime often fail to dissipate,' as Norman Douglas says in *An Almanac*, undoubtedly hung around me, and it took ten years and a second marriage to rid myself of it. At heart I was shy and painfully introspective, awkward with women and incapable of carrying on a light-hearted conversation with a new acquaintance. My manner, I'm afraid, was supercilious, my smile mocking, my laughter

forced. I was supremely fitted not to get married, yet that
was what I intended to do. Before doing so, however, it was
necessary to find a job. A girl's parents look awkwardly
at a suitor who hasn't got one, unless he has a sizeable
unearned income by way of substitute. My future in-laws
were no exception.

In the cluttered sitting-room of No. 21 I discussed the
matter many times with my father and mother. My mother
was unhelpful and optimistic; it seemed to her a foregone
conclusion that her son could start a career in any walk
of life through which he chose to promenade.

'What do you *want* to be, darling?' was the theme of her
conversation. My father, of course, took a more down-to-
earth line, though his suggestions were not very practical
and were marred for me by his constant harping on my
folly in having abandoned science. My grandmother was
called in for advice, and an uncle or two. On balance the
family urged me to go in for banking, to train in New
York or Hamburg in the Warburg strongholds of wealth
and become a man of money. My grandmother's protests
that my health would not stand the strain of so arduous
a career were over-ruled, on the grounds that my life at the
front proved that I had a toughness of fibre that the previous
generation had unfortunately been unable to acquire.

To me, however, a career in banking seemed ridiculous.
It was true that I had little or no conception of what it
would be like, but I was convinced that it was unsuited
to the philosopher I foolishly imagined myself to be. My
thoughts rose like a helicopter above such a mundane
affair. The great Felix Warburg, the original Kuhn Loeb
partner in New York, had referred in his will to the fatal
tendency to *drift* that he noticed among the younger
generation. He meant, of course, the drift away from the
solid reality of the accumulation of wealth. He was not

78

concerned in this, his final utterance, with the London branch of the family, though his words had a particular relevance for them. Drifters to a man, the London Warburgs of my generation have made their marks anywhere but in the field of banking. As the eldest son of the eldest son, I was the first to go astray and so set an awful example to those who came after me.

But whither was I to drift? Though I had a strong aversion to banking, I hadn't any alternative in mind. A vague urge to become a doctor, even perhaps a surgeon, vanished on reflection. To me, who had endured so many illnesses as a child, the ailments of others made too personal an appeal. There was, of course, the law, into which Basil Herbert was plunging. But the gift of oratory, despite my excellent translation of Quintilian, had been denied me; I had not even dared to make a maiden speech at the Oxford Union. The rosy uplands of the post-war world of 1922 stretched deceptively ahead as I pondered which enticing eminence to climb. But I made little progress; all prospects pleased, but none decisively. A job, however, I had to find, and soon. The pressure was becoming too strong.

Fate—for there can be no doubt that fate was at work— came to my rescue swiftly and from an unexpected quarter, my sister's husband, A. L. Schlesinger. He and I were far from intimate, but I admired him for a quality which I knew myself to lack, the know-how about money. I was capable of living with ease on any income amply sufficient for my requirements. No spendthrift I, perhaps even a little on the mean side. But if you had asked me then how to provide myself with an income, or how to increase an income which was insufficient, I should have been without an idea in my head. This valuable knowledge, whose practicality I shrank from, was possessed by my brother-in-law in full measure.

79

At this time Schlesinger was working in the publishing house of George Routledge & Sons Ltd. He was a few years older than me, and his job was a minor one with prospects. But he didn't enjoy it. It was not only that his interest in books was slight or even non-existent; there was, I am certain, a more fundamental reason for his desire to get the hell out. He knew unerringly that no one but a fool went into publishing to make real money. In his view there could only be two reasons for becoming or remaining a publisher, that you were dotty about books or that you couldn't find a better job anywhere else. There can be little question that he reckoned me an ideal publisher on both counts.

For reasons obscure to me, Schlesinger deemed it unethical to leave his job without providing a substitute. Perhaps it was because he was related to the owners, the Franklin family, and felt that his position had other than a commercial significance. Possibly he was genuinely anxious to find me a place in life which I could fill without making a fool of myself. 'It will suit you down to the ground,' he told me, 'books, books, books, all day long. And those blasted authors always wanting something you can't give them. You'd better go and see old Stallybrass.'

Schlesinger's definition of publishing has not yet attained the widespread currency of Professor Parkinson's laws, yet it is not without its merits. Partial admittedly, crude perhaps, but there is many a publisher today in Henrietta Street or Holborn, on Madison Avenue or Boston Common, who would say that it has the ring of truth about it. Not myself, I hasten to add, not by any manner of means; none of my authors are blasted.

Unperturbed by his remark, if without undue enthusiasm, I agreed to allow myself to be interviewed by the manage-

80

ment, and an appointment was made for me to see 'old Stallybrass', the senior Managing Director.

William Swan Stallybrass—Mr. Stallybrass as he was and will always be to me—was born in 1855 and died at the age of seventy-five in 1931. Intended for the medical profession, he had begun his studies, only to find that 'the operating theatre and dissecting-room proved more than his sensitive nature could endure'.[1] He soon became a publisher, and during the long span of his life must have done as much as any man of his time for the advancement of reading, the enhancement of scholarship and the practice of bibliography. Of medium height, with iron-grey hair over a high and broad forehead, he had a face with strong features, as if chiselled from stone. A nervous mouth, surmounted by a bushy moustache, revealed a diffidence which perhaps prevented him from reaching the eminence his talents deserved. His eyes, large and dark-brown, had a look of fanaticism. And indeed a fanatic he was, a fanatic for work.

First to arrive at the office at 9 a.m., last to leave at 5.30 p.m., he took home with him in a large case the bulky manuscripts on which he would labour that evening. A product of the Victorian age, work was his pleasure and enlightenment his gospel. He set me an example which I shall never forget, though I cannot hope to equal it. Happily married to a wife who shared his tastes, with an unmarried daughter living at home, he pursued the work of publishing and his own literary work after hours in his residence in Linden Gardens, Bayswater, with the help of

[1] This quotation and other details of the career of W. S. Stallybrass, before I knew him, are taken from an interesting monograph, *From Swan Sonnenschein to George Allen & Unwin Ltd.*, published by the latter firm. It is written by F. A. Mumby, the great historian of the book trade, and Frances Stallybrass, his daughter. William Swan Stallybrass changed his name in 1917 from William Swan Sonnenschein. Stallybrass was his mother's name. His father came from Moravia, Austria, in 1848, and was in due course naturalized.

these two devoted women. His son, the late Dr. W. T. S. Stallybrass, became the Principal of Brasenose College and Vice-Chancellor of Oxford University.

Little did I know of all this when I paid my call on Mr. Stallybrass at his home one Saturday morning. To me he was simply an elderly gentleman who 'ran Routledge's' and might offer me a job. With this job I could get married and live happily ever afterwards. The job was in publishing, but I had no idea what publishing was or what publishers did. My classical education and the study of Aristotle had convinced me that 'the well-educated man' could deal effectively with any problems presented to him. I had no doubts about my ability to be a publisher. Smug and intellectually arrogant, I presented myself and found that I had encountered a master of his craft. It is to my credit that I recognized this immediately and behaved myself with reasonable humility. Had I not done so, I should never have entered the world of publishing, to pursue a career which has absorbed me.

I cannot now remember what I said to Mr. Stallybrass that Saturday morning or what he said to me. Perhaps he talked of his early days as an apprentice in Henrietta Street with Williams & Norgate, publishers and book importers. Perhaps he told me about the foundation of his own firm, Swan Sonnenschein, long, long ago in 1878. Maybe we discussed contemporary European thought and scholarship, and the masterpieces of German literature which he knew so well. Perhaps he said a word or two about the science of bibliography and his experiences as a second-hand bookseller; certainly it was said of him that he 'became so expert that he could always cover his holiday expenses in those early days, if he wished, by the bargains he picked up in the local bookshops'.[1] I cannot

[1] From *Swan Sonnenschein,* page 15.

remember, and it does not matter. What matters is that Mr. Stallybrass must have seen in me some sense or sensibility that he could kindle into a flame; must have believed that this ex-second lieutenant, this ex-undergraduate of Christ Church, Oxford, this ex-simpleton had it in him to serve as a link in the great chain of publishing, handing on the experience and knowledge I was to absorb from him to a newer generation. At least I have attempted to do so.

When I left Linden Gardens, the job was mine. I had blundered into publishing through the casual proposal of a brother-in-law and the sympathetic understanding of a man old enough to be my grandfather. It was a lucky stroke, and not the last lucky stroke in my life. Without my luck, I should undoubtedly be today bankrupt, in prison, a failure, and unhappy, or, if it were possible, all four simultaneously.

It was as a married man, occupying with my wife a small house in Chepstow Villas, Bayswater, that I started out to become a publisher. Every morning I left the house at 8.30 a.m. to reach my office in a narrow street, Carter Lane, E.C.4, one minute's walk from St. Paul's. Routledge in the early nineteen-twenties was an old-fashioned firm, highly respected and of substantial size. The building inside was large and rambling. On the ground-floor was the trade counter, to which aged men carrying huge sacks came from the various London bookshops to obtain the books ordered by customers which were not in stock. These men were known as collectors. They had long lists of their requirements, which they read out in a monotonous voice in a system of pronunciation as mysterious as Tibetan. Tolstoy's well-known novel, for instance, became 'Annie Carrie Nina'. Often they could not read their own writing, and long confabulations would take place between them and the manager. The atmosphere round the counter was relaxed, no one hurried, excellent dirty stories were told, the gossip of the trade was exchanged. Here you could obtain a worm's eye view of the London book trade. One thing only was unpopular, the best-seller; it made their sacks uncomfortably heavy. This splendidly old-fashioned system is still, I believe, in vogue, and must add a good deal of expense to the overheads.

At the back of the trade counter were the invoicing, export and packing departments. Here books were sent out in all kinds of quantities, up to the big shipments in wooden packing-cases, specially manufactured, of thousands of copies to New York. A steep staircase led to the first floor, where all the main offices were located. Here clerks sat on high stools at sloping counters working on the various ledgers, like characters in a Dickens's novel. Above, two huge floors were racked up to the ceiling to carry the vast stocks of books over the whole range of the firm's catalogue. Telephones were few and far between; one had the impression that they had been installed with reluctance. Mr. Stallybrass certainly disliked them as a new-fangled horror, and shouted down the mouthpiece when conversing as if afraid of them. Typewriters too were in vogue, though I doubt whether there were more than two typists when I arrived on the scene. I sensed that the copying of letters by hand was a recent memory, and the use of blotting paper in lieu of sand a new custom grudgingly adopted.

Mr. Stallybrass's agreement to my joining the firm as an apprentice was embodied in an ancient form of indenture, entirely appropriate to the surroundings I have described. This was my passport to publishing, possibly the last ever to be signed by a still active publisher. This remarkable document, written on parchment, is worth attention. It reads (in part) as follows:

'Witnesseth that the Apprentice of his own free will put and bind himself Apprentice to the Master to learn the Trade of Publisher, and with him after the manner of an Apprentice to serve for the term of two years . . . during which term the Apprentice his Master faithfully shall serve, his secrets keep, and his lawful commands obey; He shall do no damage to his Master or to his Goods or Premises, nor suffer such to be done by others, and shall forthwith give notice to his Master of the same if necessary; He shall not waste the Goods of his Master nor lend them unlawfully to any person, nor do any act whereby his Master may sustain any loss; and shall not without the consent of his Master buy or sell during his Apprenticeship, nor absent himself from his Master's service unlawfully; but in all things as a faithful Apprentice shall behave himself towards his Master and those having authority over him during the said term.'

I cannot believe that, even in the earliest weeks of 'the said term', I regarded these solemn words, these onerous and exacting duties, with the respect due to them. Probably I kept my Master's secrets, since I knew hardly anyone to whom they would have been of the slightest interest. Certainly I obeyed his lawful commands, since they were given in a firm and conversational tone, and I had no wish to be fired. Nor did I damage his goods and premises; arson has always been foreign to my nature, and the defacing of books hardly worth the trouble. But I did 'buy or sell' during my apprenticeship, though whether unlawfully or not I'm uncertain, since I don't know precisely what the words imply.

85

In consideration of all this 'and of the sum of two hundred and fifty pounds sterling', the indenture continued, 'the Master shall receive the Apprentice . . . and by the best means in his power shall teach and instruct him in all the branches of his Trade and in all things relating thereto.' At this point the indenture made some small concessions to modernity by striking out the words 'finding the Apprentice sufficient Meat, Drink, Lodging and all other proper necessaries during the said term'.

It is easy to laugh at the long-winded and legalistic sentences of an out-of-date document. Yet there is a simple straightforward sincerity in the words which today I find admirable. Out of his ripe experience and in the goodness of his heart the Master will pass on to the young Apprentice the fruits of his wisdom. True that there is the little matter of 'a consideration', but the Master, we may suppose, has spent a lifetime in learning and adapting and perfecting his trade. It has cost him dear in hard cash, it may have affected his health and strength. What's a few hundred pounds, even worth what it was in those good old days, in exchange for something impalpable and unique. I do not grudge the money paid over, especially since it was my father who paid it, for my Master was one of the best Masters an unruly and conceited Apprentice could desire. To him I owe a debt I can never repay, though I have become fully aware of it only in the last few years. Had I neglected the majority of his precepts, I should have been out of business long ago. Had I followed others, the results might have been somewhat unsatisfactory, for Mr. Stallybrass was not sympathetic to all branches of literature, at least when I knew him. His attitude to novels and *belles-lettres* was less than enthusiastic; he hated literary agents; he regarded an advance in excess of £25 as positively damaging to an author's morale.

My first tasks at Routledge were of a trivial nature. I wrote addresses into a card-index of people who wanted to receive our catalogues. I pasted reviews for reference on to large sheets of cardboard. I copied the names of authors and the titles of their books into gigantic stock sheets with many ruled columns. I fiddled about in the production department with specimen pages and devoted hours to the designing of a title-page. I discussed binding brasses and examined the manifold colours and makes of cloth for binding. One department saw me rarely as a visitor in those early days, the finance department with a sardonic company secretary who disliked me. Perhaps I was discouraged by Mr. Stallybrass from entering this holy of holies, and my ambivalent attitude to the money side of publishing may date from this period.

My desk was in the large board-room, occupied by the two managing directors. Mr. Stallybrass exercised his power from the S.E. corner; Cecil Franklin, son of the company's chairman, exercised his from the N.W. My own humble duties were performed in the S.W. corner. What occupied the N.E. corner I can't for the life of me remember, but a huge table filled the centre of the room, usually littered with books, ledgers and manuscripts. The decor was dingy, hideous, and to me immensely impressive.

The room gave off a busy hum of activity. To my left Franklin would carry on long and largely incomprehensible conversations on the telephone with printers, binders, papermakers, travellers, the bank, booksellers, carriers and heaven knows who else. In front and facing me sat Mr. Stallybrass, his desk usually piled high with manuscripts on which he was working. From my earliest days, right through my apprenticeship and on till 1931, one book dominated all others, the great work written and compiled by Mr. Stallybrass himself. This work, which was his life work and which was ultimately to kill him, was known as William Swan Sonnenschein's *The Best Books:* a contribution towards a Systematic Bibliography; a Reader's Guide to the Choice of the best Available Books in every department of Science, Art and Literature, with Dates of First and Last Editions, and the Price, Size and Publisher's Name (both English and American). Published in quarto, and bound in boards, it consisted eventually of six vast volumes, dealing with (1) Theology and Philosophy; (2) Society, Geography and Travel; (3) History and Biography; (4) Science and Art; (5) Literature and Mythology; (6) Index. This gives only a much abbreviated list of its contents.

The mind boggles at the almost superhuman labour required for such a project. Probably, when it was begun, it was one manageable if enormous tome. But, as authors wrote and publishers published new and excellent books all over the world, Mr. Stallybrass's bibliography got out of date, had to be revised, enlarged, and finally republished. It was rather like the labour of the Augean Stable, which gave Hercules so much trouble, but in reverse. The faster Mr. Stallybrass extracted the *best* material from the book stable and incorporated it into his vast bibliography, the faster poured new worth-while books out of the world's presses. It must have been an exhilarating but backbreaking task, and he stuck to it with a single-minded maniacal devotion to the end. Only a man with his iron constitution, obstinacy, and devouring interest in everything that appertained to the workings of the human mind could have continued, while simultaneously managing the complex affairs of a substantial publishing house. The bibliographers and the scholars of the world owe him a debt of gratitude. Without this self-imposed burden, which brought him little financial reward, he could have lived to be a hundred without any trouble at all.

Facing this battlefield, where Mr. Stallybrass wrestled with the Best Books of all time, I received a lesson in industry and concentration which I was never to forget. In those early days I was basically a learner, though within a few months I began to grasp the elements. Soon I was permitted to prepare copy for the limited amount of advertising deemed essential by my Master. But, most important of all in my instruction, was what I heard, as Mr. Stallybrass talked to Mr. Franklin, and each of them talked to their visitors. Sitting mouse-like and apparently absorbed in my work in the S.W. corner of the board-room, I listened eagerly to what went on. Sometimes I was sent from the room when matters of supreme consequence were to be discussed, or during the monthly board meetings. But I returned in due course to resume the endless process of listening, listening, listening. I became a publisher by osmotic absorption, sucking in the wisdom of my elders through the sceptical filter of a mind trained in the metaphysical hair-splitting of an Oxford course in Greats. There is no better method of learning known to me than this, and I have tried to practise it inside my own business on the rising generation. Only the future will show with what success.

Visitors there were in plenty, of the most varied types. Dr. Bronislaw Malinowski, father of the modern school of anthropology, came frequently to discuss the problems of one of his numerous books. He had published his well-known *Argonauts of the Western Pacific* shortly before I joined the firm, and it had established a great reputation. Mr. Stallybrass used to tell me how he had been working at the office one Saturday morning, when Malinowski had rung up and asked him if he could bring round the manuscript of his *Argonauts* for submission. It was his first book. Before he left the office that morning, Mr. Stallybrass had accepted the book for publication and terms had been fixed. Mr. Stallybrass used the incident to impress on me the importance of working on Saturdays. 'You can never tell,' he told me, 'when an author may bring in a really important book. If I had not been at my desk when the 'phone rang, he might have called up another publishing house and we would have lost a most valuable author.' Deeply impressed I realized that the first-class publisher was one who was in the right place at the crucial moment, and capable of making up his mind without flurry or delay. Since those days I have never been backward in accepting instantly manuscripts which I regarded as worth while, often to the amazement and sometimes to the horror of my colleagues.

Another caller in those early days was Prince D. S. Mirsky, who published with Routledge two of the best books on Russian literature ever to appear. Later he was to go back to the U.S.S.R. to give communism a try-out, but matters shaped disastrously for him and his end was tragic. Another Russian writer with whom I was friendly was S. S. Koteliansky, with a quizzically humorous face and short black curly hair over a skull-like cranium. A friend of Katherine Mansfield, and many of the leading literary figures of the day, he was one of the few authors who ever expressed his doubts about the commercial success of his books. When I told him one day that we should be delighted to publish his edition of *The Letters of Tchehov*, or whatever it was, he said with charming candour in his Russian-accented English: 'But, Warburg, such a book cannot pay you know; it will stay in your stock-room and lose much money.' It was he, too, who told me that

I looked much too young to be a publisher and talk to persons like himself. 'You should grow a beard like mine,' he said. 'It will make you look five years older, and then the authors will think they are dealing with a most important executive.' For many months afterwards I worried about my youthful appearance, but I never grew a beard— I had hated my father's too much.

Among English authors who came was Dr. Hugh Dalton, then a lecturer at the London School of Economics, and author of a best-selling textbook, *Principles of Public Finance*. We did not know then that he was to become Chancellor of the Exchequer and put his principles into practice. There was the eccentric Montague Summers, whose *History of Witchcraft*, torn to pieces by the reviewers, had a big sale none the less, since books sell, not because they are well reviewed, but because readers are interested in their subjects. There was the venerable and gallant H. W. Nevinson, with red face and snow-white hair, whose exposure of the Belgian Congo atrocities many years before had made him world famous. With Routledge he published *Rough Islanders*, one of the best books about England ever written, which analysed with a fine irony the snobbish element in the English character. Another expert on England's past and present, who published with Routledge, was Esmé Wingfield-Stratford. His enormous book, *The History of British Civilization*, was said to be the first Tory study of British history to be made for half a century. Not long after its first issue, it was re-issued in one volume of 1,352 pages, measuring nine by six-and-a-half inches, at a price of fifteen shillings! There were certainly bargains to be bought in those days!

Among all the personalities who came to Carter Lane the most frequent visitor was C. K. Ogden, valued by many as the last of a long line of English eccentrics. In my first years, rarely a week passed without a call from him. The high domed forehead, the deep-set serious eyes behind their spectacles, the thin mouth, the prominent chin, gave him a slightly vinegary look, and he could be sharp and tetchy when annoyed, which was not unusual since his relations with my Master were somewhat up-and-down.

How he met Mr. Stallybrass in the first place was never revealed to me by either of them. But I suspect that it was Ogden who approached the firm a year or two after World War I. His base of operations then was Cambridge, where he owned and ran the Cambridge Bookshop. Here during the war as a pacifist he had issued a weekly news-letter, giving little-known scraps of information on foreign policy and war news calculated to infuriate the ultra-patriotic. But with the war over, he sought fresh fields for his energies and found it in publishing. Before I arrived on the scene he had already been appointed editor of the great International Library of Psychology, Philosophy and Scientific Method, published by Kegan Paul, Trench, Trubner & Co., the twin imprint of Routledge and in effect inseparable from it.

Ogden was not merely eccentric, he was hard-working, learned, witty and highly mysterious. I never heard from him of a father or a mother, though he was only in his early thirties when I first knew him, and his parents could well have been alive. He gave the curious impression of having been a man in his early thirties all his life, nor did he appear to age at all during the fourteen years of our acquaintance. His activity was immense, and his range of friends prodigious.

It is said by some that Ogden had no private income, and surprise has been expressed that he was able to maintain himself with ease and some magnificence in the 'twenties and 'thirties. It is true that he made contributions to philosophical journals, though not under his pen-name 'Adeline Moore', but these naturally produced no money. Kingsley Martin, editor of the *New Statesman*, has suggested that Ogden's expensive wardrobe was the gift of an American millionaire in reward for philosophical instruction, and this might be true, though personally I doubt it. Certainly Ogden made money by supplying American libraries with rare books, which he picked up for a song on the market stalls of Cambridge. But, to the best of my belief, it was the need for an income which turned Ogden's attention to the world of publishing, to Kegan Paul and to my Master.

The value of Ogden to Kegan Paul was immense. He put them among the most important publishers of the day in the wide fields of psychology, theoretical and practical, philosophy, ethics, psychopathology, educational theory, and scientific method. He persuaded with ease and celerity most of the greatest academic minds of the period to contribute to his library. The first volume of the series was a reprint of the famous but unobtainable *Philosophical Studies* of G. E. Moore. Soon came the epoch-making work of Ludwig Wittgenstein, *Tractatus Logico-Philosophicus*, surely one of the most forbidding titles ever to be bestowed even on a metaphysical book. Another early volume was Ogden's own book, *The Meaning of Meaning*, written in association with I. A. Richards, a pioneer study in semantics. In due course, volumes by Bertrand Russell and C. D. Broad, C. G. Jung and Alfred Adler, Sir Richard Paget and Jean Piaget, and a score of others appeared. Volumes by Professor W. Koehler and Solly Zuckerman on the mental and social processes of apes were not the least successful contributions to an enormously varied series. Between 1921 and 1934 no less than 114 titles

93

appeared in the International Library, a tremendous publishing achievement for those or any other days. My share in this venture was a minor one, but it taught me once and for all the advantages and the drawbacks of academic publishing, and the need for patience before any return could be anticipated on the money invested.

Such was Ogden's contribution to the prestige and prosperity of Kegan Paul. But in return he exacted a price, a small over-riding royalty, in addition to the author's, on every copy sold of every book introduced by him to the firm. As the years passed, the amount earned by him in this way mounted, and the Ogden commission account, as we called it, reached quite a substantial figure by the second half of the nineteen-twenties. This perhaps consti- tuted at least in part the missing income which has puzzled so many. The mystery which Ogden spread over all his affairs probably covered the commission account as well. He was not the man to reveal the workaday facts of his publishing activity; indeed, he may have felt that to do so would injure his standing with the authors he introduced. Later, he invented Basic English, which boiled down the infinite complexities of the English language to 850 simple words which did not fit together very well in speech, though they could all be printed, if I remember correctly, on a postcard. He became in the 'thirties a British institution, with a large house in Bloomsbury crammed with his collections of books, clocks, masks and music boxes. Here he turned night into day and day into night, practising the art of which he was a master, that of a latter-day magician. With his death in 1957 something unique and unrepeatable was removed from English life, and even I who had long lost touch with him mourned his passing.

So continued around me the slow processes of growth of a firm which, under the redoubtable Mr. Stallybrass, ranked high among its competitors. But, young and ambitious, I sought for books and authors of my own, books which I hoped would sell much faster and in much greater numbers than the *International Library* or the almost equally important *History of Civilization Series*. One day, looking at the pile of manuscripts submitted for our consideration, I spotted one written in a beautiful, sloping spidery longhand, a translation into lively English verse of the complete love poems of the Palatine Anthology. It was called the *Girdle of Aphrodite*, and contained a long introduction on love in Greek literature, and the problem of translation of Greek and Latin classics into English. The translator was F. A. Wright, of the Classical Department of Birkbeck College, later to become Professor.

This collection fascinated me. The poets of the anthology may not be major artists, and their verse can often be regarded as merely erotic. But in the original Greek the words sparkle like diamonds, and in Wright's translation the effect was most pleasing. He used as his models the kind of poetry written in England between 1550 and 1650, before the Puritan blight withered the budding shoots of English literature. Here was the voice of ancient Greece reheard in the English accent of Jonson and Donne, Waller and Lovelace, and above all Robert Herrick.

As I read on, filled with a growing excitement, I felt certain that I had discovered a book worth publishing. I was in fact experiencing for the first time the symptoms of what is usually referred to, sometimes contemptuously, as a 'publisher's hunch'. The symptoms of those suffering from this occupational disease are easy to recognize. The breathing grows faster, the cheeks are slightly flushed, there is tension in the pit of the stomach and an urge at all costs to do something sensational on behalf of the manuscript you are reading. Since those early days I have experienced the feeling many times—for instance, with certain chapters of Lewis Mumford's *The Culture of Cities*, with George Orwell's *1984*, with Angus Wilson's first collection of short stories, *The Wrong Set*, with Alberto Moravia's *Two Women*, and a score of other books. Often, as is well known, at least to publishers and publishers' readers, the feeling of enthusiasm is misplaced. The manuscript that has aroused it is neither a masterpiece, nor a big seller, and in due course the publisher discovers this, often after publication and to his great financial loss. Nevertheless, a publisher's hunch is to me the keynote of publishing, whether it is regarded as the forerunner of success or an occupational hazard. Now, in the first months of my apprenticeship, I was having my maiden experience, and an exquisite one it was, comparable to a first sight of the Parthenon, or the gasp of admiration sometimes heard in the theatre when the curtain goes up on an exquisite *mise-en-scène*.

When I had finished reading the manuscript, I got up and carried it across to Mr. Stallybrass. I stood there waiting while he finished some intricate work of his own.

'What have you got there?' he asked, at last.

'Something worth publishing, I'm sure it is,' I stammered nervously, 'A verse translation of the Greek Anthology.'

'Warburg, you shock me,' my revered Master said, severely, 'we'll never make a publisher of you if you believe we can sell verse translations from the Greek, and dirty ones at that, if I remember the Anthology with exactitude. Let me have a look at it.'

Mr. Stallybrass took the foolscap sheets from me, and idly turned the pages. I no longer remember which poems he read, perhaps it was:

Automedon's The Jewel of Asia

"There's a girl just come to town,
    Not a week ago;
Every trick in love that's known
    To you she will show;
Every mood of wantonness
    In the dance she can confess
        Swaying to and fro,
Passion in her finger tips
Pliant arms and bending hips.

Better still she does not scorn
    With disdainful head
Suitors just a trifle worn
    Given up for dead;
Flattering caresses tries
Till they from the tomb arise
    Back to vigour led;
And returned to life once more
Voyage to Cythera's shore.[1]

Perhaps it fell on a poem of Meleager or Rufinus or Antipater of Thessalonica. Who knows, and today who cares? Nor did I care then, for I could sense that Mr. Stallybrass was impressed, and had no intention of telling me that I had wasted his time.

A week or two later Mr. Stallybrass informed me that *The Girdle of Aphrodite* was certainly a possible book. 'We'll publish it,' he said, 'if you feel really enthusiastic about it. It's the first book you've found for yourself and recommended for publication. It will give you confidence

---

[1] My thanks are due to Routledge & Kegan Paul Ltd. for permission to quote this naughty poem.

in your own judgement, and it is a book you need never feel ashamed of having picked. All the same,' he added sadly, 'it can't possibly sell. As an isolated book it has a poor chance of success. Put with other classical translations it might do quite well.'

I was overjoyed. To have found a book worth publishing, to have picked it out of the quantities of rubbish that pour into every publishing house, and so soon after I had joined the firm, stimulated me to further efforts. I had no intention of allowing *my* book, my ewe lamb, my first-born, as it were, to perish miserably for lack of companionship. Feverishly I set my mind to work, at first without success. Then, in a blinding revelation, the great idea came to me, my first publishing inspiration, the one that marked me out—though naturally I did not realize it then—as at least of the stuff of which publishers are made.

Not long before I had started my apprenticeship, Routledge had issued a racy English translation of *The Satyricon* of Petronius by J. M. Mitchell who was, I believe, at the time the librarian of the Carnegie Institute in Edinburgh. The book had been well received and sold a thousand or two copies. Mr. Stallybrass had insisted on the deletion of the most indecent passages, of which there were quite a few, and this may have harmed its sales. But now the idea came to me to re-issue it with *The Girdle of Aphrodite* in a uniform style, to find or commission other translations, and not only from Latin and Greek, but from French, Italian, Spanish, yes and Russian too, and to edit a series of books which would now perhaps be described as 'off-beat', and so bring off a publishing coup of no mean order. I took the idea to Mr. Stallybrass and, behold, he said it was very good. I asked him might we not call it the *Broadway Translations*, from the name of the Routledge building—Broadway House. And so it was. And that evening and that morning were the sixth day of my delight, and all the hosts of the translations began flooding into my mind. Such was the genesis of the series, and I felt god-like.

I set to work eagerly. I rushed to Shakespeare, as publishers so often do in moments of excitement, for a motto to be set on every half-title page: 'Age cannot wither her, nor custom stale her infinite variety.' This was to be my tribute to literature. There was to be a title-page in two colours, the second colour to vary with the language from which it was translated, blue for Greek, green for Latin, maroon for French. The binding case was to be of an imitation cream vellum, with a coloured leather label bearing the name of the author and his book, also the name of his translator.[1] The end papers were marbled. The shorter volumes were published at 7s. 6d. and ran to about 360 crown 8vo pages; the longer ones ran to between 500 and 600 demy 8vo pages, and were 12s. 6d. Today these prices would be at least three times as high.

Immense discussions took place between Mr. Stallybrass and myself about what should be included in the series, who should translate, who edit them. Mr. Stallybrass treated me throughout as an equal who needed a little advice perhaps, but who was in definite control of the affair. His immense resources of knowledge about what had already been done, coupled to my enthusiasm, got the series going without more than a few months' delay. My confidence grew, my head swelled a trifle. At last I was truly a publisher. Orders originating with me were being carried out; translators and editors were being commissioned to do work because I had had an idea; money was being spent on printing, binding, paper, blocks, all the minutiae

---

[1] In recognition of the importance and difficulty of the art of translation, it is only decent to print prominently on the title-page, or the page facing it, the name of the translator—at least when the translation is a good one.

of book production, to satisfy my whim. It was marvellous and it made me. After that there could be no looking back.

There was, however, a spot of bother over Petronius. My Master wished the translation of *The Satyricon* to appear in the original expurgated version; his apprentice wanted it all in English. The struggle continued for days, while I put forward the arguments that have been batted to and fro so often since then. An author's work, especially when it is a recognized classic, should appear precisely as he has written it, not a word put in, not a syllable left out. Anyone who was shocked by strong language was a vulgarian, and anyhow the shockable could give the book a wide berth. What was good enough for the Romans was good enough for the British. Had I not recently fought in a war for human freedom? But Mr. Stallybrass, enlightened though he was in so many fields, had something of a blind eye on this issue. Besides, his knowledge of publishing history was extensive, and he knew, though I did not, the menace that lurked in the office of the Director of Public Prosecutions. The battle was drawn in his favour; all the 'objectionable' passages appeared, but they were in Latin! So early was it in my career as a publisher that I approached the subject of obscene litera-ture, but my finest performance in this field was not to be seen till 1954, when I starred in the role of criminal at the Old Bailey with a fine supporting cast and was acquitted.

After *The Satyricon* and *The Girdle* new titles appeared regularly in the Broadway Translations. Richard Aldington, then a young literary man, did several for us, probably his first paid work in the world of letters and for that reason of considerable importance to him. He translated *Candide* and other short stories of Voltaire; the little known *Voyages to the Sun and Moon* of Cyrano de Bergerac; Marivaux's *Game of Love and Chance* with three more

100

eighteenth-century French comedies; and perhaps most interesting of all, Choderlos de Laclos' cynical study of the game of love, *Les Liaisons Dangereuses* (Dangerous Acquaintances). He also edited, and in part translated *A Book of Characters* from Theophrastus through Overbury to La Bruyère. But it was F. A. Wright, my original discovery, who displayed an unequalled rage to translate— in Latin, Ovid (twice) Plautus, Catullus and Martial; in Greek the Anthology (twice), Alciphron, and Heliodorus— in all, no less than nine beautifully edited books came from his work-desk in some five years, a remarkable record.

The Heliodorus was a revised and corrected version of Thomas Underdowne's richly coloured translation (1587) of *An Ethiopian Romance*. It was dedicated to me in the following words: 'There are those perchance who will think but lightly of these imaginings: yet some folk deem a blood-red rose, or a lark's song, to be more precious than a king's coronet.' Long and proudly I puzzled over the source of this quotation, but it eluded me. Finally I felt obliged to reveal my ignorance and ask Wright where it had come from. 'Out of my head,' he replied.

Forty-eight titles in all were issued in the Broadway Translations. Mr. Stallybrass himself entered the lists, and gallantly edited Esquemeling's little-known work *The Buccaneers of America*, 'containing the excessively rare fourth part, with facsimiles of all the original engravings, maps etc.' I have never been sure precisely what the word 'etc.' designated, but the full phrase on the title-page had an alluring sound to it. Mr. Stallybrass also made himself responsible later on for the modernization and editing of *Reynard the Fox* in the 1481 version as printed by William Caxton. Indeed, it became clear to me that Mr. Stallybrass was far happier when engaged in the profession of scholarship than in the trade of publishing.

Only the necessity to earn a worthwhile income held him back from his heart's desire. It was in all probability the scholar hidden within him that prevented him reaching the summit as a publisher. For a publisher of the first rank must concentrate on publishing, and not allow himself to go whoring after false gods.

But in those days such diversion of energy was possible and perhaps permissible. Publishing was still a quiet backwater, and publishers could spend long hours after lunch at the club dozing in the library or playing whist or auction bridge till the late afternoon. We were still gentlemen then, pursuing an occupation fit for gentlemen with minds attuned to the placid march of events of the pre-1914 era. Book jackets were optional and were called dust wrappers, merely because they served to keep the dust off the books, not to fascinate potential readers with dazzling if misleading designs. But only a few years ahead lay the new era of sensation. It was to start in 1928.

The Broadway Translations were well received. The *London Mercury*, under the editorship of J. C. Squire, at that time exercising a powerful literary influence—alas, that he and his magazine are now both dead—wrote: 'Messrs. Routledge are putting us deep in their debt with the Broadway Translations. We wish this series luck. It is really covering fresh ground.' The series had luck and was successful, though perhaps not wildly so. It anticipated the far more elaborate and comprehensive Loeb Library and the more recent Penguin Classics. The Broadway books were lively, unconventional and scholarly. They were *mine*, my first creative effort in publishing and in some ways my best. I was proud of them then, and I remain proud of them now. The wear and tear of events, and the thievish propensities of friends have removed all but nine of them from my shelves. It is high time I went out and picked up

the missing thirty-nine volumes in the second-hand
bookshops.

A budding publisher must learn not only where to
discover books he can publish, but how to sell them when
he has published them. Selling books, other than textbooks,
never has been and probably never will be, an easy task,
for even today in England a laughably small proportion
of the population are book buyers, or even book readers.
But books published in England are sold all over the world,
and not least to the U.S.A. The Routledge and Kegan Paul
business sold many thousands of pounds worth of books
to American publishers. Foremost among these was John
Macrae, head of the large house called E. P. Dutton, from
the name of its founder. The ceremony of selling books
to Macrae took place once a year.

John Macrae was a short sturdy man with keen brown
eyes and a short black spade beard. A native of
Virginia, with a Southern accent, he had risen in the firm
step by step to the top. Macrae was no scholar-publisher,
like my revered Master, but a gambler on the big scale.
Poker player, cigar smoker, a stickler for the etiquette
demanded of a Southern gentleman, he rarely read the
books submitted for his consideration, but merely glanced
at them, touched them, and on occasion smelled them.
Instinct was his guide, and it often failed him. The annual
visit of Macrae to the office gave me an unrivalled opportunity of studying the technique of selling to the vast
U.S. market.

Many hours were spent at Routledge in preparation
for the arrival of this unique and powerful individual, a
close friend and business acquaintance of Mr. Stallybrass
and Cecil Franklin, and in due course myself. First, the
huge boardroom table was cleared of the clutter normally

piled upon it. Next, a list was made of all the books published since his last visit, which had not already been disposed of to America. Great tomes at 30*s.* and 40*s.* a time, little pamphlets at 1*s.* or 6*d.*, illustrated and unillustrated books; books on gardening, metaphysics, sport, travel, mysticism, science, flower arrangement, cookery, history, biography; good books and bad books and mediocre books; recondite and popular books; silly books and wise books; *all* the books were listed, and the list was handed to the stockkeepers upstairs, to be looked out and carried down by the score to the board-room. Here they were piled on the table, waiting for Mr. Macrae's arrival.

In due course, the short dapper figure would be announced and greeted by Mr. Stallybrass, Cecil Franklin, and myself. Mr. Stallybrass and Macrae would sit down side by side at the head of the table, comfortably relaxed, and discuss at length the manifold problems besetting the British and American publishing trades in that year. Always they agreed that 'things were not as good as they used to be', that 'far too many books were being published', that 'every fool today thought he could become a publisher without taking the trouble to learn the trade', and that 'the authors don't write nearly as well as they used to'. This conversation took some time, and was of a ritualistic nature, since it became clear to me as early as the second visit that neither man had the least interest in what he was saying, but was intent only on what each knew was to come.

My place was half way down one side of the table. In front of me lay sheets of blank foolscap paper; in my hand was a fountain pen; it was my duty to write down a complete and accurate record of the titles bought by Macrae, the numbers of copies of each title, and the price. The session lasted for many hours, usually with an interlude for lunch at a local chophouse, for in those days the great did not find it necessary to convey themselves to smart and expensive West End restaurants for refreshment.

The procedure was unvarying, and would start with Macrae picking up the book nearest him, turning to the title-page, and reading out the title, which I immediately wrote down on my foolscap sheet, *Elements of Mahayana Buddhism* or whatever it might be. Macrae would riffle through the pages, sometimes pausing to read a few sentences here and there, then turn to Mr. Stallybrass. 'How many of this one, d'you think, Stallybrass?' he would inquire, 'seems like five hundred copies to me.' Looking solemn as an owl, Mr. Stallybrass would consider the matter swiftly and accept the number proposed if he thought the order a good one. If he did not, he would suggest a larger one. Usually Macrae agreed with Mr. Stallybrass on the number to be bought, and the matter took a bare half minute; sometimes he did not, and there was argument. Occasionally Macrae would decline a book altogether, and nothing could shift him. At other times, impressed by what Mr. Stallybrass told him about the sales potential, he would decide to manufacture the book in the United States in a large edition, instead of shipping a few hundred copies across the Atlantic in bulk. It is perhaps worth mentioning that Mr. Stallybrass had never visited the U.S.A. and that his advice to Macrae on how much to buy was strictly second-hand.

Usually the business was concluded after a cup of tea about 4 p.m. Macrae would shake us all ceremoniously by the hand and take his leave. As soon as he was out of the door I began, with the assistance of a ready reckoner, to multiply out the individual totals of books purchased, and add them all up. Within a quarter of an hour I would inform my Master of the grand total, which would run to some thousands of pounds.

For years Macrae had dealt in this manner with Routledge and two or three other London firms close to him. But in 1926 E. P. Dutton in New York flooded the market at bargain prices with up to a million copies of books bought mainly in London. It was the largest remainder sale ever in the history of the American book-trade and it ruined the market for months to come. But it did not bring ruin to the house of E. P. Dutton. Every year, and sometimes twice a year, Macrae, the great gambler, found among the hundreds of not-much-good books he had imported, a best-seller to save him. Disaster may have been waiting for him in the wings, but it never came upon the stage. About twenty years later, when he died, the firm was still very much in business, and it still is today, buoyantly directed by his son, Elliott. A true chip off the old block, Macrae junior too conjures up a best-seller a year to startle his rivals and to consolidate his balance-sheet, but he does not follow his father's footsteps in the bulk-buying of hundreds of miscellaneous titles. And for an excellent reason. It doesn't pay.

L'Affaire Casanova must have taken place in the second half of the twenties, a bitter-sweet episode which made a deep mark on my publishing mind. Soon after the 1914–18 war, a young man, John Rodker, of pleasant appearance and soft voice, with a sensitive literary intelligence, decided to enter publishing in a special field, that of exotica or (as some might say) erotica. Certainly, if this country had wished to create a new governmental post in a Ministry of Entertainment, Rodker would have had my vote as Pornographer Royal. He knew the literature; he had taste and judgement, and a fine flair for producing a handsome volume; he fully understood the distinction between distinguished erotica and merely coarse obscenity. The two

106

main ventures on which Rodker embarked were *The Memoirs of Jacques Casanova*, twelve volumes, in the standard translation of Arthur Machen, one of the liveliest autobiographies ever written,[1] and a new version of *The Thousand Nights and One Night*, often called *The Arabian Nights*.

For many years Burton's translation of the *Nights* had held the field. Painstaking, cumbersome, and cluttered with learned footnotes of exceptional indecency, it was an almost perfect example of a book which 'no gentleman's library should be without'. But recently there had appeared in France a new translation by Dr. J. C. Mardrus, in which the gaiety and narrative swiftness of the original found colourful expression. Could a first-rate translator be found to turn Mardrus' French into lively English? Rodker thought so, and persuaded the remarkable and eccentric Powys Mathers to try his hand. Mathers was a prose stylist of no mean accomplishment—later under the pseudonym of Torquemada he composed the famous crossword puzzles in *The Observer* with which he tortured the addicts once a week—and his version was a success. Rodker printed it in four large volumes, and put it on the market.

These two great ventures, and a small number of miscellaneous books, made up the stock-in-trade of the Casanova Society. But sales were slow, Rodker's capital small, the published prices of the volumes perhaps too low, and Rodker got into grave financial difficulties. The time came when, unable to raise new capital, he found himself forced to sell. He offered the Casanova Society, lock, stock and barrel, to Routledge.

Mr. Stallybrass and Franklin immediately realized the value of the enterprise. A quick check on the stocks, and an offer was made which Rodker accepted. It was, in my

---

[1] A new edition of this translation is in course of publication by Elek Books Ltd.

view, a poor one, and I decided that Routledge had picked up a bargain which would profit them for years to come. But I had reckoned without my Master's puritan conscience. No sooner had the deal gone through than a sense of guilt took hold of him. He began to believe, without so far as I know a shred of evidence, that the Public Prosecutor had his eye on him. Panic reigned in the office. 'We must get rid of the *Casanova Memoirs* immediately,' Mr. Stallybrass groaned, 'There would be no defence if an action were brought.' Vainly I argued in their favour. 'A standard work,' I said, 'a recognized classic, a masterpiece of autobiography.' My Master would not listen. 'Young girls in their 'teens,' he muttered hoarsely, 'utterly corrupting, the Old Bailey, never hold my head up again, grave responsibilities, can't think what induced me to buy, filthy, utterly filthy.' Within a week, Casanova in twelve finely produced volumes had been sold for a pitiful price to the great remainder dealer of those days, Grant of Edinburgh. Soon they were on the market at much less than half the price Routledge would have charged. The young girls, whose corruption my Master feared, could now buy them twice as easily as before. But honour was saved, though the profits went by the board. There was no prosecution then, or since. As for *The Thousand Nights and One Night*, Mr. Stallybrass never looked at them. It was just as well. They were at least as 'filthy' as Casanova in the sense that he used the word. They remain to this day in print on the Routledge list, enjoying the steady sale which their merits deserve. I wish Routledge would issue a one-volume selection of the best stories at a reasonable price and send me a copy. I lost my own set long ago. Now I should like to read it again, and run whatever risk of corruption this enterprise involves.

5   Today and
Tomorrow

IN NOVEMBER 1923 Routledge published, under the
imprint of its identical twin, Kegan Paul, a little book of
101 pages called *Daedalus, or Science and the Future*. It was
written by J. B. S. Haldane, and is probably today a
forgotten book. Yet then it received glowing reviews and
made an impact on the public which was electrifying.

The book was based on a paper read to the long defunct
Shaftesbury Society at Oxford in June 1914, and in modified
versions to other societies in Oxford between 1919 and 1922.
I heard it myself when I was up, and marvelled at its
prophecies. But I was not a publisher then, and no thought
of printing it occurred to me. Nor did I remember the
paper when I entered Routledge as an apprentice, much
as I would like to be able to claim the honour of introducing
it to the public. It was C. K. Ogden, with his numerous
acquaintances in academic circles, who brought it in to
Mr. Stallybrass and suggested that it might be printed as a
sixpenny pamphlet. My Master read it and thought it
interesting, and so did I, indeed I thought it in many
ways the most sensational thing I had ever read. I therefore
pressed for its appearance as a book rather than a pamphlet,

bound in cloth or paper boards, at the comparatively high price of half-a-crown. This was agreed, and the little volume lies before me now, bound in dark purple-brown boards with a white label pasted on it announcing the title and the author's name. There was no jacket. At half-a-crown the margin of profit per copy was above average, but no great sale was expected and the first printing was a mere 2,000 copies. Within days of its publication *Daedalus* began to sell like wildfire; impression followed impression, each of about 2,000 copies in the cautious tradition of the respectable firm which had issued it. In all, over 20,000 copies were sold, bringing in a revenue of some £1,700, of which perhaps £1,200 was gross profit. This profit, equivalent today to about £4,000, was derived from a book of less than 13,000 words! The common publishing adage 'short books never sell' is today, as it always was, absolute bunkum.[1]

There were many remarkable and some shocking things in *Daedalus*, but what undoubtedly gained it a large circulation was its general attitude to science as a force that would completely transform the world in a future that was only just round the corner. Not since the days of H. G. Wells's early novels, many of which would now be described as science-fiction, had a young but reputable scientist dared to speak so plainly and with such authority about the role of science and scientists in a universe which people even in 1923 still tended to regard as static or at least slow-moving. Motor-cars and aeroplanes and telephones were, it is true, taken for granted. But radio was in its infancy and television was not to be born for a generation; the talking film and the colour film were ten years and more ahead; and even the knowledge that the atom had been split, with all its incalculable consequences, was

---

[1] One of the biggest sellers of my lifetime, *Animal Farm* by George Orwell, 1945, contained under 30,000 words. It was rejected by a number of American publishers, mainly on the grounds of its length.

known only to a few outside the society of initiates. But in *Daedalus* Haldane brilliantly revealed many unexpected secrets of the scientific laboratories. Not a few readers were disgusted, but all were excited.

At the outset Haldane pictures three Europeans in India, guests at a large dance, looking at a great new star in the Milky Way. Haldane himself is one of the guests. What, Haldane inquires, was the origin of this cosmoclastic explosion, and answers: 'Perhaps it was the last judgement of some inhabited world, a too successful experiment in induced radio-activity on the part of some of the dwellers there. Perhaps . . . what we were watching that evening was the detonation of a world on which too many men came out to look at the stars when they should have been dancing' (page 4). In the age of the H-bomb his hypothesis may be said to be bang on the target. Is there any hope of stopping the progress of research? Not, he says, if our present economic and national systems continue. In the age of competition between the U.S.A. and the U.S.S.R. inter-continental missiles and sputniks, Haldane was right again. On page 9 Haldane quotes H. G. Wells in *Anticipations* (1902) as being singularly modest when he gives 'his personal opinion that by 1950 there would be heavier-than-air flying machines capable of practical use in war. That, said he, was his own view, though he was well aware that it would excite considerable ridicule. *I propose in this paper to make no prophecies rasher than the above.*' The italics are Haldane's and served to give a tremendous and well-deserved verisimilitude to what was to follow.

After a tribute to Einstein, Haldane discusses future sources of power, a prerequisite for continued human progress. 'Ultimately,' he says, 'we shall have to tap those intermittent but inexhaustible sources of power, the wind and the sunlight. . . . I do not much believe in the commercial possibility of induced radio-activity.' Here Homer-Haldane certainly nodded, but recovered quickly to give on pages 37–68 a fascinating account of the world as he foresaw its development up to about 2070. In this section he made his famous prophecy about the breeding of babies outside the human uterus (ectogenesis), which sent a thrill of horror through the society of the 1920's. We are tougher nowadays, or more accurately perhaps, more thoroughly indoctrinated. But Haldane fully anticipated the dangers ahead. He remarks, on page 82, 'man armed with science is like a baby with a box of matches,' and is aware that 'the question of what man will do with these powers is essentially a question for religion and aesthetic.'

This wonderful little book made a tremendous impression on me, and indeed on all who read it. In many ways it altered the thinking of at least part of a generation. Pandora's box of science had long been ajar; now it was clear that it was being forced wide open. I saw a little of Haldane in those days, a tall and powerful figure, with a mass of chestnut hair rising over a high forehead. At the back of his head the hair was snow-white in the shape of a small equilateral triangle. His knowledge was vast, and his memory extraordinary. It was said that he could speak fifty Indian dialects, and could recite *Paradise Lost* by heart. I have no doubt this was true. He was singularly unselfconscious. Sometimes, when I had tea with him in a café, he would begin talking about ectogenesis in a voice that reached to the farthest corners of the room, and I saw middle-aged women shuddering away with horror But he never noticed, and I didn't care. People should be strong enough, I thought, to hear the truth without wincing.

Some of the most tremendous successes in publishing are unexpected and unplanned. It is the mark of a great publisher to exploit them at a moment's notice. Of course, we at Routledge and the shrewd C. K. Ogden had as yet no idea of the extent of the market we had unwittingly tapped. But we realized without delay that a follow-up to *Daedalus* was called for, and soon. Ogden found one. He induced no less a person than Bertrand Russell to write a companion volume, which appeared within weeks. *Icarus, or the Future of Science* was even shorter than *Daedalus*, but it too was a brilliant essay and it got off the mark on the first page. 'Much as I should like to agree with Mr. Haldane's forecast,' wrote Russell, 'a long experience of statesmen and governments has made me somewhat sceptical. I am compelled to fear that science will be used to promote the power of dominant groups, rather than to make man happy. Icarus, having been taught to fly by his father, Daedalus, was destroyed by his rashness. I fear that the same fate may overtake the populations whom modern men of science have taught to fly.' These wise words of 1924 sound with the authentic ring of prophecy twenty-five years later. *Icarus* sold well too.

By now it had become clear that there was a considerable market for books about the future, and we discussed the possibility of a whole series of little books and a title for it. After a good deal of deliberation, the clumsy but not inappropriate title was found, the Today and Tomorrow Series. Authors were approached and books commissioned from them, often in my opinion the wrong books and the wrong authors. Some of these sold much less well. But *Daedalus* and *Icarus* continued their headlong career, and carried many of the others along with them. Most of the titles were classical names, and the device worked well. The series continued in full spate for six years and more, an unprecedented time for what were really short essays. But the mood of the series harmonized with the desire of

113

the public for debate and information. The Great War was behind us; something new and better would surely follow it; what was it to be? Perhaps the Today and Tomorrow Series would tell them. Before it was finished over one hundred volumes had appeared. It was a unique publishing event.

Many now distinguished personages made their debut in this series or contributed an early work. Others belonged to an older generation. The almost legendary Vernon Lee wrote on the Future of Intelligence, E. J. Dent on Music and the Future, J. F. C. Fuller on Transport, J. W. N. Sullivan on The Tyranny of Science, Gerald Heard produced An Anatomy of Clothes. There was J. D. Bernal with his horrific *The World, the Flesh and the Devil;* J. D. Woodruff with a remarkably witty satire, *Plato's American Public;* George Malcolm Thomson on Scotland; Winifred Holtby on the Pulpit; James Jeans on Astronomy; J. F. Roxburgh on the Public Schools.

One of my favourite volumes, which was issued in February 1927, was *Lars Porsena, or the Future of Swearing and Improper Language,* by Robert Graves. Written three years before *Goodbye to All That* (1929) it was funny, good-humoured and perceptive. It had an excellent sale, and contains as much sense today as when it first appeared. I cannot resist a short quotation from page 53. 'This book is written for the Nice People. . . . Observe with what delicacy I have avoided and still avoid writing the words X—— and Y—— and dance round a great many others of equally wide popular appeal. I have yielded to the society in which I move, which is an obscene society: that is, it acquiesces emotionally in the validity of the taboo, while intellectually objecting to it. I have let a learned counsel go through these pages with a blue pencil and strike through paragraph after paragraph of perfectly clean writing. My

114

only self-justification is that the original manuscript is to be kept safe for a more enlightened posterity in the strong room of one of our greater libraries.' The case against pruriency could hardly be better put, and it is significant that even today it is doubtful whether the full text of *Lars Porsena* could appear without an outcry . . . and a prosecution! After an able defence of James Joyce's *Ulysses* and a biting reference to the pose of the respectable that Shakespeare's sonnets are either the 'extravagant flattery of a patron or an academic exercise', Graves closes his book with the following words—I wish I had remembered to quote them in my evidence before the Select Committee of the House of Commons in 1957, when a new Obscenity Bill was under discussion. 'Joyce is read,' writes Graves, 'as obscene instead of successfully past obscenity: Shakespeare instead of being read as past lust is not even read as lusting.'

The Today and Tomorrow Series was an outspoken series, and I fought like a tiger to preserve this precious quality against the fears of Cecil Franklin and my Master. That I was successful is proved by the frequency of attacks on individual volumes, mainly due to the unflagging zeal for purity displayed by the late James Douglas, writing in the *Sunday Express*. In the beginning, when he thundered his comminations against the sexual explicitness of one or other of the books, alarm and despondency was created in the board-room. But soon we became inoculated against attacks, and smilingly ordered another printing of 2,000 copies on the Monday morning following an outburst. Douglas helped a good deal to make the series a thumping success, though his campaigns against British immorality had dangerous consequences for other publishers.

Before leaving these bold little books on great themes, I must refer to one other title not yet mentioned, André

Maurois' *The Next Chapter*: The War Against the Moon, published in September 1927. *The Next Chapter* is written in the form of a fragment of Universal History, published by the University of C—mb—e in 1922. There had been a world war in 1947 lasting six years (a good guess this) causing over thirty million casualties. The five great newspaper proprietors have gained control of public opinion and hold 'a weekly meeting by telephotophony' to discuss policy. At the end of 1962 a grave crisis has arisen, since the important new discovery of how to derive power from wind-machines has led to a struggle for the limited number of suitable factory sites. The workers are disturbed. 'The miners knew that within five years—or ten years at most—they would no longer be needed.' There's a familiar ring to this sentence. A new world war seems inevitable. M. Alain de Rouvray, a steel man from Lorraine, the French press-lord, suggests to the British press-lord, Lord Frank Douglas, an old Etonian of course, that a common enemy must be found, since 'it is regrettable but true that hatred is the only thing that can unite mankind'. Douglas suggests the Moon, and is laughed at for his pains. But soon it is clear that no alternative plan exists, and with the concurrence of the aged Joseph C. Smack, Dr. Macht and Baron Tokungawa, the American, German and Japanese press-lords, a fake campaign is arranged, and the world press begins to report the mysterious obliteration of various small (but inaccessible!) towns. All newspapers print the banner headline THE WORLD FIRST, and the popular song of the days is

> Oh, stop tickling me,
> Man in the Moon;
> Stop tickling,
> Stop, ah! stop!

All goes well, until Ben Tabrit, a top scientist of Marrakesh University and the inventor of the wind-accumulator, not himself privy to the hoax, suggests that Moon-Beings must actually exist and devises a long-distance ray with which to attack their universe. The weapon is constructed and brought into action; new craters appear on the Moon. The World is wild with joy, until . . . the Moon hits back. What a horrid topicality this satire has acquired in the age of the sputniks and moon probes.

The Today and Tomorrow Series was the most lively, most successful and most enjoyable publishing enterprise with which I have ever been connected. It showed that the essay form was still a useful weapon in social, scientific and political controversy. It showed also that the highbrow, when he can be persuaded to write for the multitude, does a much better job than the popularizer and the hack.

6   Divorce and
the Sack

IN THE AUTUMN of 1930, the long and glorious reign
of Mr. Stallybrass was drawing to a close, though no one
then knew it. By now I had been with the firm eight years,
and learnt a lot. My apprentice days were over, I had
risen to near the top. As junior managing director, I was
of course a member of the Board. Covered by Mr.
Stallybrass's experience, I felt ready to do great publishing
deeds. In fact, I felt strongly the necessity for them,
since times had changed in the publishing world, and Mr.
Stallybrass had not changed with them. At least, so I
believed.

The trouble had begun some years earlier. The 'pony-
and-trap' period of English publishing, virtually unchanged
for fifty years or more, had been superseded by the 'auto-
mobile' epoch. Chief among the internal combustion engines
was Victor Gollancz, with a very high horse-power. With
the foundation of his firm in 1928, the revolution may be
said to have begun. Then we saw the shape of things to
come. Instead of the dignified advertisement list of twenty
titles set out primly in a modest space, there was the

double or triple column, with the title of one book screaming across it in letters three inches high. The forces of modernity had been loosed, the age of shouting, the period of the colossal and the sensational, had arrived. It was not to die down till World War II checked its frenzies. Though Gollancz was the great innovator and the lettering of his advertisements the biggest and blackest of all, his competitors did not lag far behind. Hutchinson, Hodder and Heinemann, Cassell, Chatto and Constable, beat the big drum in an ever more shattering tattoo. Amid all this clatter, how could the quiet whisper of a Routledge advertisement, the gentle nudge of a Routledge promotion, be heard or felt by an over-stimulated public. If the merit of books was now to be measured by the height of the letters that advertised them, publishing, it could well be said, was no longer an occupation for gentlemen, but a real business, even perhaps a rat-race.

The Routledge business, it is true, had a magnificent back-list, books published years before that continued to sell so many hundreds or thousands of copies each year. There was, for instance, *Heaton's Ready Reckoner*, an indispensable reference work for banks; there was the *Ideal Cookery Book*, suitable for chefs and wedding presents; there was Hoyle's *Games*; there were ready reckoners, gardening books, language manuals, and the great standard works in the various series. These, and a hundred others, were the source of its strength, as of every publishing house that has been in existence long enough. But the Routledge current list depended a great deal for its success on the sale of large editions of the new books to the United States publishers. The purchasing sessions of John Macrae were sensational examples of this form of trading. Macrae still visited us each year, but he bought far fewer books. The crash of the bull market on Wall Street in 1929, and the great depression which followed it, exercised a disastrous effect on the policy of bulk purchases by American publishers. Even the great International Library of Psychology, handled by Harcourt Brace in New York, and the History of Civilization Series, handled by Alfred Knopf, were seriously affected. Orders diminished, some titles were passed over completely. The writing was on the wall, and vaguely I discerned it.

But to Mr. Stallybrass matters appeared otherwise. It was not possible for him to imagine that the well-tried recipes of fifty years of publishing were now inadequate, as I believed them to be. The balance-sheets told a story of slackening profits, but to my Master this suggested merely that more work needed to be done, and to Cecil Franklin that in a period of recession strict economies must be enforced in the overhead expenses. But to me, the junior managing director, filled with the boundless optimism of youth, the times seemed ripe for a new deal. I began to press for the hiring of a sales manager and an advertising executive, even if the latter had to shout as loud as his rivals on half their budget. I began to think in terms of a livelier list than the honest, scholarly, no-nonsense-about-it list built by Mr. Stallybrass. I began to dream of finding books more suitable for manipulation by the resources of modern promotion. I even considered that the time was approaching when Routledge should publish novels. This shocking view found little favour. It was regarded by my Master as a heresy, and by Franklin as a dangerous speculation. Like many a young publisher before me, I was in revolt against the powers that be. Innocently I imagined that my arguments would be accepted, if only I repeated them often enough. But it is no easy task to change the fundamental pattern of an established publishing house, as I was to discover within five years.

In January 1931, Mr. Stallybrass died, and the most momentous year in my life till then got off to an ominous start. Returning prematurely to the office after a severe attack of influenza, he had a relapse and was dead within a few days. His ending was in character. Mr. Stallybrass, deaf no doubt to his wife's pleas that his convalescence should be prolonged, came back to his desk to get on with the firm's business and his own work. But at the age of seventy-five, even his gallant spirit could no longer drive his weakened body to further efforts. He perished of exhaustion, in harness, as he would have wished. His work was his life, and his work was great. Modest, shy, a trifle puritanical, learned, energetic, with broad interests, determined, humorous and honest, I do not see his like among us publishers today. He belonged to the age of heroes, and in a publishing Valhalla he must surely have his being now, seated at a vast mahogany desk, peering through iron-rimmed spectacles at the clutter of books and MSS. before him, delightedly conscious of the eternity stretching before him in which he can pursue the twin tasks of his choice, the pursuit of knowledge and the reduction of chaos to order.

So passed the greatest scholar-publisher of his day. Deprived of his sturdy figure, the board-room seemed empty, and I mourned him for a time. I had lost not only a Master but a friend. But the young have short memories, and their egoism is often disgusting. My own was no exception. Within a few weeks my recollection of him began to fade into the past, and I think more often of him now than I did in the years after his death. Certainly there was much work for me to do, as I grappled with the problems he hitherto had effortlessly disposed of, and pondered the methods by which I might bring the blessings of modernity to what appeared to me a thoroughly old-fashioned outfit.

About a year before the death of Mr. Stallybrass, a young girl of my acquaintance, Pamela de Bayou, had decided to open a bookshop in Hampstead. The decision was sudden and the venture ill-advised, since she had omitted to obtain from the Publishers Association a licence, without which she was unable to obtain books at a discount from the publishers. Nothing daunted by this trivial contretemps, Pamela de Bayou had sought and obtained an appointment to see me at my office one afternoon in the autumn of 1929, for the purpose of persuading me to back her application for a licence as a bookseller. In due course, the hour for her arrival came, but Pamela did not come. Ten, twenty, thirty minutes passed, while I sat fuming at my desk, essaying with all the realism at my command the role of an important executive kept waiting by a chit of a girl.

Suddenly from the outer office there was wafted to my ears an immense hubbub; a male voice held colloquy with a deep female voice which announced loudly: 'I want to see Fred Warburg. Where is he?' The male voice inquired nervously whether she had an appointment. 'Of course I have,' the female voice replied irritably, 'and I want to see him at once. I have another appointment in half an hour.' A moment later, the board-room door opened, and Pamela advanced towards me, like a yacht in full sail.

'Am I late?' she inquired apologetically, extending her hand.

'That depends on when you intended to arrive,' I said.

The riposte checked her only slightly, and she sat down calmly enough in the chair by my desk.

'My taxi got held up in a traffic block,' she began, 'and then of course the driver couldn't find Carter Lane. I'm really not surprised. What a horrible little street it is, so narrow, and it smells of cheap scent.'

This was true. A well-known perfume manufacturer had his offices only a few doors down the street, and a delicious scent of lavender often contended with the smell of petrol.

'And what dreadful stairs.' Pamela continued, 'I caught my heel in the lino and nearly fell down. Why don't you have them repaired? They're frightfully dangerous.'

'I'll see to it tomorrow morning without fail,' I replied, with a hint of sarcasm.

'I most certainly should,' she said, ignoring the sarcasm, if indeed she noticed it. 'As a matter of fact, the whole place wants doing up. It's shabby and dirty. A well-known publisher like you oughtn't to have an office like an old warehouse. Why don't you let me redesign the whole place?'

Taking advantage of a brief pause in the torrent of words, I asked what her problem was and in what way I could be of assistance to her.

'Well,' she said, immediately, 'we have this bookshop, Helen Fletcher and I. Only very *good* books, of course, poetry, *belles-lettres*, a few of the best novels. It's got rather a small window, and I arrange just three or four books in it at a time, with a single white rose. It looks marvellous. A lot of people come in and admire it.'

'And are you selling a great many books?' I inquired.

'Indeed we are. Only yesterday afternoon, three people came in and they all bought something. But we simply must get a bookseller's licence, otherwise it's so expensive.'

'How do you mean, expensive? You surely don't buy the books from the publishers at the full net price, and sell them to the public at the same price?'

'Don't be idiotic,' Pamela remarked, sharply, 'how on earth could we make a profit if we did that? We get the books from Simpkin Marshall, the big wholesalers, you know. But they won't give us a proper discount, because they say we ought to have this licence. That's why I've come here today, to ask you to give me a recommendation or a reference or whatever the thing is called. Can you do it?'

'Certainly I can endorse your application,' I said, rather pompously, 'if you have the proper qualifications. I expect you know what they are.'

'You must be mad,' Pamela exclaimed, with genuine astonishment in her voice, 'of course I don't know. It's all a lot of red tape, anyhow, Why should one need a licence to sell books? They're not like wines and spirits and tobacco.'

'One of the most important qualifications,' I interrupted, sternly, 'is about stock. A bookseller is expected to carry a representative stock of books. How many volumes have you got in stock?'

'I haven't counted them for a week or two,' Pamela said, 'but we had nearly two hundred books last time I did. It seems an awful lot to me. Isn't it enough? There's not room for many more.'

'It's not nearly enough,' I said. 'I should think a minimum stock would cost you about two hundred and fifty pounds, say one thousand volumes of one kind or another. The argument is that a customer must be given a reasonable chance of finding a book he wants when he comes in.'

'But that's utterly ridiculous,' Pamela retorted. 'For one thing, Helen and I haven't got two hundred and fifty pounds or anywhere near it. For another, there are thousands and thousands of new books, no shop could possibly have all of them. Why, we'd need a place as big as Buckingham Palace. What we do is this. When a customer wants a book we haven't got, we get it for him immediately.'

'Very right and proper,' I remarked primly, 'but how exactly do you do that?'

'Easily enough,' my budding bookseller said, 'I take a cab to Simpkins, buy the book, and bring it back within an hour or two. That's a marvellously efficient service, isn't it?'

'But rather an expensive one,' I said.

'Of course it is. Every time we sell a book that's not in stock, we lose money, several shillings every time. It simply can't go on. That's why you must give me the strongest possible backing. You will, won't you?'

The plea wrung my heart strings, and I promised to do my best. To refuse this beautiful if lunatic girl what she asked would have been as difficult as withholding a crust of bread from a starving child. But, wisely, despite my warm and disingenuous recommendation, the Publishers Association refused the application. Pamela's bookshop ended its brief and exceptional life within a few weeks, while its owner directed her pulsating energies else-where.

The year 1931 was a watershed in my life. At its beginning I was a man without worries; by December there was hardly a department of my life and character that did not cause me anxiety. At the beginning I was comfort-ably off, without serious responsibilities, and contented in rather a dull way; by the end I was hard up, bowed down with the burdens of life and work, and deliriously happy.

The end of an era is hard to identify at the time, especially for an optimist like myself prepared to believe that my affairs are in pretty good shape, and likely to remain that way. I have never egged my friends on to play the role of Cassandra in my company, and have easily resisted the blandishments of palmists and crystal-gazers to share with me for a consideration their estimate of my fortunes. To me the future is unknowable. Indeed, to have foreknowledge of it would in my view transform it, and probably for the worse. I do not fear it, but I regard it with a certain scepticism, like an uncracked egg whose freshness has not been guaranteed. 'Hope for the best' has always been my motto, 'and don't be too startled if it lets you down.'

But I have to admit that on 1 January, 1931, I was prepared to put a much bigger stake on the future than the circumstances warranted. Nelson put one blind eye to the telescope at the Battle of Copenhagen, but at least he kept the other one open. It seems to me now that I had both eyes securely shut against the events sailing rapidly into my life. Had I foreseen the alarms and the perils which the next five years were to bring upon me, I should excusably have faltered. Even the supposed stoicism of a Jew, the stiff upper lip of an ex-public school-boy, the sunny temperament of a man who has had it easy (or fairly easy), would have been strained.

My grandmother, authoritarian head of the Warburg clan, had died some years before. My Aunt Agnes had moved from the family stronghold at No. 8 to No. 52 Porchester Terrace, a nice enough house with a better garden, but definitely not a stronghold. The hothouse atmosphere of a well-run matriarchy belonged to the past. The old taboos were weakening. My mother was dead also, and I realized too late that I had never shown her the warmth of affection which I had felt for her and which she had so badly needed. My father waited a decent interval to mourn, but he disliked being a widower and married a childhood friend whose husband had long been dead. The family was breaking up. The fatal tendency to drift was spreading, and in my own case to the most intimate sphere of all, the conjugal.

There is little written in this book about my first wife and our marriage. I am no Rousseau to publish my *Confessions* to the world. The marriage lasted nine years, quite a long time by modern standards, and was perhaps neither much better nor much worse than a million others. There were three children of the marriage, David, Hew and Jeremy, now all grown up, busily living the lives that suit them. They should do well. But the break-up of a home has an ugly side, and the two parties to the marriage contract rarely see eye to eye about the reasons. Between my first wife and myself, there were divergences of temperament leading to disagreements. To me the remedy was a simple one, less nagging and more courtesy between husband and wife. To my wife a different remedy suggested itself, nothing less than a course of Freudian analysis. This seemed to me absurd, expensive and unnecessary, for I could see no reason for an attempt to alter my character structure, which appeared to me adequate, more or less, for the purposes of my life. But my wife thought otherwise, when our differences came to a head, and after much argument I allowed myself to be persuaded. I went to the eminent and sympathetic J. C. Flugel, then Professor at London University, later the author of *The Psychology of Clothes*. On his couch I lay peacefully for fifty minutes four times a week for nearly four months.

Psycho-analysis was a theory with which I had been acquainted since my days as an undergraduate. The news out of Vienna had reached the philosophers of Oxford and been greeted with howls of derision. It was almost too easy to show, the philosophers told us, that the theory was untenable. For one thing, it rested on a belief in the unconscious mind. Now if a mind is unconscious, it follows that it is impossible to be conscious or aware of it. Therefore, it is impossible to know how it functions or even whether it exists. Q.E.D. So argued the philosophers, blissfully unaware of the devastating effects the doctrine of the unconscious mind was to have on society and culture during the next generation.

My own difficulties at Oxford had been concerned with the unreality of the metaphysical concepts with which we were supposed to juggle in Greats. But I was able to accept an unconscious mind with, if the word is appropriate, insouciance. When I came to Routledge, I found the list cluttered with learned tomes on the subject—Freud, Jung, Rank, Adler, Stekel and others. I read extensively, and became as adroit at spotting the phallic significance of a bunch of bananas as any analyst alive. My interest, however, was purely intellectual. No urge to rid myself of inhibitions visited me.

On Professor Flugel's couch, however, the situation was different. Now I was paying out real money for therapy which might conceivably do me a bit of good. After all I was not so conceited as to regard myself as without imperfections. No doubt I had as many inhibitions as the next man, and now was the time to rid myself of them. I put my back into it—an appropriate phrase perhaps— dreamed the dreams required of me and worked out their symbolism with all the verve of a crossword addict hunting up his clues. It was a pleasure too to have a sympathetic listener paid to hear only one side of the story, *mine*. Indeed, it would be true to say that I was able to hear my side of the story for the first time without interruption. The result could have been foretold by even a second-rate fortune-teller who had lost her crystal ball. I discovered within weeks that I was in love with another woman, the impetuous girl who had come to me for help in the matter of a book licence. But I had no reason to suppose she was in love with me. In this matter, Professor Flugel, excellent analyst as he was, could do nothing to aid me.

With my Master dead and my marriage collapsing, 1931 had got off to an ominous start. But there was yet more to come. Now my father lay ill of a fatal disease and was not expected to live much longer. He died, in fact, in November, leaving a substantial portion of what remained of his wealth to my stepmother and her son. In the world of affairs the Labour Government of Ramsay MacDonald was in the throes of the crisis that was to explode in August and lead to the formation of the so-called National Government. The position of sterling was jeopardized, citizens were careful of their money, and this was bad for trade, and for the publishing trade in particular, since it was said, not without justice, that this trade felt a slump first and a boom last. Since it was I who had a major share of editorial responsibility at Routledge, now that Mr. Stallybrass was gone, the Routledge list absorbed more and more of my time.

Distracted rather than bowed down by my responsibilities, I decided to break off my analysis. There were three excellent reasons for so doing—I no longer had the time; I had ceased enjoying the radical revision of Freud's theories which occupied me on the couch, it was after all none of my business; and I was in love. By now relations between my wife and myself were at breaking-point. As so often, and for simple enough reasons, psycho-analytical treatment had led to results unexpected by those concerned. I left my wife, my children, and my home. There was nothing else to do. To court the woman of my choice seemed to me an inescapable necessity, and I pursued it with ardour and inefficiency through the late spring and summer of that year. The combination proved acceptable to Pamela. In the autumn my wife started divorce proceedings against me which I did not defend. These did not go smoothly at first, and I have always feared that Warburg, M. N., versus Warburg, F. J., has become a standard case in the legal textbooks on the subject, though I have never dared to examine them. At any rate, the proceedings closely resembled those so splendidly described in A. P. Herbert's novel, *Holy Deadlock*. But on 14 January, 1932, a decree *nisi* was granted my first wife, which was made absolute on 25 July. I was a free man again, technically that is, for in fact I was more enslaved than ever before.

What kind of a woman was my second, and I trust my last, wife? I will not say much about her here, since she figures abundantly in the latter pages of this'book, where she speaks for herself with an unmistakable voice. A talented dress-designer and a bold painter in the expressionist manner, she was primarily an artist in temperament. She had at least three qualities which I associate with the creative spirit. Spontaneity—what she had seen or experienced was immediately available to her, and was expressed absolutely without inhibitions. Intensity—her reactions to events were overwhelmingly powerful; if, for instance, she heard a slight noise, barely perceptible to me, she would be immediately agog with interest or even alarm. Decisiveness—she knew what she liked, what she wanted, what she despised, with a certainty that I often envied.

Pamela was the daughter of a French father, who had lived most of his life in England, and a French mother who had not. Dark hair cut in a fringe framed a face that was heart-shaped. A pale skin, slanting blue eyes, a full mouth, and high cheek-bones paid tribute to her Irish and Russian as well as her French ancestry, for her father's

mother was an Irishwoman, and her great-grandmother a
Russian. Her mother died within a few days of her birth,
and the first six years of her life were spent in Paris with
her French grandmother. Soon however her father married
again, and she returned from France and spent the rest
of her life in England. French in her basic attitudes, but
with an apparently English surface, she spoke English
with a pronunciation more precise than those who have
never known another language. Her outlook on life was
basically pre-industrial, indeed almost feudal. Like the Red
Queen in *Alice Through the Looking-Glass,* she was capable
of an 'off with her head' to those who offended her, but
below the fierceness of her manner was concealed a heart
kinder than all but her closest friends suspected.

Virtue, according to the ancient Greeks, consists of
following the mean between two extremes. For those who
accept such a view, Pamela must be considered the most
unvirtuous of women. When first I knew her, she was
able to pass from a mood of blackest melancholy to a
state of delighted exhilaration, from good humour to rage,
from wild extravagance to shrewd parsimony in a matter
of moments. She is not much changed to this day. It was
perhaps her father who was responsible in some degree
for this waywardness. Only nineteen when she was born,
he had indulged her whims and encouraged her excesses.
When she was to be sent away to boarding-school, he had
told her that if she did not like the atmosphere of the school
she should advise him instantly so that he might make
better arrangements. Armed with such a licence, it is not
surprising that Pamela attended in succession half a dozen
of the best educational institutions in the land. Bored at
last with such a variety of instruction, at sixteen she ran
away to contract her first marriage. Its duration was brief.
Her second marriage lasted not much longer. About a

year before my analysis began she married a painter, a man a good many years older than herself, whom she had known since she was a girl. This second husband died of tuberculosis within a few months in tragic circumstances. The experience brought maturity to her. Many traces of the wilful girl remained, but now she was a woman, with whom I had fallen in love and whom I hoped to marry.

In December, 1931, Pamela and I moved into a house in St. John's Wood and set up housekeeping together. It was a reputable or respectable affair, but it was not yet marriage. It was however expensive, for Pamela decorated the place magnificently but with scant regard for the size of my income or the amount of my capital. She also engaged a butler and cook, a devoted married couple who were unaware that their master and mistress were not yoked in holy matrimony, and a personal maid, Inge, a Norwegian woman who had been with her for many years. When the decree *nisi* came through in January, without a moment's delay I proposed marriage, to take place of course six months later when I expected to be free to remarry. Pamela's answer was a negative, politely formulated but unequivocal. 'Naturally,' she said, 'I shall live with you all my life, but marry you, certainly not. You know how I hate being tied down.'

It was true that I knew how Pamela hated being tied down. There was, for instance, her account of reading *Gulliver's Travels* at the age of eight. Arrived in Lilliput, it will be recalled, and finding no one around, Gulliver lay down for a good night's sleep on the shore. The next morning, when he woke up, he was unable to move, since the Lilliputians had tied him to the ground during the night with a myriad strings. This scene had been realistically illustrated in the edition of the book read by the

132

eight-year-old Pamela. On examining the picture of Gulliver bound, horrified at his helplessness, the child had been seized with a violent fit of trembling, which had recurred for many days afterwards. Freedom to move, liberty of action, the ability to come and go at will, these were the breath of life to the grown-up as to the youthful girl, and marriage, as she made clear to me, might frustrate them. The argument lasted days and weeks. Urgently I implored her to make an honest man of me. Vehemently, and often angrily, she refused. 'You're like all the others who wanted to marry me,' she complained, 'you want to tie me down. I won't be tied down by the idiotic laws of this country.' The debate continued. I brought forward the view of one of my men friends to prove that it was I who should have doubts about the wisdom of marriage, not she—'As soon as you marry the girl,' he had told me, 'she gives up trying.'

'Your friend's a fool,' Pamela said, 'I shouldn't give up trying, what ever the silly phrase means. I should simply leave you at once.'

'But how do you know?' I demanded.

'Why should I tell you?' she replied, 'it's obvious. Can't you leave well alone?'

One day, after the divorce had finally gone through, I was summoned by the chairman of Routledge to an interview. He inquired delicately, but firmly, when I intended to marry the charming girl with whom I was living. 'As soon as possible,' I replied. 'But surely,' my chairman said, 'the decree has been made absolute? Why is there all this delay?' 'There's no delay on my part,' I said, 'it's simply that she refuses to marry me.' 'Why on earth not?' my chairman asked incredulously. Flattered that he considered me so eligible, I shrugged. What could I say? He would never have believed me if I had told him the truth.

Married or unmarried, Pamela threw herself with vigour

into the enterprise of publishing. She designed book jackets for the list of children's books I was issuing at Routledge. She entertained learned authors at our house, and questioned them irreverently about their fundamental beliefs. A friend of authors before we came together, she rapidly migrated into the opposite, the publishing camp, and was called a blackleg for her pains. 'Before I knew Fred,' she would say to her friends, 'I always thought that publishers were bloodsuckers, mean men who ground the faces of the poor hard-working authors into the dust. Now I think they're far too generous to authors, simply giving them money in advances for books they never write. No wonder publishers' salaries are so rotten. Why don't you ask for a rise in yours?' It was certainly my own view either that my salary was too low, or that our expenditure was too high, but to Pamela I dared admit nothing, since had I done so, she would have pressed for some drastic action on my part which I was not yet prepared to take.

So for six months we lived together, experiencing all the grandeurs and miseries of married life, without however being married. But in May Pamela became pregnant, and by July there was no room for doubt that she was having a child. When my first wife's decree was made absolute, I determined to broach the subject of marriage to Pamela in a manner as firm as it was persuasive. I must admit that in the circumstances I expected only slight opposition. I should have known better.

'You're hopelessly conventional,' Pamela remarked, with some acidity, 'there's a horrible bourgeois side to your nature which I absolutely detest. I've told you before that our relationship will break up if we get married. Don't you *want* to remain with me?'

'Of course I do,' I said, hurriedly racking my brains

for arguments with which to convince this obstinate girl, 'but with a child, my position as well as yours will become very vulnerable, very dubious.'

'Don't worry about my position,' Pamela said, 'it's quite all right for me. And you can't expect me to sign away my freedom just because you're too cowardly to face the world and all its filthy innuendos.'

I tried a new tack. 'Consider the baby itself,' I said, 'it won't bear my name, it'll be illegitimate. Perhaps it will take after its father and be as conventional as you say I am. In that case, it will be furious, when it grows up, that you didn't marry me.'

Pamela looked slightly shaken, then with an expression of extreme seriousness on her face, she voiced her inmost thought. 'If we do get married,' she said, 'and if for any reason I should feel obliged to leave you, who would the child belong to, me or you?'

I hesitated. I wasn't quite sure of the correct answer, and I made a bad error of judgement. 'If you left me,' I said, 'for another man, I imagine the courts would award custody of the child to me.'

'Exactly,' Pamela said, triumphantly, 'they'd take my baby away from me. It's a man's world. If I don't get married to you, the baby's mine whatever happens. Can't you *see* that?'

I could, or I thought I could. But in any case I realized that the battle was lost. Perhaps I could fight a new one in other and more favourable circumstances.

In January 1933 Hitler became Chancellor of Germany, with the aged Hindenburg as president. The uncertain political situation in Europe had taken a turn for the worse. Though the future was still obscure, a cloud of fear, as yet no bigger than a man's hand, appeared in the sky. The foundations of the civilized world began to shake almost imperceptibly. But Pamela's political intuitions ran deep. I have often wondered whether the rise of Hitler did not play a part in her change of mind. On the surface, however, it was not so.

One evening, as we sat discussing the day's events, Pamela suddenly put on her most serious expression. 'I met Mrs. B. in the street today,' she announced, 'and we had a long talk. She told me she thought it's disgraceful that we're not married.'

'Exactly what I've been saying myself for months,' I said, 'what a sensible woman she must be. Who is she?'

'An old friend of my family's,' Pamela said, 'you don't know her. She thought you'd be better off if we got married.'

'Financially better off?' I inquired, cautiously.

'Better off in every way,' Pamela replied with finality. 'We'll get married at once. How long will it take?'

'Am I to understand,' I asked, 'that you're proposing marriage to me after all these shameful months?' But Pamela was no longer listening. 'They don't value you properly at Routledge,' she said, pointing an accusing finger at me, as if it was my fault, 'you must do something about that. Ask them to double your salary.'

The next day I rang up the registrar's office. A week later, we were married. When we returned home from the registrar's, we told cook and butler what we had been doing. They didn't turn a hair. 'Madam must have a wedding breakfast,' they said, and went away to prepare it.

In February 1933, after three agonizing days of labour, our baby was born. He died of a cerebral haemorrhage twenty-four hours after his birth. It took my wife many months to recover from the physical and mental shock.

That summer our house in St. John's Wood began to fall down, and it cost a small fortune to prop it up again. Disillusioned by its behaviour and reluctant to remain in a place that had acquired such sad memories, we sold it and moved out to a rented house in Great Missenden, Bucks. Meantime, Hitler consolidated his position in Germany, and I continued to build up a new kind of list for Routledge, which in my view of the publishing situation was a necessity. In the winter of 1934 my Board decided to send me with my wife on a publishing trip to the U.S. and we sailed to New York in January.

As we arrived off Manhattan Island in a temperature of 14 degrees below, I remember looking in astonishment at immigrants from Europe clad in flimsy cotton dresses staring hopefully at the promised land. But the flavour of that first trip has gone, it simply remains in my mind as a four weeks' whirl of exciting events, interrupted by prodigious snowstorms which made the streets almost impassable. Memory is as obstinate as a mule, and will disgorge only the secrets it sanctions. But one thing, or rather one person, stands out from the snowy background of this 1934 visit, a striking figure, of medium height, with dark-brown hair, a strong aquiline nose, and the eyes of a seer, Lewis Mumford. Born in Flushing, Long Island in 1895, he had graduated from New York University and served in the U.S. Navy during World War I. His first book, *The Story of Utopias*, had appeared in 1922 and been followed by others, including his pioneer work on *Herman Melville* in 1929. But his greatest books were still to come when first I met him, and it has been one of the privileges of my life to have been their English publisher.

Mumford was and remains a disciple of the great scientist and sociologist, Sir Patrick Geddes, who died in 1932. Like his master, he has worked in a great variety of fields and it is the breadth of his scholarship which gives his work much of its special quality. Determined, like H. G. Wells before him, to take all historical cultures for his studies, he has avoided the limiting effects of a university chair, though many have been offered him, and indulged his passion for research in accordance with his desires at any given period of his life. A small inheritance, which came to him as a young man, allowed him to buy a house in Amenia, N.Y., a few yards from the Connecticut border, and there, embattled among his books, he has pursued with selfless devotion and the aid of his wife Sophie a course of reading and writing unique in American letters. Unaffected by literary fashions, equally unmoved by failure or success—though he naturally prefers the latter—he has weathered the economic storms of American life without damage. 'With a house of my own, furniture and a stock of clothes,' he has told me more than once, 'I can work as I please and write as I wish. I can always earn enough by journalism to buy the family its food.' For many years he has written the Sky Line section of *The New Yorker*.

Many books and proofs poured into my hotel suite on that trip. But Mumford's new book I remember with clarity, and for a reason. It was a set of enormous galley proofs[1] pulled on shiny paper. I placed them over the padded arm of my chair to read, but the slightest imprudent movement caused them to slide inexorably to the floor, from where I had to pick them up and sort them out again. Inexperienced in the handling of galleys at Routledge, who rarely made use of them, it maddened me.

The book I was reading was *Technics and Civilization*,

---

[1] A galley proof is about 30 inches long and 7 inches wide. It normally contains about two-and-a-half pages of type, but continuous, that is, before the type is divided (made up) into pages. In this form, proof corrections can be made by the author more easily and more economically.

sent me by Donald Brace, of Harcourt Brace, so long associated with Routledge and Kegan Paul in the publication of Ogden's *International Library of Psychology*. As I read, I realized that here was a book of unusual quality, though Mumford's name was unknown to me then. But I also realized that the subject was no easy one, both because it was novel and because it clearly did not fit into any university curriculum. *Technics and Civilization* dealt with the development of the machine during the last thousand years and its effects on society. Mumford put the questions he proposed to answer in the first lines of his work: 'How did this come about? Where did it take place? What were the chief motives that encouraged this radical transformation of the environment and the routine of life. . . . What unexpected values have arisen in the process?' There were chapters that struck my imagination then and strike it again today when I re-read them. The disciplinary influence of clocks; the effect of war on techniques; the degradation of the worker, especially the miner, in the early phases of the industrial revolution; the necessity of socialization in the production and consumption of goods. The book was stuffed with ideas and little known facts and unfamiliar episodes of history. But what impressed me most was the humanist intelligence that shone through every sentence. Seller or non-seller, this book meant a lot to me, and I secured the rights in it from Brace. Before returning to London, my wife and I lunched with its author at Schrafts, and so began one of the closest friendships of my life.

Back in England in March, I brooded on the experiences I had had in New York. This great source of books, written in English, lured a man like myself, restless, eager for the new, ready to take a chance. In 1935 I made a second trip, expecting to return yet again in 1936 or 1937. In fact, it was twelve years before I was to go back. The furies were on my heels, and in the autumn of 1935 they were to catch up with me.

The first signs of their approach had been visible in January 1934 when Routledge celebrated its centenary with a huge dinner. Publishers, booksellers, authors, critics, agents and distinguished men and women of all kinds attended. There were perhaps two hundred and fifty guests. Among half a dozen others I was to make a speech. It was the first time I had been called to this abominable task on so public an occasion, and I cast about for a theme to animate my discourse. Only too soon inspiration was vouchsafed me, and I started on the slippery path to my doom. In those days of slump and unemployment, with the economists pursuing a rigid deflationary policy whose social effects they rarely viewed where they were visible, the doctrines of social credit were having a vogue. The social credit bug had bitten me, which was not surprising. My unenthusiastic attitude to banking made me a sucker for any theory which attributed a high proportion of the world's ills to the machinations of bankers. This remarkable theory, I decided, should be the mainspring of my oration. On the appointed day I rose from my seat at the high table and poured out with passionate ineptness a speech of exceptional stupidity. When I sat down, there was a scattered round of clapping, probably from those hard enough of hearing not to have grasped precisely what I said. I was appalled. Too late I realized that I had made the wrong speech in the wrong place.

The next speaker to rise was the never-to-be-forgotten David Roy, high executive then of the W. H. Smith & Son organization, now alas dead. With the rich Scottish accent cultivated by so many who have lived for years south of the border, he proclaimed that the future of the book-trade rested in the hands of its young men. Much had been said, he continued, about the eminence of Routledge directors past and present, but he for his part wished to expatiate on the virtues of the junior managing director who had just sat down, etc. I listened with joy and astonishment as he sang my praises. Slowly the blood returned to my cheeks. I sat up and began to look almost cheerful. It had been a near thing.

As I left the great hall with my wife when the affair was over, I said to her 'Thank God for David Roy'.

'I told him,' she replied, 'that it was absolutely disgusting the way the speakers were talking about the old fogies, and not one mention of you. After all, what on earth would Routledge be, if you didn't give it a bit of life? Everybody knows that.'

'And what did he say?' I asked.

'He said "Just wait till I get on my feet and I'll show them where they get off".'

The evening had ended far better than it had begun. Partisanship is one of the greatest gifts from a wife to her husband.

Meantime in Europe the madman with the raucous voice grew stronger. In June 1934 Hitler purged the Nazi Party, and murdered many members of the brownshirt left wing. I rejoiced at their death, but could scarcely approve the manner of it. In July there was the affair at the radio-station in Vienna and the murder of the Austrian prime minister, Dollfuss. All through the day, Pamela and I sat glued before a radio, listening to the harsh voices and horrible news of a real-life melodrama. At the end of the year old President Hindenburg died and became a totemic symbol to the German people. Hitler became Führer, a word barely known to me till then, and began his debauchment of the most powerful nation in Europe.

As it was with Hitler in the international field, so in my tiny publishing plot it was with me—those whom the gods wish to destroy they first make mad. My madness began one evening after dinner, a period of the day when a husband, weary after a hard day's work, lies back in his armchair and attempts to give his mind a rest. On this particular evening certainly, I had no thought for the Nazi threat to peace, the rise of anti-semitism, the futility of whoever was British Prime Minister at this juncture. I was dreaming of a holiday due to take place before long. Relaxed and cheerful I was off guard when the first rumblings of the storm came to my ears.

'Did you say I was complacent?' I inquired, startled at a sudden tendency in the conversation to become critical of me.

'Of course you're complacent,' my wife said, 'in fact, I'd call you smug.'

'That's a dreadful accusation to make,' I replied, 'just because I haven't yet got around to asking my Board for a rise in salary.'

'I'm not thinking of your cowardice about salary,' Pamela said.

'You're not? Then what are you thinking about?' I asked, by this time seriously alarmed.

'You're getting to be a bore,' came the answer, in a voice that sent shivers down my back.

My wife has a strange and strong personality, rather like a volcano that bursts into sudden and destructive eruption after years of inactivity. The difference between my wife and a volcano is that in her case the activity is more frequent, occurring every few months or even weeks. When such an outburst occurs, it develops a force not easily resisted, and flight is usually the most prudent remedy, indeed one that I have often adopted. But no man with any self-respect can retreat before the charge of being a bore. The accusation is so grave, so wounding, and so fundamental that a retreat might easily become a rout. I decided instantly to take up the challenge and stand my ground. This decision, made in haste, was repented at leisure.

'What on earth do you mean by calling me a bore?' I asked, rather angrily.

This rhetorical question also turned out to be a mistaken tactic, for my wife hastened to tell me. The firm for which I worked, it appeared to her, lacked the indispensable quality of glamour. 'No poetry, no *belles-lettres*, no book any normal human being could possibly read with pleasure. And you,' she added irritably, 'are getting as dull as your books.'

Mildly, I pointed out to her that we published many of the most important philosophical, psychological and historical works of the day, as well as a wide range of general literature. But this too proved to be an unwise remark, for she proceeded to concentrate with unfair precision on what she believed to be a weak point in my defences. 'Take all that psycho-analysis on your list,' she cried indignantly, 'you know what I think of that! What good does it do? Of course people have a disgusting side to their natures which they repress, but there was no need for Freud to help them indulge it to their heart's content.'

'Without psycho-analysis,' I remarked, tentatively, 'we might never have got married.'

'What nonsense,' Pamela replied, 'it wasn't Professor Flugel who removed your inhibitions, it was me. All that money you spent with him was absolutely wasted. Have you no *ambition*,' she went on, switching disconcertingly to a new line of attack, 'no urge to publish the great books of the day? Are you prepared to spend the rest of

143

your life mouldering at Routledge? Are you really satisfied with nothing but cookbooks, ready reckoners, and guides to gardening? Of course you aren't!' After this magnificent if misleading flood of rhetoric, she relaxed triumphantly. The storm was over, but the damage to my ego was grievous, and I was not unaware of it.

As the weeks passed, I took stock of my position. The arguments I had used five years ago came back to me. Then my revered Master had still been alive, and a rebellion against his authority had been unthinkable. But now all was changed; at the least I was five years older and, I considered, five years wiser. The editorial health of the firm was in my hands, not Franklin's, according to my way of thinking. One by one I went over the ideas that came crowding into my head—the publication of novels, readiness to pay big advances for big books, a more literary list, fewer slow-selling academic works, stronger sales and promotion organizations. The thoughts that had been dormant, pushed into the background of my consciousness for so long, came to life, released through the waving of my wife's magic and over-efficient wand. They were dangerous thoughts, though I was naturally unaware of the fact that they were to lead me into wholly uncharted waters.

The first thing to do, I decided, was to write a memorandum embodying the Warburg Plan for Livelier and More Profitable Publishing. I set to work without delay and soon completed it. The habit of writing memoranda is a favourite of mine, but it is attended by risks which I have come to understand better since 1935. The risks are twofold. In the first place, a memorandum has to be reasonably short, to make its point pithily and somewhat dramatically. This brevity carries with it the danger of distortion and exaggeration; you say, as it were, less than you might but more than you ought. In the second place, a memorandum nearly always convinces the writer of it. Fascinated by his own skill and originality, his enthusiasm for whatever the project may be is doubled and tripled. But this boundless enthusiasm cannot always or even often be conveyed to those who read it, with the result that the gap between the writer and his readers may become so great as to be unbridgeable. So it was with my memorandum. As I committed to paper the words that were to change my publishing life, my appetite for a new policy increased. Visions of a Routledge transformed, glamourized, modernized, filled my mind. I completed my draft and presented it proudly to my Board. It was not received with the degree of sympathetic understanding that I had anticipated.

As opposition developed to my ideas, so my devotion to them grew. My frustration, too long pent up, broke through the normal barriers of politeness. Reticence turned to volubility, suavity gave way to pugnacity. What looked at the start like a storm in a teacup soon became an argument at a board meeting. Insults and counter-insults were flung across the table. The quarrel settled my hash, for soon, as was inevitable, the legal aspects became paramount. Within two weeks I was out on the streets, without a job, salary, or prospects, a miserable victim, in my own youthful opinion, of a vicious and degenerate capitalism.

So nearly always are new publishing houses born, though I did not realize it in those frantic days. The pattern is well defined. Youth attacks age and experience, and is expelled by them, to start as often as not a new firm and ultimately a new orthodoxy. Such I imagine to be the nature of progress.

7

It's the First
Step that Counts

THE LOSS OF A JOB to which I had devoted thirteen years of my life and an enormous amount of energy filled me with dismay. There, on the Routledge list, were authors I had found, books I had commissioned, series I had invented. It was intolerable that I should be forcibly separated from them. I felt empty and panic-stricken. From being a managing director in a distinguished firm I had become unemployed, all in a matter of days. I was dimly aware, too, of the most depressing fact, that the more important the job you lose, the more difficult it is to find a new one of equal importance. Self-righteous and self-pitying, I went home to break the shocking news to my wife. I expected from her sympathetic understanding of my tragic plight; what I got at first was displeasure and even alarm. 'It's just like you to go too far,' was the mildest form in which she manifested her annoyance. But she recovered soon enough, for her optimism on the subject of her husband's inevitable progress was buoyant and unbounded. Her attitude to those so recently my colleagues, she summarized in the memorable phrase: 'You were far too good for that mouldy crew.' This was balm to my wounded ego. She then began to paint a picture of my future so golden as to be almost unbelievable, ending with the sentences: 'We don't know yet where it is, but there's a wonderful job waiting for you. Why, there isn't a publisher in London who won't jump at the chance of obtaining your services!'

Stimulated by these visions, we sat down to an excellent dinner, ignoring for the moment the undoubted fact that they did not add up to a policy. Yet a policy was needed, and without delay. My capital resources were slender, my income had come to a stop, while expenditure seemed likely to remain much as before. As a matter of fact, it somewhat increased during the weeks that followed, since Pamela, though aiming at a rigorous economy, took infinite trouble to provide me with all kinds of extravagances to boost my morale. The situation required swift and masterful handling, but it did not receive it.

In those days before World War II, the London publishing trade was situated in two widely distant neighbourhoods, near St. Paul's and especially in Paternoster Row, later to be destroyed utterly by fire-bombs, and in the district round the British Museum down to Henrietta Street, Covent Garden. These districts I came to know only too well, as I walked from one well-known publishing house to another seeking a job. The experience was humiliating. Elderly and middle-aged gentlemen received me kindly by appointment and listened while I gave them a brief résumé of my career and qualifications. I was, after all, not a completely unknown figure in the publishing world of 1935. But when I came to expound my plans for the future, they turned me down flat and with unanimity. After a time it became obvious, either that my charm of manner was less effective than my wife had led me to believe, or that they divined my secret wish to turn their businesses upside-down to make room for my own ambition. Despondent after some weeks at my renewed failures, I put the problem of what to do next before my wife.

'I can't afford to make another mistake,' I told her solemnly, 'after the years spent at Routledge to no purpose. If I fail again I shall be forced to go right out of publishing.'

This admirable young woman had no qualms. 'I've always told you,' she remarked, briskly if inaccurately, 'that it was a sheer waste of time asking those poor old dodderers for a job. I've met them at cocktail parties, and they're no use to you at all. Why, they haven't the brains to engage an office boy without help.'

Genuinely shocked at this cavalier description of the pillars of my trade, I protested that I had in fact been interviewed by several of London's leading publishers. But my wife waved me aside. 'You're much too good for them,' she said, 'and they know it. That's why they won't give you a job.'

'A very unsatisfactory position for me to be in,' I suggested grimly.

'Not a bit of it,' Pamela answered, 'don't bother with them. *You must start your own business*. In three years' time *you*'ll be offering *them* jobs.'

The idea pierced through my gloom like a ray of sunlight on a cloudy day, or perhaps like a sharp knife through butter. Struggling to assume a calm which I did not feel, I thanked her for the confidence she felt in me. It was, I said, a rare and beautiful thing for a wife to think so highly of her husband. 'It's not that I think so highly of you,' she replied, 'it's that I think so little of the others.'

The idea of starting up on my own had occurred to me more than once since I had lost my job, but I had set it aside on the grounds that it needed far more capital than I possessed. The history of publishing made it clear that new firms usually developed by means of a fission process. The disgruntled young partner, furious that 'the establishment' would take no notice of his plans, got out and started a new firm that overshadowed the one that trained him. It was in this way, for instance, that young Willy Heinemann, debonair and adventurous, forsook the ageing house of Trubner & Co., to found the large and distinguished firm that still bears his name. Why should not I do the same? The answer came pat. The time for establishing new publishing houses was past; there were too many already. Besides, to direct even a well-established firm was, I knew, a complicated and hazardous process, comparable to gambling on the Stock Exchange, trading in furs, or running houses which are not homes.

Confidently, I put before my wife the insuperable difficulties which beset the course she proposed, but she returned a dusty answer. 'Of course,' she said, 'if I've married a coward, there's no more to say. You could find another job easily enough, but I married you as a publisher. You'd not suit me so well if you were anything else. As for the money,' she continued blithely, 'you can raise that easily enough. But you must ask for plenty of it. They won't give you any at all if you ask for too little.' Marvelling at my wife's appreciation of this nicety of financial behaviour, I inquired who she had in mind when she referred to 'they', those persons unknown, at least to me, who were prepared to hand out thousands of pounds to a fanatic in search of a publishing house. Did she not know, I said sternly, that publishers were going bankrupt every month or two? My wife neither knew nor cared. 'You won't go bust, once you've started,' she said emphatically, 'everybody thinks you're a wonderful publisher. Anyone would finance you—

149

printers, binders, paper-makers, your bank, of course. And there's always your Aunt Agnes.'

Stunned by these ruthless improvisations, I sat silently pondering her words. How easy she made it sound, how hard it was in fact to achieve. Before I could voice my gloom, she had left the room, confident that she had as good as solved the problem, an Eve who has offered Adam the apple and has no fear about his taking a big bite out of it. But could I? Were my teeth strong enough? Would I dare take the risks? What printer or paper-maker would lend me a farthing? How would a banker react to a request for an unsecured loan of £5,000 to £50,000? How much did I need anyway? Would my Aunt Agnes think well of it? To these questions I returned no answers, not knowing any.

About this time I had become aware, as a result of my unsuccessful explorations in the world of publishing, that a small and most distinguished firm, Martin Secker Ltd., had recently failed and fallen into the hands of a liquidator, Mr. Harry Wingfield of Fairbairn, Wingfield & Wykes, accountants specializing, among other more impressive matters of commerce, in the re-sale or winding-up of publishing firms that had come a cropper. In those grievous days when Hitler was ranting his way through Europe and Chamberlain whispering appeasement into ears only too open to receive it, the casualty rate among publishers was so high that the possibility of disposing of all of them to those willing and able to revive them was negligible. Most of them sank without trace, their lists absorbed by the giants of the trade, their policies, when they had any, lost for ever.

But Martin Secker's firm was an exceptional one. He had founded it in 1910, and had been a publisher of sorts before that, a reader for Mr. Eveleigh Nash. Through his hands and under his trained eyes had passed the never-ending stream of misbegotten manuscripts which flow in and out of all publishing houses, pretending unsuccessfully to be books. Being a good reader, Secker naturally rejected, with the contempt it deserved, all but one in a hundred of this trash. But from time to time he perceived, or thought he perceived, a nugget among the dross, whereupon he would write a note to Nash recommending acceptance of the manuscript, and Nash, not himself a great reader, would deposit the book with his mistress for a final report.

Around 1909, Martin Secker had read a novel about which he had formed so high an opinion that he had recommended it unhesitatingly to Nash, who had passed it on to this distinguished and powerful personage. She had read it and disliked it, so the book had been rejected. In 1910, Secker had left his job and started up on his own. Remembering the fine novel he had read and admired the previous year, he had written to its author, Mr. Compton Mackenzie, offering to publish *The Passionate Elopement* on his first list. Mackenzie was only too happy. The book appeared, took London by storm, and Secker was made. Young and distinguished writers flocked on to his list— Frank Swinnerton, Francis Brett Young, Hugh Walpole and others, urged on by the grateful Mackenzie. The firm flourished but never grew big. Secker was perhaps less than energetic, somewhat unambitious, or maybe he had insufficient capital. But from the beginning he had an eye for talent—*South Wind* and other early books of Norman Douglas, the poems of J. E. Flecker, Thomas Mann's *Buddenbrooks*, Franz Kafka's *The Castle*, Lion Feuchtwanger's *Jew Süss* and all the later works of D. H. Lawrence, these were but a few of the brilliants that sparkled in his publishing crown. His firm was a literary sensation, but it never succeeded in consolidating itself financially. Twenty-five years after its foundation, it collapsed, and Wingfield was appointed by the creditors to dispose of it. This was the firm on which I had cast my eyes, as an excellent foundation on which to build a publishing house of my own.

Fired by my wife's enthusiasm and unwilling to accept from her the damaging appellation of coward, I began seriously to consider the possibilities. Optimistic as I was by temperament I could not but be aware, however vaguely, of the formidable nature of the task. To set up a new business in any branch of trade means to compete with the flourishing houses already established. But a brand-new publishing house encounters at the start a snag which does not seem to be present to the same extent in other trades. That snag is the scarcity of the raw material.

The raw material out of which the finished publishing article is made does not grow in the open, like tobacco or rice or cocoa beans. It is not mined from the bowels of the earth like coal or iron or uranium. Nor can it be bought in the open market at a generally agreed price. The raw material of publishing is unpublished books, that is, flimsy and often unattractive-looking typescripts with corrections and additions in ink made by the author in an illegible hand. These books or typescripts or manuscripts, good, mediocre, bad and unspeakable, share one quality in common. They are written. It is writers who are the kings and queens of the publishing trade; the publishers, uncharitable people might believe, are the knaves. Without the writer the publisher would have nothing whatever to manufacture and sell.

The ability to write well is scattered sparsely throughout the population. It is arguable that it is commoner than the ability to paint, sculp or compose music. But whether it is so or not, there can be no doubt that good writers are scarce and even indifferent writers hard to find. Since all the writers of any merit whatever are already off the market, comfortably placed with publishers whom they have learned to love, or at least to tolerate, they are not for sale to a new firm, except perhaps at a prohibitive price. The problem of finding worthwhile books to publish was, I knew, the most difficult of all the problems that faced me. The purchase of the assets of Martin Secker might go some way to solving it. It would also, I hoped, give me a small back list, and a name known and respected throughout the literary world. This, I decided, was just what I needed to give me a run for my money, or, as seemed inevitable, for someone else's.

Without delay I communicated the facts about the Martin Secker business to my wife, who became so excited as to lose temporarily her powers of speech. Rapidly recovering from this brief attack of aphasia, she told me that this was the most wonderful idea I'd had in my life, though it was a pity I hadn't conceived it earlier. She added that she did not intend to allow me a moment's peace until I had secured the firm, which she considered was ideal for my requirements. 'Why,' she said, referring to her discreditable adventures as a bookseller, 'I used to buy more books from Martin Secker than from anyone else.'

That evening we spent some hours, which my wife at least thoroughly enjoyed, planning a golden future. It appeared to her that, within a brief period of time, a wide range of masterpieces in all manner of literary forms would be assembled under my direction, and launched auspiciously on a world hungry for good books. Established authors would leave their miserable publishers to join the rising firm. Unknown but brilliant newcomers would rush to

153

have their books included on my first, or at least an early, list. Martin Secker Ltd., was to be re-christened at a champagne dinner as Martin Secker & Warburg Ltd., to rise as a publishing phoenix from the ashes of liquidation. Naturally, also, a salary would be paid me more in accord with my deserts than the feeble pittance provided by my recent employers. If these Utopian dreams stimulated me rather less than they did my wife, it was because I remained intermittently aware that the Martin Secker assets might already have been sold, or that my bid for them, assuming that I was ever to be in a position to make one, might prove unacceptable.

Such technicalities occasioned Pamela no misgivings whatever. Indeed, I hardly had the heart to mention them. For her it was unimaginable that a plan on which she had set her hopes should be incapable of realization almost within a matter of days. What gave her as much pleasure as a baby derives from a new rattle was the thought that I could soon launch a fine new English translation of the works of Colette. 'I was brought up on Colette,' she said to me, reminiscently, with a glow of satisfaction which memories of her girlhood never failed to induce, 'especially the *Claudine* books. Every girl should read them at school. Colette knows more about men and women than any other living writer. I simply can't understand why English girls aren't given her to read.' I forebore to tell her, since I had no wish to spoil the evening's roseate glow or to attract to myself the accusation of being perversely and hopelessly Anglo-Saxon.[1] On this evening we would feed on hope, washed down by rich draughts of ambrosia. It was after

---

[1] In 1950 I published the first volume of a collected edition of Colette's works in new translations, starting with the immortal *Chéri*, the author's favourite novel. The series had a big success. Eleven volumes have appeared to date, containing seventeen of the original French titles. A large selection of her short stories appeared in one volume in 1958. I hope to give an account of my visit to Colette in Paris in 1951 at a future date.

midnight before we retired to bed. I had become aware that, if my stupidity or lack of enterprise were to deprive me of the glittering prospects dangled before me by a beneficent providence, my wife would feel inclined to abandon my society in disgust. Next day I paid a visit to the offices of Martin Secker at 5 John Street, Adelphi, just off the Strand by Charing Cross.

Martin Secker, in 1936, was a man in his early fifties. Round-headed, fresh-complexioned, with jet-black hair, short and slim, he spoke with an almost imperceptible drawl, and laughed heartily but not very often. He wore a pepper-and-salt tweed suit. To me, nearly twenty years his junior, he appeared somewhat elderly, a slightly fabulous figure from a distant age, a personality belonging with the eccentric, brilliant and adroit publisher-editors of an earlier period—John Lane with his *Yellow Book* and Grant Richards (a personal friend of Secker's), the discoverer of *The Shropshire Lad* and founder of the World's Classics. From Secker's desk, which was otherwise unremarkable, rose the faint musty odour of the *Yellow Book* itself, with vague aphrodisiac traces of Aubrey Beardsley.

Greeting me amiably, Secker sat me down in front of a big coal fire—it was a cold day in February—and we discussed the situation at length. He was obviously proud of the business which had now collapsed after twenty-five years' work, and regarded me as a potential rescuer. He hoped, no doubt, that I would maintain the list on much the same lines as before, with himself as a senior adviser. Certainly, whether he intended it or not, Secker and his firm fascinated me. For ten years I had been practising the science of publishing, now I was listening to a survey of the art. And a tricky art it was, heaven knows. Though Mr. Stallybrass had been dead for five years, his influence still lay heavily upon me. Despite the brave words of the memorandum which had gained me the sack, it yet sounded to me immoral to hear casual mention of an advance of £250 here and £500 there. The expenses involved in launching a best-seller—the advertising budget, the shower of free copies, the poster and show-cards, the cocktail-party send-off, the huge printing—were terrifying to a publisher of the school of Mr. Stallybrass. With sagging jaw and startled eyes, I heard the names of the literary giants, D. H. Lawrence and Thomas Mann, Lion Feuchtwanger and Frank Swinnerton, men known personally to Secker, but to me brilliant stars in a distant firmament. I sat hypnotized by the spells woven by Secker, delivered in a flat throw-away manner which enhanced their power.

How was it possible, I wondered, that I could have frittered away the best years of my life in the dull routines of academic publishing? I had been living like a monk in the cloister; it was high time for me to venture out as a knight into the world of pageantry and jousting. More than ever I realized the intuitive wisdom of my devoted wife in demanding something more adventurous, gayer and more romantic from her husband. It was a fabulous bit of luck, properly viewed, that I was out of a job, for it allowed me to risk my all on something worthy of my talents, even if, as I half suspected, I fell flat on my face in the attempt.

Concealing as best I could from Secker's shrewd eyes the strength of my feelings, boasting and telling a few thumping lies in the process, we examined together the eight brand-new unpublished titles, which would constitute my first list, if ever I became the owner of the business. Five of them at least seemed to me attractive. There was, for instance, Erskine Caldwell's *Tobacco Road*. In those days Caldwell's was not a name to conjure with; it is only in the last decade that his sales in the U.S.A. in paper-back editions have reached the colossal total of nine or more million copies. There was a volume of the short stories of Thomas Mann, *Stories of Three Decades*. Already the reputation of Mann, author of *Buddenbrooks* and *The Magic Mountain*, was fabulous and he had won the Nobel prize for literature in 1929. There was a novel by a popular woman writer of the day, Elinor Mordaunt, called *Prelude to Death*, on which I was astonished to learn that an advance of £250 had to be paid. Arnold Zweig also figured on the list with *Education Before Verdun*, the grim second volume of the great trilogy begun some years before with the famous war novel, *The Case of Sergeant Grischa*. Grischa had sold, Secker told me, over 40,000 copies and had been the biggest of all the books of the 1914–18 war until Remarque's *All Quiet on the Western Front* had swept the records of all other war books into the discard.

These works of fiction excited my cupidity and satisfied my judgement of value. But there was still another ace up Secker's sleeve, a book by an unknown French writer, Gabriel Chevallier. As Secker described the book to me, this novel began to give off a strange radioactive gleam. It was certainly an unusual novel, Secker said, and perhaps this was why it had been declined by a dozen other publishers before being offered to him. Readers had reported mournfully and monotonously that it was too long, poorly written, strictly for the French market, definitely obscene, and untranslatable into the bargain. But he had taken it, *tout de même*, perhaps, I thought unkindly, because so few good new books had been offered to a business known to be in such dire financial straits. The novel, Secker went on, dealt with life in a small village of the Beaujolais, devoted to the production of wine. It concerned the feud between the village's Catholic priest and the local atheistic schoolmaster, which had arisen from the proposal to construct an essential utility, in fact a public convenience for men, in the square facing the church. *Clochemerle*, Secker opined, might sell pretty well. It was my view, also. If the scales needed tilting yet further on the side of my buying the business, *Clochemerle* certainly tilted them. From then on, I was wholly converted and began to display the traditional zeal of the recent convert.

Infatuated as I was at the prospect of controlling this splendid, if bankrupt, business, I remained sober enough to recall that I had still to find the means of obtaining the price of admission, or even to discover what it was likely to be. Secker might have useful information about how much his assets would realize. Assuming the demeanour I imagined appropriate to a man about to ask a rather unimportant question, I put it to him. 'About five thousand pounds,' he replied. Instantly, as a reflection of Pamela's words, the idiotic thought flashed into my mind: 'The bank will never lend me as little as that!' It was followed by another, more realistic and more depressing: 'Five thousand pounds is far more than a man in your financial position will be able to raise.' Tentatively I indicated to Secker that to secure £5,000 in a hurry might present me with a problem of some difficulty. At this he seemed put out, for his expression was that of one disappointed to find that he has been talking to a man of straw rather than one of means. Waving my hand in the air, to convey that the solution of complicated financial problems was practically a cinch for an experienced man of affairs like myself, I asked whether there had already been potential buyers in the field. 'Several,' Secker replied; 'there are at least two firms keenly interested, but I should much prefer a publisher like yourself to take charge. You would have a more sympathetic understanding of this type of business than the others would.' Despite my pleasure at his flattery, I was disconcerted by the news that competitors were active, especially when Secker told me their names. Each of them could have bought ten businesses the size of his without noticing the drain on their bank balances. My earlier elation drained away. My own ambition and my wife's dreams seemed remote and inaccessible. Vaguely my thoughts dwelled on the substantial sums I had squandered, with her enthusiastic aid, over the purchase, decoration and furnishing of our St. John's Wood house, only three years before when we had started our almost-married life. What fun it had been! How mistaken it now appeared!

But there is always a storm before the silence; otherwise the human race would live in a perpetual and uneasy equilibrium. Secker's voice broke into my reverie, and startled me out of my gloom. 'The business,' he said, 'will be auctioned to the highest bidder on March fifteen. Bids should be in the hands of Fairbairn, Wingfield & Wykes by three p.m. on that day. If you feel that five thousand pounds or some such sum is rather more than you can afford on your own, there's a Mr. Roger Senhouse who seems quite keen on buying the business.'

I gaped at him. 'Roger Senhouse,' I said. 'Who on earth is he?'

'A connoisseur of books,' Secker replied, 'with a library of his own to which he seems deeply attached. He's never had any experience of publishing. In fact, that is why he is rather doubtful about the wisdom of buying a publishing house.'

'Do you mean,' I asked Secker, 'that Senhouse and I might go into partnership and buy the business jointly?' I wanted to get my facts absolutely straight.

'Certainly,' said Secker.

The idea seemed to me ridiculous. How could Senhouse and I, two men who were probably poles apart in taste and

159

attitude, come together at short notice and spirit the business away from two great firms who had already cast covetous eyes on it. It was too much to expect. Yet, as I pondered the matter, what other solution lay open to me? It was hardly likely that anyone would give me anywhere near £5,000 with which to start a business. Grasping at the straw, I obtained Senhouse's address. A week later we met in the Martin Secker office.

Roger Henry Pocklington Senhouse, when he appeared, was a man of about my own age, the descendant of a long line of Senhouses of Maryport in Cumberland. Unmarried, good-looking, and physically powerful, he was a product of Eton and Magdalen College, Oxford. Steel-blue eyes and a firm jaw promised, I thought, decisive action in whatever direction appealed to him. As soon as we began to talk, I was held by his beautiful speaking voice and a charm of manner calculated to win him many friends in and outside of business. This was a man who could perhaps help me surmount the countless difficulties which lay irremediably in front of me.

Soon after Secker had introduced us, he left us alone in his private room. Excited and suspicious of each other, we exchanged those meaningless pieces of information which serve as a substitute for that real knowledge of another person which only time can create. Our educational backgrounds were similar, but we had few mutual friends and differed on politics. I learnt that Senhouse had worked for some time as an assistant to Lytton Strachey, whom he obviously admired as among the greatest of contemporary authors. With this view I had no quarrel; *Eminent Victorians* seemed to me in those days a brilliant work. More recently, it appeared, Senhouse had been employed at Hay's Wharf in the London docks on the mysteries of a

My father and mother about 1896, at the time of their engagement

(Below, left to right) Aunt Agnes, Aunt Lily, my grandmother and my mother

The author prematurely practising his art, aged eight

The author as second-lieutenant

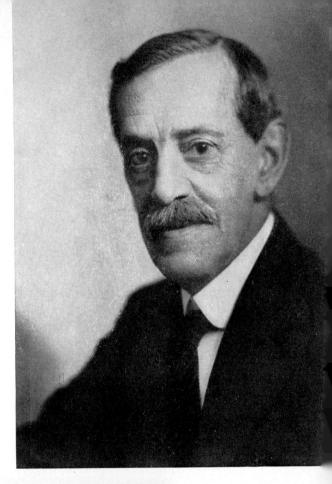

William Swan
Stallybrass, the
author's Master

John Macrae, American
publisher — oil by
Nikol Schattenstein,
about 1933

The author's second wife, Pamela de Bayou, in 1938 —
from an oil by Ethel Gabain

Roger Senhouse, the author's first partner, as a young man

Martin Secker
about 1945

J. G. Pattisson, in his twenties

Gabriel Chevallier,
author of *Clochemerle*

Tanya Benckendorff,
in her twenties, read-
ing a manuscript

Thomas Mann, Nobel Prize winner

George Orwell, John McNair and others, in 1938. Orwell is in the middle of the back row, and McNair, right front row

Lewis
Mumford

Pamela de Bayou in 1959

The author in 1959

H. G. Wells
from an unfinished oil by Pamela de Bayou, 1943–4

great import-export firm. This appeared to me to guarantee at least a minimum of business acumen, though I wondered why he had left. Intently I stared at him, seeking those strains of feeble-mindedness, dubious integrity or down-right criminal tendency which the average man prefers his partner to be without. Failing to detect them, I became comparatively cheerful and we began to get on rather well. Clearly Senhouse regarded me with some degree of respect as a knowledgeable publisher. To me he appeared as a gifted amateur, keen on books, well read, with a staggering assortment of friends in and outside the literary world. We said good-bye and agreed to meet for lunch a few days later, when we had had time to think things over. Mean-while I returned to Pamela, who was waiting eagerly for my report on the interview.

'Well,' she said, as soon as I got within speaking range of her, 'is it all fixed up?'

'No,' I said.

'Why not? Hasn't he got the money?'

'I really don't know.'

'Is he business-like?'

'H'm!'

'Does he want to buy the business with you?'

'I'm not sure.'

'Good gracious!' Pamela said. 'Do you mean to tell me you've been talking to Senhouse for three hours without having found out *anything* important at all?'

'I've found out a lot,' I said. 'That he's a man of integrity, full of charm and fond of books, but I must admit he seemed a trifle vague, uncertain of what he wanted to do or not to do.'

'If only I could have been there!' Pamela said, waving her hands desperately in the air. 'You probably didn't ask him one direct question, so of course he didn't give you a direct answer. All too gentlemanly, both of you, beating about the bush, not saying what you meant.'

'It was the first time we'd met,' I said apologetically, 'and to tell you the truth, his character was as opaque to me as a London fog. But we're meeting again on Wednesday.'

The conversation continued for a long time, but it got us nowhere. My wife's object was to establish a state of certainty where none existed; mine to leave the whole affair misty and obscure, to develop as it would when the time arrived.

Fortunately for my wife's sanity, the time arrived only four days later. We met at the Gargoyle Club in Dean Street, Soho, where I had long been a member. Sitting down to lunch in the glass-walled restaurant, I attempted to put my case to Senhouse briefly and sensibly. 'New publishing houses,' I said to him, 'require publishing knowledge and cash. I have the former, you have the latter. At the start the publishing side will be left to me, though naturally I shall pass on to you to the best of my ability the accumulated wisdom garnered from ten years' work in the publishing jungle. In due course you will become a first-rate practitioner, but to begin with you will have to be the financial brains of the new under-taking.'

'But,' Senhouse interposed, 'I don't believe I have a good financial brain. I fancy myself more on the literary side.'

The answer flabbergasted me. In the first place it was unexpected; since I had cast Senhouse in the role of financier and promoter, it seemed disobliging of him not to play the part. In the second it seemed to me unreasonable; if Senhouse had no experience of publishing, at least, I thought, he had some business experience. In the third,

I was only too well aware that any financial ability I might possess was, let us say, under-developed; at Routledge this indispensable quality had been provided by Franklin and others.

Recovering as best I could, I passed hurriedly on to a new aspect of the matter. 'A new publishing house,' I told him, with something of the magisterial pomposity of the schoolmaster addressing a promising pupil, 'requires authors. To find them will be difficult. Naturally,' I went on, warming to my task, 'I should hope to persuade some of the learned and brilliant authors I know to publish with us in future. Unknown writers are scarce, but I feel sure I can discover one or two promising novelists as soon as we have a firm to introduce them to.'

'I know several writers,' Senhouse remarked dreamily, 'Raymond Mortimer and Harold Nicolson and Stephen Spender and lots of others. But I'm not sure I should wish to ask them to publish with us.'

'Why not?' I asked in surprise. 'You mean they already have their own publishers?'

'It's not that so much,' Senhouse said, 'but one doesn't want to be under any obligation to one's friends, does one?'

'I don't know,' I said, too horror-struck to think of a proper answer. It occurred to me that it would be difficult to build a list if Senhouse and I refrained from asking for books from those most likely to heed us.

Summoning up my last reserves of energy, I told Senhouse that I was prepared to work day and night for the success of the new firm and that I was confident that within five years we could be one of the most distinguished publishing houses in Great Britain, and practically ready to retire. Forestalling any comment from him which might depress me further or convey doubt as to the possibility of the rapid progress I anticipated, I came to the heart of the matter, which was that he should invest not less than £5,000 in this promising and attractive speculation.

'But I haven't got it,' was Senhouse's reply.

Silenced at last, I sat staring at the wall, while the waiter changed the plates. So this then was the end of all my hopes; Secker & Warburg was not to be born; my wife would leave me; and I could start work as a junior executive in some piddling but prosperous publishing house stupid enough to employ me. But at this stage in my desperation, Senhouse took up the running. He sounded cheerful.

'I could easily raise the cash,' he began quietly, 'even though I haven't actually got as much as you say you want. Three thousand pounds, perhaps four. But a director of Martin's Bank, an old friend of mine to whom I've shown the figures, tells me that the scheme is unsound and that publishing is far too risky a speculation for me in these critical days. My fortune-teller, on the other hand, is strongly in favour of my going ahead, and I've never known her give me bad advice in the past.'[1]

I could hardly believe my ears. Was this man serious or was he pulling my leg? If serious, could he be regarded as the ideal partner for a professional publisher? If he was pulling my leg in a matter, to me, of life and death, was he not an unmitigated sadist? I regarded him narrowly, but he remained as poker-faced as ever, and seemed to think it was my turn to speak. With difficulty swallowing my indignation, I made a final bid for a deal. After all, without Senhouse, where was the financial backing, however flimsy,

[1] A story is told by Arthur Waugh of an English millionaire, seeking a new field for his activities in the late thirties, who conceived the crazy idea of making a corner in the publishing trade. He sent his clerk to Somerset House to make copies of the balance-sheets of all the publishers who were bound by law to deposit them there, and retired to his inner sanctum to plan his coup. Emerging a day or two later he shrugged and remarked that he had made a thorough investigation, but unfortunately there was 'nothing in it'. Post-war millionaires and crack financial institutions have come to a very different opinion, and many London publishing houses today are financed and controlled directly or indirectly by them. This anecdote is derived from Jonathan Cape's quarterly magazine, *Now and Then*.

to build my house of cards? 'All right,' I said, with as much calm as I could muster, 'we can do it. You put up three thousand pounds, I will put up a thousand pounds. We'll split the profits fifty-fifty. Do you agree?' Senhouse thought for a moment. 'Agreed,' he said. We shook hands on the deal while I prayed under my breath that Aunt Agnes would display more belief in her nephew's ability than she had ever done before. I ordered double brandies, and we drank a toast to the future of the firm we were to found. After this triumph of economic planning, we went our separate ways. The die was cast.

It must be rare in the annals of business enterprise for two men, not overtly certifiable, to have come so rapidly to such an idiotic decision. A modern electronic brain, had this fearsome invention then been fully developed, could doubtless have worked out our chances of success in one-millionth of a second. They were slim. For the financial situation of the new company, if it were ever to be incorporated, would be ludicrous. In those far-off days it was said that it took £10,000 and all the luck in the world to set up even a publishing doll's house.[1] The publishing trade was in the doldrums, as never before or since. Indeed, it was believed that overall it was making no net profit whatever. With £4,000 between us, and no arrangements made for further financing, we proposed to buy a business reported to be worth £5,000. No doubt any small change left over after the transaction would be available to pay the staff, the authors' advances, the bills for paper, print and binding, and the advertising expenditure. It also had to provide salaries for Senhouse and myself and the interest on the capital. Nevertheless, after this fateful lunch, I must admit that I experienced hardly a twinge of misgiving, but

[1] Today, the corresponding figure in England would be £50,000 and in the U.S. about $250,000.

was concerned exclusively with the question, would I or would I not succeed in extracting the essential £1,000 from my Aunt Agnes? It was to this task that I turned my attention without delay.

My Aunt Agnes was in 1936 a spinster in her middle sixties. Sympathetic to me at the time of my divorce, she yet had thirteen other nephews and nieces in which to take a benevolent interest. True that I was the oldest of them all, but I was not as close to her as some of the others, and my father had certainly not been the favourite of her three brothers. Nor was she by any means an avid reader. Worse still, she was an ardent Conservative, and regarded me, not without reason in those days, as a radical, or even worse as a socialist. However, she agreed to see me without delay. Over a cup of afternoon tea, I set before her with all the eloquence at my command, the whole tangled situation. Repressing the intrusive thought that I was behaving like a con-man with a credulous victim in tow, I spoke of the experience I had gained as a publisher at Routledge's and my abrupt dismissal; of the possibility of snatching victory out of defeat by grasping an opportunity that might never recur; of the maturing of my character, the growth of my abilities, and the plans already elaborated to ensure the success of the new venture. I described to her the brilliance and integrity and sense of realism to be discerned in my proposed partner, Senhouse, and his substantial backing of the firm-to-be. I depicted—and this at least was no over-statement—the enthusiastic support extended to me by my wife.

While a hostile critic might well have described my remarks as fraudulent misrepresentation, my aunt listened patiently to this farrago of nonsense, then quietly asked a pertinent question or two. 'It seems to me,' she said, 'though I really have no head for business, that you will not have nearly enough capital for your enterprise.'

It seemed to me that this maiden lady had hit the nail on the head, but there could be no retreat now. 'Once we've started,' I said, falteringly, 'we'll get all the money we need. *It's the first step that counts.*'

Aunt Agnes regarded me sceptically. 'You're being a trifle rash,' she remarked, 'but at least you know what you want. So many of the young men nowadays, it seems to me, just take the first thing that is offered to them. But,' she went on, inexorably, 'you and Mr. Senhouse have known each for so short a time. How can you tell that you will get on with each other as partners?'

It was, I thought, a good question, one that I should have expected from so commonsensical a woman as Aunt Agnes. Suppressing the feeling that I understood Senhouse as little as I did the binomial theorem, I assured her that there would be no trouble on that score.

Tensely I awaited the next question. I felt like a witness with a poor story to tell being cross-examined by a keen-minded counsel. I was nearly ready to throw up the sponge and call the whole thing off. But, thank heavens, the pressure had relaxed. 'It's probably idiotic to give you the money,' Aunt Agnes said primly, 'but your grandfather had great financial acumen, and no one can be sure you may not have inherited some of it. It would gratify me to see the family name on a flourishing business. I'll let you have one thousand pounds whenever you want it, but please don't ask me for any more.'

I stammered out my thanks, as my mind hurried ahead to the next step. Aunt Agnes smiled, almost she might be said to have grinned. 'You're going to do well,' she said, 'at least, I *hope* so.'

I raced home to tell my wife. She was pleased, but not

as impressed as I had expected. 'I've always told you,' she remarked, 'that Aunt Agnes was the only worthwhile member of your frightful family. But,' she continued, with the air of a professional adviser on the flotation of industrial enterprises, 'anybody could get a thousand pounds out of Aunt Agnes. She's got all the money in the world. You ought to have asked for more.'

By now the day was approaching when the bids for the assets of Martin Secker Ltd. had to be in the hands of the liquidator. Senhouse and I had agreed that we could not afford to offer more than £3,000, leaving the balance of £1,000 free for the running and development of the business. Even today, after all this time, the remembrance of our recklessness, makes my blood run cold. We wrote our bid down on a single sheet of notepaper, signed our two names underneath, placed it in an envelope, sealed it and, fearing to entrust it to His Majesty's mail, deposited it in person on the morning of 15 March in Wingfield's office. It was about eleven o'clock, four hours to go. Senhouse and I repaired to the Grosvenor Hotel, Victoria, to wait and discuss our chances. These in my opinion were poor.

My pessimism was in no way alleviated by the décor of the hotel, whose gloomy lounge contained us. But Senhouse was cheerful. Three thousand pounds was, he thought, a lot of money for the business, which had after all been in the market for months without finding a buyer. Almost everyone, he continued, had advised him against going ahead, and even at this last moment he wondered whether we had not offered too much and should withdraw. I looked at him in amazement. Did he mean what he said? If so, could I express to him the horror I felt at this crucial time? Possibly, I told myself, he's preparing to console us both, in case our offer is rejected, by demonstrating that it would have been folly to go ahead in any eventuality. At this my heart warmed to him as a friend in need, a man of sympathetic intuition. But I was and remained uncertain which interpretation was the correct one.

Slowly the time passed; we had lunch; it was two-thirty; we took a taxi and drove to the offices of Fairbairn, Wingfield & Wykes, 67 Watling Street, E.C.4, near to St. Paul's Churchyard. At two-fifty-five we paid off the driver, and hung about outside for five minutes. At the stroke of 3 p.m. we went in and asked for Mr. Wingfield. The waiting was over. After the months of agony, effort and indecision, I felt as calm as a man about to receive a death sentence after a long-drawn-out trial.

Wingfield received us standing behind a table in a small office. He seemed amused at our coming in person. Senhouse and I faced him across the table, like two schoolboys up for a caning by the headmaster. 'Have we got it?' I asked rather loudly, in a voice barely recognizable as my own. 'I have two bids, each for three thousand pounds,' Wingfield replied. I exchanged glances with Senhouse. Throughout the whole absurd affair, a tie had never been envisaged. What, for God's sake, did we do next? 'Why don't you raise your offer?' Wingfield said slily. Before the words were out of his mouth, I shouted out 'three thousand, one hundred pounds.' I looked round wildly, as if expecting a voice out of the blue to overbid me. 'Accepted,' said Wingfield. We made the alteration in our written bid. Subject to contract, the business was ours. Senhouse and I were in publishing! I shook hands with Senhouse. I shook hands with Wingfield. 'Why did you allow us to raise our bid?' I asked him. 'Because you took the trouble to come here and see what had happened,' Wingfield replied, 'and because Martin Secker's firm deserves an able publisher to revive it.'

169

When I told my wife the good news, she was delighted. 'I was never the least bit worried,' she said, with that disregard for historical truth which alone makes life enjoyable to most women. 'I always knew you'd get the business. Soon you'll be the most famous publisher in London, and conceited beyond all bounds.' Without a tremor she poured out the drinks to celebrate the occasion. She was smiling all over her face. As I drank the toast I thought to myself: 'With this exceptional woman directing operations behind the scenes, even a broken-down selling-plater could win the Derby.'

8   Year One

THERE IS, I SUPPOSE, never an ideal time in which
to start a publishing house; the odds are inevitably against
so rash an undertaking. But, of all conceivable periods
during the last hundred years, the spring of 1936 was the
most unfavourable of all. Mussolini's conquest of Abyssinia
was complete, and an uneasy truce prevailed in the
Mediterranean. In March, a month before we began to
function as a firm, Hitler marched into the Rhineland in
defiance of the Versailles Treaty, and France looked to
Britain for support in a strong counter-move. She should
have known better. The British Government, with Stanley
Baldwin as prime minister, returned a dusty answer, and
the last chance to bottle up the Nazi menace was gone.
We published our first book under the proud new imprint,

MARTIN SECKER AND WARBURG LTD.

on 4 April. It was a library novel by Elinor Mordaunt,
with the appropriate title, *Prelude to Death*. Within three
and a half months the Spanish Civil War had begun, and
death stalked the sierras and city streets of Spain. Publishing had to be pursued in the midst of tragedy and high
drama. The task was not easy. With a partner whose

171

reactions were unpredictable, at least to me, and employees I did not know, I felt lonely, but eager to have a go.

Problems surrounded me on all sides, but after five months' unemployment it was wonderful to be working again. No more moping at home, no more visits to prospective employers who spurned me. Like a willing galley-slave, if such there be, back on his trireme after an enforced absence, I sank my oar into the ocean of work and pulled with a will. I was chairman, managing director, sales manager, promotion executive, advertising manager, supervisor of production, and many other things as well. In the interests of morale, I pretended to a sureness I lacked. My experience at Routledge was an untrustworthy guide to the conduct of a firm one-tenth its size and fragile as an eggshell.

The problem of finance I left to Senhouse. It was a brutal decision, but it seemed to me an inevitable one. The publishing side of the business had to be restarted; only I had the necessary power and authority to do it. Besides, I was only too well aware that my gifts as a money-raiser were negligible. In the months that had preceded the foundation of the new firm, I had secured a mere £1,000, and that from an aunt who had her nephew's well-being at heart. It was not impressive, as my wife had told me in unmistakable terms. There was, of course, a more or less permanent financial crisis from the very beginning, and Senhouse coped with it as best he could. I used to hear him talking in his room next door to mine to representatives of printers, binders, paper-makers and the rest. The conversation had a certain monotony, ending with words spoken in a tone of mild reproach, 'You really must wait another month; you know how slowly booksellers pay their accounts these days.' It was amazing to me that our creditors were so patient. They must have believed that the potential resources of the firm were vastly bigger than in fact they were. Every Friday morning we sent round to Simpkin Marshall, the great wholesalers, to collect the cheque due to us. It wasn't very large, but without it, as often as not, we could not have paid the week's wages.

But Senhouse's friends were devoted to him. They rallied to him in his need, and subscribed £500 here, £1,000 there. The trouble was that there were not enough of them. Of the £10,000 share capital we had specified in our articles of association, only £8,300 was found. After that, Senhouse and I began to lend money to the company, pretending that the time was not far distant when we would be able to repay ourselves. But of course that time never arrived. In spite of this amateurish financial muddling, we did hold firm against one of the most damaging courses a new and hard-up publisher can pursue, the appointment of new directors. In return for an investment of £1,000 or some lesser sum, your proposed benefactor wants a job and a salary, though he knows nothing of the business and probably intends not to do a stroke of work. I have known publishing houses where there are ten or more directors on the board, and barely enough capital to run a teashop. The temptation was great, but we resisted it. It was the one sensible financial decision we took.

Soon after the new business became ours we were forced to move. The lease at 5 John Street, Adelphi, had run out; the building was to be demolished to make room for one of those neo-Georgian monsters, which have since become such a boring feature of post-war London. It was Senhouse who found the new offices at 22 Essex Street, Strand, and as soon as I inspected them, I fell in love with them; they had a ramshackle charm much in keeping with the firm that was to occupy them.

Essex Street runs south from the Strand, leaving it a few yards east of the church of St. Clement Danes, the famous church of the nursery rhyme, 'Oranges and lemons, say the bells of St. Clements.' Perhaps Orwell's grim use of the rhyme in *1984* twelve years later can be put down to the frequency with which he was to pass it on the way to our office. The south end of Essex Street, a narrow little road, culminated in the Essex Steps, a steep flight of about eighteen stone stairs leading to the Thames Embankment. Over the steps rose a fine arch; half-way down on the left lay the Steps Restaurant, where meals were served by ladies who knew their publishing executives ranked as sweated labour. I often lunched there. No. 22 was the last house but one on the right-hand side going south. As you went in, there was the trade counter. On the first floor were the four rooms which housed what brains and energies the new firm commanded. My own office was long and rather narrow, with a window looking out across the gardens on the Embankment and over the Thames itself to the South Bank. There I sat at my desk, brooding on the world's chaos and the jam we were in.

Looking back, it seems to me impossible that I should have accomplished so much in the forty-one months before World War II began. Yet I cannot remember that I was ever in a hurry, as I am so often today. Were the processes of publishing less complex and demanding than they are now? Hardly. Was I perhaps so unaware of the necessities of the situation that I had time to reflect? Certainly I can remember idle half-hours, staring out of the window at the Thames muddily flowing past Essex Steps to the sea. The great river soothed me and gave me a badly needed intimation of permanence, with Europe in flux, as Hitler hammered on its groggy defences. Nor was the eternality of Secker & Warburg any too obvious, even to my deliberately hopeful eyes.

If finance and premises were Senhouse's problems, practically everything else was my concern. There was, for instance, the staff. It was tiny—Senhouse and myself, Martin Secker who was responsible for manufacture, Ridgewell, a plethoric little man who was in charge of the trade counter, and a young clerk called Pattisson. Lean, lanky, fresh-faced and curly haired, J. G. Pattisson was then in his early twenties. Forced by the death of his father, a solicitor, to leave school prematurely, he had gone into Secker's firm as an office boy. Intelligent and industrious, he was well on his way to mastering the technical details of a publishing house, and must have done more than most of us to carry out those menial but necessary tasks without which a business simply falls to pieces however well directed it may be. In other words, he was indispensable. Since he is still with me, as a director, it can be assumed that he remains so.

One other member of the original staff remains with me today, our London traveller, C. R. Roth. In 1936 we shared him with one or two firms as small, though perhaps more significant then, as ours. Now that we have prospered, he works for us alone. Roth was a man nearing forty, a serious and thoughtful socialist, ex-member of the Independent Labour Party with which we were soon to get entangled. His job, of course, was to carry our books to all the bookshops in London and persuade them to buy more than they wanted. Difficult as this would have been at the best of times, in 1936 it approached the impossible. Booksellers do not normally regard the offerings of new publishing houses with enthusiasm. Bombarded with books they have no leisure to read from the established firms, they groan at the thought that another publisher has emerged to waste their time and ruin their tempers with unsaleable offerings.

Yet for us Roth's job was a vital one. Nearly half the total turnover of a general trade house derived in those days from London. Without a first-class representative, we might as well have put the shutters up without more ado. But in Roth we had struck lucky. His modesty, sincerity and lack of boastfulness had already endeared him to his customers. His unusual intelligence and literary sensitiveness soon recommended him to me. Roth was a godsend, an ideal representative for the kind of firm I intended to create.

Roth had only recently started work as Secker's traveller. His predecessor, whom, alas, I never met, was a Mr. G., a man of advanced years and companionable temperament. G. was a friend to the bookseller and the bookseller was a friend to him. They drank together, and the drink was too much for G. He would arrive at the office intoxicated, sink into a chair, and fall fast asleep. It was the duty of Pattisson to search his pockets for the precious orders, the life-blood of the firm, and decipher them for execution 'at earliest'. The genial G. was a good traveller, up to a point. He remembered, as a rule, to obtain the orders for new books from the great houses of the day, Mudie and Boots, W. H. Smith and Simpkin Marshall, Hatchard, Bumpus and the Times Book Club. But he forgot, as often as not, to record and pass them on. Two days before publication it was again Pattisson's duty to ring round the trade and discover what had been done, or left undone. At last the strain became too great, and G. was sacked, a victim of his own exuberant temperament.

This was the staff. But where, I asked Martin Secker, is the typist?

'We always typed our own letters,' Secker told me.

I was flabbergasted. As a managing director at Routledge, I had but to call and secretaries ran to do my bidding.
If I required production costs, depreciation figures, stock
lists, all was prepared and brought to me in a jiffy. Now
you did it yourself, or it wasn't done at all. But to be
without a typist was asking too much of me, I thought,
especially as I could not type even with one finger. How
could I write the hundreds of letters necessary to get
things moving?

'We must hire a typist at once,' I told Senhouse.

'We can't afford one,' he replied, 'there's hardly any
money left in the bank.' This phrase, used then for the
first time, was to become nauseatingly familiar as the
months and years rolled by. Gloomily that evening I went
home from the office. My wife noted my depression. 'What's
the matter?' she asked.

'Everything's the matter,' I said, 'I haven't got a typist,
and Senhouse says we can't afford one.'

'Can't afford one?' Pamela said, with a grimace of
horror wrinkling her forehead, 'you can't be serious. You
must get one immediately, a first-class one. It never pays
to economize on essentials. No one ever made a fortune
without taking risks. Look at old Rockefeller!'

'I'm not old and I'm not Rockefeller,' I broke in,
hastily, 'and where on earth is the money to come
from?'

'That's your affair, you must save it in other ways,'
my wife remarked grandly, and began at once to discuss
suitable candidates for the post. It was, of course, soon
after this that I hired a typist, Tanya Benckendorff, who
was to play an important role in our affairs.

In her early twenties, with a pale complexion, high
Slavic cheekbones, pointed chin, blue-gray eyes, and dark

177

hair brushed back untidily from a lofty forehead, Tanya was good-looking. The daughter of Baroness Budberg, known to many in literary and film circles in London by her Christian name of Moura, she was Esthonian by birth. Like her mother she spoke many languages, including French, German and Russian. English she spoke with a not quite perfect accent. Untrained in any secretarial college, she spelt indifferently, typed irregularly, and formed her shorthand signs in accordance with no known method. With Pattisson's help, it is said that she reconstructed the fragmentary scrawls in her notebook into letters not too unlike the ones I dictated to her, as palaeontologists reconstruct long-extinct animals from a few bones. She was, in fact, unlike any previous secretary of my acquaintance, a fact which endeared her to me in an office wholly unlike the vast organization from which I had been expelled.

Tanya ran her affairs, as she ran mine, with spasmodic violence and unusual powers of forgetfulness. She made so many minor mistakes that they could not have been counted, but never a blunder. She had understood what none of my colleagues except Senhouse understood, that Secker & Warburg was not so much a publishing business as an editorial office with a political branch, not so much a commercial enterprise as a 'movement'. It followed that 'public relations' was the most fundamental of our activities, and as a P.R.O. Tanya was unexcelled, everybody liked her.

There can be no doubt that in 1935–6 the publishing world was having a difficult time. The daily newspapers had been selling huge quantities of books at give-away prices in a frantic effort to increase their circulation above those of their rivals. 'An entirely new, exclusive and unique edition of the *Plays* of Bernard Shaw', for instance, could

be procured from the publishers of the *Daily Herald* for
3*s*. 9*d*. (postage extra) plus six coupons. These sales, and
many others like them, which did not pass through the
bookshops, were damaging to booksellers and publishers
alike. Remedies for this state of affairs were hard to find.
As Mr. (now Sir) Basil Blackwell himself said, at a dinner of
the Booksellers Provident Institution in February 1935:
'Publishing, that trade whose members can always be relied
upon to agree—to agree to differ.'[1] While confusion reigned
in the booksellers' shops, the publishers were stunned by
the successful prosecution of James Hanley's novel *Boy*
before Mr. Justice Porter at Manchester Assizes on obscenity
grounds four years after its publication. The fine alone
amounted to £400 and led to the rapid collapse of Messrs.
Boriswood, the publishers; £400 was an awful lot of money
then.

However, hope sprang in the hearts of some publishers
besides myself in 1935–6. Mr. (now Sir) Allen Lane was
to produce in June 1935 the first ten titles of a new series
of cheap reprints, bound in strong paper covers, to sell at
6*d*. per volume. The series was to be called 'The Penguin
Books'. Lane concluded his *Bookseller* article on the subject
with perhaps the most faulty prophecy in the history of
publishing—a trade in which faulty prophecy is naturally
endemic—when he wrote 'I would be the first to admit that
there is no fortune in this series for anyone concerned. . . .'

The late Mr. Michael Joseph was also an optimist in
1935. He had recently resigned from the well-known Curtis
Brown agency to start a publishing house of his own. He
engaged a Mr. Robert Lusty from Hutchinson as editorial
and production manager. Lusty was the youngest man in the

---

[1] These and other facts referred to here are taken from the Centenary issue of
The Bookseller, 3 May, 1958, pages 1614–16. *The Bookseller*, edited by Edmond
Segrave, is the premier organ of the British book trade, a lively and often brilliant
weekly, with an appeal far wider than a trade appeal. Indeed, it is read all over
the world, wherever books are bought.

trade at that time to hold so important a position. But he made a success of it and became deputy chairman.[1]

In 1936 several more new publishing houses were optimistically started, of which mine was one. As *The Bookseller* wrote at the time: 'Another company has come into being this week. The firm of Martin Secker Ltd., which during the last twenty-five years has contributed in no way meanly to the literature of the period, has been taken over by Mr. F. J. Warburg and Mr. Roger Senhouse, and will be known henceforward as Martin Secker and Warburg Ltd.' This as it were official confirmation of the fact of our existence gave me an exquisite pleasure when I read it, and I resolved to contribute also 'in no way meanly' to the publishing activities of the next quarter century. In order to do so, an editorial policy was necessary, and this I had. Strangely enough, it was the one thing about which I was never in doubt from the beginning.

An established firm needs no policy. It has its own authors, its prestige, its contacts. New books are attracted to it by a force accurately describable as publishing gravity. It can get along almost, but not quite, without effort. A new firm needs a policy, because its authors are few, its prestige not yet earned, its contacts still to be made. Without a policy it may never emerge into sufficient prominence to have a chance of success. A policy, a personality, an aura of some kind is the first essential of a new publishing house. This at least I knew in 1936, and I was well aware of the difficulties in achieving it. But, as usual, I was not without hope.

An author's books are not only his bread-and-butter,

[1] Twenty years later he resigned, after accepting an invitation to return to Hutchinson as chairman and managing director. In this capacity, he asked me a year ago to allow him to publish this book.

but the dream-children of his imagination, dearer to him in all probability than the disappointing and often unappreciative offspring of his loins. Why should he, or his agent, entrust these precious objects to an untested organization whose financial strength is almost certainly inadequate to the demands likely to be made upon it? Well, there are reasons. Otherwise, no new publisher would remain in existence longer than the time required to dissipate his initial capital. The old steadies would continue unexcitingly to rule the roost.

A new imprint can offer something novel to an author in more ways than one. It can, for instance, develop hitherto unused and exciting methods of promotion; in this way Gollancz advertised himself to success with huge spaces and types at the end of the 1920's. It can devise an exquisite format for its productions, as the Nonesuch Press in the years of its magnificence also in the 1920's. It can aim to exploit new markets by producing books so cheap that the poorest reader can afford to buy; so it was that Allen Lane with his Penguins earned himself a fortune in the 1930's and in due course a well-deserved knighthood. Lastly, a new imprint can establish itself by its willingness to publish books so unusual or so unpopular that the established houses won't touch them with a barge-pole. It was mainly by this method that Secker & Warburg came slowly to the front.

And this was no accident. In rejecting what I thought of as the coarse commercialism of so many of my rivals and plumping for a quality list which verged on the highbrow, I was not actuated by any high-flown or ethical motives. There was little or no priggish feeling that 'we needs must love the highest when we see it', as Emerson untruthfully remarked. The fact was that a high-class education in classics and philosophy, and a decade of

181

training under Mr. Stallybrass had rendered me incapable of estimating what the bulk of the population wanted to read. Since I didn't know and dared not guess, I regarded it as merely prudent and indeed inevitable to issue what I admired myself, and leave hokum to the addicts. In the short run, this policy was to create shocking financial problems. In the long run, it paid off handsomely.

What were these quality books that were to form the basis of my list? Here again the answer came pat. We lived, I thought, in an age of politics, where dangerous ideologies were driving the world mad. It was desirable to inoculate the British public at least, against the madness that was infecting it. This suggested that our list should be anti-fascist, and probably anti-communist as well. Not only was the age a political one, it was one where the forces of change and revolt were loose, broken like jinns from the bottles that had so long confined them. This indicated that our list should be radical, anti-conservative and unorthodox. In the literary sphere, my views were not less definite. The Martin Secker tradition of foreign translations appealed to me strongly. I had read and enjoyed the great best-sellers on the old Secker list from Zweig's *The Case of Sergeant Grischa* to Feuchtwanger's *Jew Süss*. Why should we not emulate them? I decided to do my best. In revolt against the Routledge policy of academic publishing, I plumped for the racy, the strictly contemporary, reportage and the modern world. Above all, I resolved to *épater le bourgeois*, to revolt against the respectable standards of a Bayswater upbringing. Egged on by my wife, whose views on morals were unorthodox if strong, I intended to shock the susceptibilities of those holding established views, to be something of an *enfant terrible*, a scandalizer, an enemy to prejudice. Despite zig-zags, we have not altered course greatly since then.

To have a policy is comparatively a simple matter. To carry it out is a labour of Hercules. How were we to persuade authors and agents to offer us worthwhile books of the quality required? This was the basic and brutal problem, the rock on which nine out of ten new publishing houses founder. Of the many misconceptions entertained about publishing by those who have little knowledge of it, the most extraordinary is the idea that good manuscripts are plentiful, and that a publisher has only to pick fastidiously from among a copious supply submitted for his approval a handful of masterpieces that suit his list. The fact is that publishers are many and worthwhile manuscripts few. Are there more than fifty well-constructed and interesting novels published in England in a twelve-month, including American novels and foreign translations, fifty out of the output of 4,000 titles? Well, yes, there are, but not many more. And about the same figure goes for books of general interest. It is easy to see that the newcomer has a hard time getting a sniff at anything outstanding.

Most of the books in a general publishing list are controlled by agents. There are half a dozen good agents in London, and their job is to act as legal and financial adviser to an author and to strike a good bargain on his behalf with the crafty and powerful publisher supposedly waiting to exploit him. Senhouse, neophyte though he was, knew about agents and had great hopes of assistance from them.

'You know them personally,' he said to me in our first weeks, in one of those halcyon periods when we were not too worried about how to pay the wages the following Friday, 'go and visit the literary agents, ask them to lunch or something.'

'Don't call them *literary agents*,' I said hastily, 'they can't endure to be called literary. Call them authors' agents.'

183

'Call them what you please,' Senhouse retorted, 'but for heaven's sake, get some good books out of them.'

I smiled wryly. 'The agents,' I told him, 'know me quite well; they probably regard me as reasonably honest and not too grossly inefficient; they may even like me personally. None of that will help. I am no longer the managing director of a respected firm, but *a new imprint*. In their opinion, we have no money to advertise the books they could sell us and no organization behind us. We lack power. That doesn't mean,' I continued gloomily, 'that they won't offer books to us; they'll offer us plenty, which will clutter up your room and mine and cost a small fortune to read and return. But these books will be worthless, the ones that have been turned down by everyone else. We shall be regarded as waste-paper-basket publishers, on whom all the rubbish is dumped.'

'Why on earth did I ever go into publishing?' Senhouse asked rhetorically.

'You went in for a career in publishing,' I told him, 'because of the glamour that attaches to it and your profound interest in literature. Bad reasons both of them. I continued with it, because I'm pigheadedly obstinate and filled with an unwarrantable optimism. Publishing is like the classical description of inflation—too many publishers chasing too few books. Nevertheless, the position is not hopeless.' But often enough it appeared so.

In Year One we published seventeen books, of which less than half derived from the activities of Martin Secker himself before we took over. There were thirteen novels and four general books. The latter were all political in character, a foretaste of what was to follow. Senhouse and I pestered everyone we knew to find books for us to publish, and books were discovered. In most cases, it would have been preferable had they not been. Richard Blake Brown's novel *My Aunt in Pink* and Richard Strachey's *The Golden Heart* were contributed by my partner to the common stock; the first, in spite of its entrancing title, made only a microscopic profit, the latter a small loss. My ventures in the field of fiction were Frank Tilsley's *I'd Do It Again* and C. L. R. James' *Minty Alley*. The latter, an account of a childhood in the West Indies, was unsuccessful, but James, a Trotskyist from Trinidad, published two important works with us later. Tilsley's novel was a success, and we accepted it as a good omen, since it was only the second book ever to be published under the new imprint.

Short and brutal, *I'd Do It Again* is the story of a clerk who stole from his employers to support his wife and children, written with such realism that I felt inclined to lock up the cash box whenever the author visited the office. The book was splendidly reviewed, and had a considerable prestige success, that is, it established the author's reputation on a high level without mitigating his chronic poverty or adding much of value to the publisher's profit. One thousand five hundred copies were printed and 1,223 sold to 31 December, and the gross profit ran to £95, of which we blued £75 on press advertising. Tilsley's second novel with us, *Devil Take The Hindmost*, was published early in 1937. It was an earlier one he had discarded, and then dolled up in a hurry after the success of *I'd Do It Again*. Poorly reviewed, it sold badly and lost money. It was the last book I was ever to publish for this strange and tormented man. He submitted next a detective story, which I started to read with excitement. There was never any doubt in my mind that Tilsley had what it took to become a big seller. The new novel began rather well. I read on and on. About the hundredth page, I came upon a passage, specially inserted, dealing with a character demonstrably modelled on myself. It was of a kind to expose me, as the lawyers say, to ignominy and contempt. I was horrified. We had no alternative but to reject the book, and by so doing we lost our option on his future work. His next novel, which was *not* the malicious detective novel, was a big book and a lively one. It appeared on the list of a famous publisher, and turned out a success.

From that day onwards Tilsley enjoyed what appeared to be a lucrative and distinguished literary career. His suicide a year or two back, twenty years after the publication of *I'd Do It Again*, shocked me profoundly, but did not come as a complete surprise. The mind of an author is complex, and his emotions bubble at times like the contents of a witch's cauldron. Perhaps Tilsley felt that he had paid too high a price for his popular success, perhaps he found that success empty or inadequate, perhaps he believed that he had exhausted the resources of his talent. The job of being a creative author can be as dangerous as removing fuses from unexploded bombs, and indeed it resembles it in more ways than one.

Apart from Mrs. Mordaunt's novel, already referred to, which sold exactly 3,000 copies and made a comfortable profit, there were four others picked by me over which it is best to draw a veil. Whatever merits they may have had, and I persist in thinking that one of them at least had merits, they did not sell well and cannot be called memorable. The fact was that, as a fiction publisher, I was a novice. In my nine years at Routledge, not a single novel had been published. I didn't know the ropes, and in spite of the melancholy warnings of Secker himself, who did know them, only too well, I went ahead. After all, I argued, a publisher has got to publish books, that is what he is for; a new publisher will hardly make a name for himself by the books he does *not* publish. So I bought my experience at a stiff price, but not quite a fatal one, as things turned out.

We naturally had more success with Arnold Zweig's new novel, *Education Before Verdun,* a grim picture of the German army in their struggle to capture in 1917 the great French fortress which barred their way to a break-through. This appeared in June. But despite our hopes, it did not repeat the success of *The Case of Sergeant Grischa,* which had sold 40,000 copies when first published some ten years before. We printed 5,000 copies of *Education,* and sold 3,676 by the end of the year. The gross profit was £350.

Probably the most important literary work to appear on our list, or indeed on any English publisher's list, that year was *Stories of Three Decades* by Thomas Mann. Awarded the Nobel Prize for literature in 1929, Mann was already famous in Europe and the U.S.A. Secker had published an English translation of *Buddenbrooks* as long ago as 1924. This was a saga of four generations in the life of a great merchant house in Lübeck, and was remarkable for the way in which Mann traced the decline of toughness and virility in the Buddenbrooks family as culture put its polish on them. The novel had been popular in England since it was published and sold a few hundred copies regularly every year. The English translation of *The Magic Mountain* was issued by Secker in 1927. This enormous novel is usually regarded as Mann's greatest work. It pictures a sanatorium for the tubercular in Switzerland, and deals with the processes of sick minds as well as diseased bodies in a Europe which the author saw, prophetically, as itself sick unto death. *The Magic Mountain* too sold well. Now Mann's German publisher had collected a large number of his short novels and stories into the big volume we were to publish, in association with Mann's regular American publisher, Alfred Knopf.

Stories of Three Decades contained some of Mann's finest work, including such undoubted masterpieces as *Mario the Magician*, the haunting *Death in Venice, Tonio Kröger*, and the famous story of a man and his dog, *Bashan and I*. In his preface, Mann describes it as covering 'almost the whole life-span of artist and man—an autobiography, as it were, in the guise of fable.' Mann was about sixty years old when he wrote these words, but another twenty were to pass before the life-span of this mountainous figure was to have run its course. Mann lived to be eighty, and four major novels, including the huge tetralogy, *Joseph and his Brothers*, were to appear on our list before death interrupted him in the middle of his most seductive book, *Felix Krull*.

In his preface to *Stories of Three Decades* Mann refers to 'that other fantastic enterprise in the shape of a novel which was to have been called *The Confessions of Felix Krull* and of which only the first book, *Childhood*, was actually written. *Krull* is in essence the story of an artist; in it the element of the unreal and illusional passes frankly over into the criminal. . . . The conception has in it the germ of truly great humour, and I wrote the existing fragment with such zest that I was not surprised to have many excellent judges pronounce it the best and happiest thing I have done. In a sense it may be the most personal. . . . *The Krull Memoirs*, however, were a difficult feat of equilibrium; I could not hold the note for too long a time without relief; and it was this seeking for variety, as I remember it, which produced the idea which afterwards developed into *Death in Venice* . . . to be written as quickly as might be, and serving as an interlude to work on *Felix Krull*. But creation has its own laws . . . I was not destined to return to *Krull*.'

So wrote Mann in 1935 about the fragment of an

unfinished novel, abandoned in 1911 twenty-four years earlier. But, as he wrote himself, creation has its own laws. Mann *was* destined to return to Krull some sixteen years later; the difficult feat of equilibrium had taken forty years to attain, but it was attained at the last in full measure. The fragment of 16,000 words became a big novel nearly ten times as long. It started with the 1911 section word-for-word unchanged. I wonder whether there is to be found in the whole history of literature a feat to be compared with this. Published in 1956 in a racy translation by the American scholar, Denver Lindley, many judges claimed it as the best novel Mann had written. But it was still unfinished, and before Mann could continue with a second and, who knows, a third and fourth volume, its author was dead. So, for ever doomed to wait, Krull, con-man and linguist, actor and thief, stands poised on the verge of that trip to South America in the guise of the Marquis of Venosta which must remain tantalizingly untravelled. It is to me the most disappointing gap in literature.

Stories of Three Decades didn't sell well in 1936, indeed it made a small loss. It was years before success came to Mann with the English reading public, a fact which I hold against that public, for Mann was surely the last of the titans.

In our fourth month of life, on 20 July, we published the 'book with the radioactive gleam' that had stirred my imagination and my cupidity at my very first interview with Secker. Gabriel Chevallier's *Clochemerle* was then an unknown book with an awkward title, but awkward titles have never hampered the sales of a best-seller, as *Kontiki* for instance has shown. In those days novels of average length, up to say 100,000 words, were invariably published at 7s. 6d. But *Clochemerle* was longer, and greatly daring

189

we priced it at 8*s.* 6*d.* But, no more than an awkward title, has price ever stopped a potential seller from selling. The advance was £100, covering the first 4,000 copies at 6*d.* a copy. The translator was Jocelyn Godefroi, and I have always thought that his version of this comic master-piece, embodying so much of the earthy tang of French village life, ranks among the finest translations of the 'thirties.

Godefroi was employed at the time in a high position in the offices of the Lord Chamberlain, concerned with matters of protocol and invitations to royal occasions. This labour, while important, was not unduly exacting. Godefroi had time to spare. In the bottom drawer of his desk he kept the paper-back original of *Clochemerle* and paper for the translation. When business was slack, and when presumably the Lord Chamberlain was elsewhere, he whipped them out and rendered another page or two into exuberant English. In this delightfully inappropriate way was executed a work that was to give less than innocent pleasure to, at a very rough estimate, ten million persons in the British Common-wealth and Empire. George VI, had he but known what his Lord Chamberlain's assistant was up to, could hardly fail to have approved a pastime so satisfying subsequently to so high a proportion of his subjects.

But these great developments were hidden in the mists of the future. To Senhouse and myself, 20 July was just another day filled with the usual difficulties, not an occasion for remembrance to be inscribed in letters of Beaujolais red on our publishing banner. Certainly we hoped to sell out the first edition in six to nine months, but that edition ran to 1,500 copies, no more and no less than the normal printing for a new and unknown writer. Mild hope rather than wild optimism dictated our policy, but success was immediate.

A reprint of 1,750 copies was made in August; another 1,000 in September, yet another 1,000 in November, and immediately after Christmas another 1,000 copies. Between publication day and 31 December we sold 4,734 copies, manna from heaven to a small business trying to make a start in life. Senhouse, entering up the figures in his great ledger, smiled, a trifle wanly perhaps, at the easement to be expected in his endless labour of paying the bills. Cock-a-hoop myself, I told everyone I met that we had published a best-seller in our first few months. My wife was not surprised. 'The English have dirty minds,' she said, 'they're only puritanical on top.' In 1937 *Clochemerle* sold another 2,381 copies, in 1938 731 copies. In the first two-and-a-half years of its life, it chalked up a grand total of 7,846 copies. But that was only the beginning.

In November 1938 we issued a cheaper edition in hard covers at 5*s*. By the end of 1942 it had sold 6,300 copies. By that time, the war had created a shocking paper shortage, and through 1943 the book was out of print, to the fury of the troops who had heard that it painted a picture of the land they were to invade much to their liking. By January 1944 we had got enough paper for a new printing of 3,000 copies, and the price had gone up to 7*s*. 6*d*. This printing was sold out in five weeks. In May of the same year we scraped together paper for 5,100 copies, all gone in a month, an example of the way in which books sold during the war years. The total sales by then amounted to 22,231 copies. Since that day *Clochemerle* has continued to sell with undiminished velocity. In 1949 we licensed the first paper-back edition in Penguin Books, where it was to sell hundreds of thousands of copies during the next decade. *Clochemerle* in English translation, as well as in the French original, has been one of the greatest sellers of the twentieth century.

The gross profits made out of *Clochemerle* before the end of 1936 amounted to a little over £700, and we spent £222 in advertising it. Enormous though this sum was for those days, at least double the maximum considered prudent by the pundits, it was probably money more usefully spent than any in the history of the firm before or since. It was the publication of *Clochemerle* that saved us from collapse in 1936, and it went right on warding off calamity through the years. It was the gift from the gods—Bacchus and Venus, no doubt, in this case—which alone enables a new publisher to survive and even to prosper, and it remains today as compulsively and agreeably readable as it was twenty-three years ago.

Of the four general books published in Year One, all secured as the result of my growing absorption in the political flux, two were flops. Neither John Paton's interesting account of his life as a socialist, *Left Turn*, nor F. A. Ridley's gloomy prophecy of the coming clash between British and German imperialism, *Next Year's War*, had the slightest success. But the other two titles, each dealing with the Spanish Civil War, found quite large publics.

Spain Today by Edward Conze appeared on 17 August. The Spanish affair had started only thirty days before, and interest was intense. Congratulating myself on my foresight in having commissioned so topical a book, I was delighted when it went into a second impression. But, of course, Conze's book was merely a short preliminary study of the conditions which made the Spanish tragedy inevitable. I decided to ask my old friend, John Langdon-Davies, for whom I had published at Routledge a book on Atoms, to write a full-length account of the Franco revolt based on personal observation.

Langdon-Davies knew Spain well, and opened his book

with an account of the May Day celebrations in Madrid, 'a city given over to the proletariat' for the occasion. But he was in England on the fatal day of 18 July. Very soon after, the *News Chronicle* sent him back as their special correspondent and he entered Spain with his son over the international bridge at Bourg Madame a week or two after the trouble began. Somehow between the second half of July and the end of September, Langdon-Davies succeeded in visiting many parts of Spain, contributing brilliant articles to the *News Chronicle*, and writing a substantial book of 90,000 words for which he provided us with striking photographs. The book was sent to press within hours of reading in the office, and was rushed out triumphantly on 23 November. It bore a sombre red, blue and black cover design by Victor Reinganum of a motorcyclist speeding on urgent business in a cloud of dust past the raised rifles of a platoon in position before some great Spanish church.

Behind the Spanish Barricades may have contained a few errors and, in the perspective of history, failed to get a complicated situation into absolutely just proportion, but it was the first authentic, on-the-spot reporting of one of the few genuine movements of the proletariat in world history. Inspired by the gallantry and self-sacrifice of the Spanish anarchists, fighting for a freedom unobtainable in an imperfect world, the author made his pages glow with colour and movement. The book was a success, of a kind. It sold about 2,300 copies in four months, and then was forgotten. We sold the American rights for a substantial sum. The gross profit amounted to £487. Of this I spent no less than £320 on leaflets and press-advertising. Since I could not fight myself in the anti-fascist ranks against Franco, it was, I felt, the least we could do to spend this large sum on promotion. Nearly three shillings a copy on

193

a book priced at 12*s*. 6*d*. with a royalty rate starting at fifteen per cent is not 'a real business'. But neither Senhouse nor I regretted one penny of it.

The great British public was lethargic about the book, as it was to its shame about the Spanish War. But those interested in the political maelstrom, whether from the right or the left, were not unstirred by Langdon-Davies' bombshell. Its political effects will be described in the next chapter.

With the *Barricades* the publishing programme of Year One was fulfilled. What had we achieved? The turnover was £7,618 during a nine-month year, one-tenth, as I remember it, of a Routledge turnover about that period. It was demonstrably too small, but it was not negligible. About one-sixth of this turnover was produced by *Clochemerle*. In fact, half of it came from only three of the new books published, an extraordinary proportion. Unfortunately, the gross profit amounted to only £1,053; it ought to have been three times as much. Under-pricing and over-printing were probably the reasons for that. The overheads stood at £4,336, of which about £1,000 was wages and salaries, £1,250 advertising expenditure, and the remaining £1,300 paid for the rent, rates, postages, packing, payment to travellers, and the host of nasty little items which make profit-making so difficult in any small business. The net loss thus amounted to £3,283, about half the capital paid up to that date. The situation was unpleasant.

We had, of course, spent far too much money on advertising, three times as much as the textbook pundits considered prudent. But it seemed to me money which had to be spent, if we were to survive. A publisher must not only publish books, he must demonstrably appear to be publishing them. Otherwise, who will know of his existence, who will offer him books? Not the flint-hearted agents who, in those days more definitely than now, judged a publisher's worth by the amount of his advertising. Not the authors who loved to see their names in print, even if the results were paltry. Besides, our rivals were spending money like water, boosting their more saleable wares at a cost known to many to be uneconomic. Even though we could scarcely breathe, I thought, we too must shout at the top of our voices, and shout we did despite the agonizing strain. Insolvent as we were, we began to be noticed. Though the greybeards muttered, 'Warburg has bitten off more than he can chew,' there were some who said, 'that's an enterprising little firm.' *Clochemerle*, *I'd Do It Again* and *The Spanish Barricades*, not to mention Thomas Mann and Arnold Zweig, had edged us perceptibly on to the publishing map.

But could we stay there? Senhouse was gloomy at times. He could not know yet how pitiable was the normal sale of unsuccessful titles. But I was not altogether without hope. We had a substantial list in preparation for 1937. We had authors, prepared to entrust their precious cargoes to us. That was perhaps the most important fact of all.

9   David and Goliath

DISTASTEFUL AND ALARMING as was Mussolini's African campaign, it was the Spanish Civil War that obsessed me in the first months of the infant firm and dominated its policy for the next three years. Franco's revolt against the legitimate Spanish Government, which took place only three months after the foundation of Secker & Warburg, roused me and many of my generation to a frenzy of indignation. Over twenty years later, it is difficult to recreate the jumble of emotions we felt then, topped by frustration at the feebleness of appeasement policy. The rise of the fascist international, as we called it, and its onslaught, with the aid of Japan, throughout the world, seemed to us to be carried out with the connivance of the British Government. The period from the German occupation of the Rhineland in March 1936 to the betrayal of Czechoslovakia in September 1938 was a nightmare one, which made us feel neurotic and ashamed. No longer was our interest centred in what appeared to be the stale old struggle in the House of Commons between two venerable, if slightly corrupt, political caucuses. It was world issues which gripped our attention, and parish-pump politics seemed irrelevant. Through the Western world travelled the deadly international viruses of Hitlerism and Stalinism, dressed up in the fancy names of National Socialism and Communism. Pacifism befuddled the minds of millions, preached by the beloved socialist leader, George Lansbury. Over their breakfast-tables normally sensible folk studied the prophecies of the numerous band of astrologers, eager to find balm for fears they dared not admit feeling. Vegetarianism and Yoga flourished. This was the age of the crank, and crankiness was the last refuge of those unwilling to face realities.

But the thoughtful could not continue indefinitely to sit on the sidelines. With the onset of the Spanish Civil War, many longed to range themselves on the side of the righteous cause, even though they were a little uncertain where it was to be found. When Nazi seeds appeared to be sprouting in the ranks of the Conservatives, it became clear enough to me, a Jew, that the party of Disraeli had little to offer the enemies of tyranny. But when I turned to the Left, I surveyed a movement where Stalinism seemed welcome as the next step in democratic development. These issues were inflamed by the Spanish political influenza and gripped a million minds, dividing families, separating husband and wife, bringing into the conventional backwaters of English life a rasp and an edge which had not been felt for half a century.

Into this political maelstrom I rushed naïvely, like a man chased by a bull. In fact, I had no choice. As the miasma of anti-semitism seeped across the world, backed by Goebbels' ruthless machine, I was bound to become more conscious than before of being a Jew and therefore vulnerable. Hitler and Goebbels were attacking *me*; it would be stupid not to resist. It was too late, even had I wished, to contract out of my birthright. Unable to believe in Jehovah, indifferent to Zionism, with few Jewish friends, an Anglican partner and a Catholic wife, I could no more obliterate my origins than a leopard his spots. 'Why,' my wife asked me more than once, 'why are you a Jew? What does it mean? You don't go to a synagogue, you can't even remember the Jewish prayers your mother taught you. You eat pork and bacon and lobster like anybody else. I don't understand how you can call yourself a Jew.'

'I don't call myself a Jew,' I replied, 'it's the others who will call me that, the Nazis, Mosley's followers, all the scum of the earth.'

'What on earth has Mosley got to do with it?' my wife said angrily. 'Don't be so absurd. Just tell me this one simple thing—what is it that makes you a Jew?'

'A caste mark on my forehead,' I said, 'indelible and invisible. The mark of difference. I am English to the core, but with a difference, the awareness of being a Jew.'

'I don't like this awareness of yours,' Pamela said, 'it seems a dangerous thing to have. What's the good of it?'

'It makes me what I am,' I said. 'A Jew is glad to be an Englishman, but proud to be a Jew. It somehow attaches him to the melancholy history of man.'

'We're all attached to that,' Pamela said. 'Why on earth do you say the Jews have some special attachment?'

'Nearly all non-Jews,' I said, 'live in boxes—called England, France, Germany, Russia. These boxes protect them from damage. The Jew has no box, or if he has it's a flimsy one, liable to collapse round him in a crisis. The Jew is in the open; it makes him proud, sensitive and wary. It ensures that he takes nothing for granted. He knows that disaster is only just out of sight round the corner.'

Pamela looked upset. 'If any disaster happened to you,'

she said, 'I should go to Germany and kill Hitler. I can't think why the Germans haven't done it years ago.'

'Because they don't want to be killed themselves,' I said.

'If you were dead, I wouldn't want to stay alive,' my wife remarked emphatically. 'Anyhow, I can't make head or tail of what you're saying, and I don't believe you can.'

'I know what I mean,' I said, 'but it's not easy to explain. It sounds melodramatic. But the Jew is committed to the world in a way that the others aren't. Whether he triumphs or whether he's persecuted, it's all a bit provisional, the luck may change. He is a man without certainties, a natural sceptic.'

'I couldn't exist without certainties,' my wife said, 'one must be sure of something.'

'You can be sure of me,' I said, to bring this dangerous conversation to an end.

In those days I believed passionately that rational thought must rule man's behaviour. But the world of the 'thirties was crammed with maniacs and nihilists, masters of irrationality, who were perverting the exercise of reason to suit their own horrible ambitions. To destroy them by force, assuming that the Western world still had the force, was to reduce oneself in the process to an identical level of barbarism. Against the ideas of evil and madness we must mobilize, I thought, the counter-ideas of sanity and health. They would have to be hammered out in words by the finest minds of our generation. To me as a publisher, the word meant the written and printed word, normally and naturally embodied in a book. My firm, Secker & Warburg, insignificant though we were, must play its part in the war of words and the clash of ideas. It was the last chance by which the civilized world could escape defeat without abandoning its own character. David would take the field against Goliath, and endeavour to get in some telling shots from a sling in whose use he was still unpractised. In this noble if hair-brained enterprise, I was assured of the support of Senhouse, no lover of barbarism in any form, and of course of my wife. Indeed, I had the greatest difficulty in dissuading her from taking the first train to Barcelona to join the anarchists, with whom she felt a deep kinship.

To be a political publisher in the 'thirties was as difficult as spotting the lady in a three-card trick. Where was the lady and who was she? Who were our friends and who were our enemies? Was Chamberlain a crypto-fascist or merely an out-of-date imperialist frightened of losing in war the booty collected absent-mindedly by his predecessors? Could the British Labour Party, backed by the ponderous strength of the trade unions, lead the struggle against a Nazi-inspired Germany? What was the real nature of the U.S.S.R., and could the Communist Party of Great Britain be a reliable ally in the battle for freedom? My mind, unused to the practice of political analysis, wobbled like a top running down.

Many on the Left believed that a front against Fascism could not be built without an alliance with the Soviet Union. Since the Americans continued to regard Europe as the ward of a fever-hospital, towards which isolationism was the only sensible attitude, the Russian Army seemed to be the only force capable of aiding the British and the French to destroy the deadly German menace. Many able and intelligent men held such views. The socialist League of Sir Stafford Cripps and the Independent Labour Party with James Maxton in charge, came together with the Communist Party of Great Britain in a United Front to promote understanding of the U.S.S.R. and an eventual alliance with her. The United Front rightly saw that only the defeat of General Franco in Spain could put a stop to the limitless ambitions of Fascism. Under the slogan of 'No Pasaran', They Shall Not Pass, the Left mobilized the idealists and the intellectuals of the day. How full we were of hope, energy and generosity. But where was the ability to organize our efforts, apart from the Communist Party, and where the goal at which we aimed, other than Communism?

Then, more than now, the Communist Party controlled an organization as hard-working as it was obedient. It had a daily newspaper, the *Daily Worker*. It commanded the services of a host of fellow-travellers, strategically placed in nearly every department of social and cultural activity. Some of these were writers. In a series of books, pamphlets, plays and reportage, as brilliant as they were unsound, they exercised an uncanny effect on all those sections of public opinion which were not too busy cultivating their own gardens, minding their own businesses, and shutting their eyes to German rearmament. These writers and publicists became grouped round the Left Book Club, set up in May 1936 by Victor Gollancz as a rallying-point for democracy and a publishing organization for the United Front. Month by month the club issued its choice, in hard covers at the usual price and in limp orange cloth at half a crown. The books sold like hot cakes; the Communist Party saw to that. Probably as many as 40,000 copies of Gollancz's succulent oranges were disposed of twelve times a year. The lucky author of a Left Book Club choice received an advance of £250, a small fortune in those days for a political work.

But, of course, there was a fly in the ointment. It was not easy for a book to become a L.B.C. choice unless it was likely to receive Communist Party approval. The temptation to writers to turn a blind eye to Soviet defects was strong. Many of the L.B.C. choices were communist propaganda, undisguised and by and large unashamed. They dominated the political thinking of the Left, converting many and confusing all, leaving no room for those who felt unable to regard Stalin as the potential saviour of liberal democracy.

My publication of Langdon-Davies' explosive book, *Behind the Spanish Barricades*, had filled the Communists with joy. This open-handed tribute to the liberalism of the Spanish Government, this paean of praise to the courage and devotion of the Spanish workers, this bitter attack on the aims of General Franco with his Moors and Falangists, was ideal propaganda for the Party line. It was the first big on-the-spot book about Spain to appear, and it created an uproar wholly disproportionate to its trivial sales. Surely its publisher must be prepared to join the Communist Party, or at least enlist as a fellow-traveller. Charming emissaries of both sexes made contact with me and my wife, to explain how all good men should rally to the service of the Party. The temptation was strong, the flattery subtle, the mailed fist daintily concealed beneath a velvet glove. If I played ball with the Party, they told me, they could turn my untried publishing business into a success almost overnight. They had connexions in every literary magazine in London. Wouldn't a spate of good reviews be a help to a firm as precariously placed as mine? Surely I had sense enough to understand that the Party was the one bastion of decency in the corrupt pluto-democratic England of Chamberlain and the Tories?

At the time this statement seemed plausible enough. *The Barricades* seemed to me a book which even a moderate Conservative could accept as valid. It argued for resistance to Fascism on genuine patriotic grounds. Yet the attack on it from the Right was bitter. When I drafted a large

BEHIND THE
SPANISH
BARRICADES

THE BANNED advertisement referred to in our leading article in this issue

On re-reading this advertisement after an interval of 23 years, I am impressed by the copy writing, which well illustrates the crusading zeal of those times, and the way in which Right and Left, Fascist or Democrat, felt themselves to be already at war.

advertisement for the *Observer*, it was refused on the orders of its then editor. To this I gave publicity elsewhere, and acrimonious arguments broke out. Tempers flared. The *Tablet*, in an article entitled 'Overhasty Propaganda', wrote that 'feeble attempts to condone—even to defend—the burning of churches; delight at the destruction wrought on the churches of Barcelona; descriptions such as that of buildings going up "in flames, well greased with monks and nuns"—these things will repel not only every Catholic, but every decent unprejudiced person, Christian or no.' Langdon-Davies brought an action for libel against the *Tablet*, and against the *Catholic Herald* who made similar allegations, and won it. The defendants in both cases were forced to apologize and pay a certain sum by way of damages.

This stormy incident threw me into the whirl of political publishing, and forced me to behave as if I had some genuine understanding of politics. Certainly I felt proud that it had been through my efforts and my firm's money that *The Barricades* had been published to strike a blow against dictatorship and the conspiracy of the Fascist powers. The role of freedom-fighter, which the Communists designed for me, seemed to be one well within my powers. I began to flex my political muscles. But my suspicions of the Communist Party ran deep. Was the Soviet Union the Utopia depicted by the Webbs in their famous guide-book, *Soviet Communism*? I had my doubts. The expulsion and vilification of Trotsky, the purges, the faked-up trials of the old Bolsheviks of the October days, filled me with dismay. Too often I had listened to the parrot-like remark of a Communist hard-pressed in argument: 'You can't make an omelette, you know, without breaking eggs.' Yet without the strength of the Soviet Union to back it, how on earth, I wondered, could the front of freedom prevail against the terrifying power of the Nazis?

One day I lunched with H. N. Brailsford, a humane and charming man and a lifelong Socialist, who stood near the selection committee of the Left Book Club. Forcibly I put my doubts to him, and his answer was clear. 'We can't altogether approve of much that is done by the Soviet Union,' he told me, 'it's a young and raw system, and at present certainly totalitarian. But, my dear Warburg, surely you will agree that, if we are forced to choose between two totalitarian systems, Nazi and Communist, we must choose the Communist? It is at least progressive and rational, while Nazism is the apotheosis of lunacy, anti-semitism and brutality.' If Brailsford can speak like that, I thought, who am I to resist? He's no Communist, but a patriotic Englishman. Yet even he feels there is no alternative to a partnership, even if only a temporary one, with the Communist Party. Gravely perturbed I took my doubts to my wife. The conversation was crucial, and it had become urgent. Not long before I had been approached by Fenner Brockway, secretary of the Independent Labour Party, with a proposition.

The I.L.P. had played a distinguished role for thirty years as a ginger group inside the Labour Party, until the ginger had become too hot for the Socialist leaders to swallow. Then it had disaffiliated, and was now a tiny political organisation, based geographically on Glasgow, where James Maxton, its guide, and the three other members of Parliament who belonged, had their constituencies. It controlled a weekly newspaper, the *New Leader*, with a substantial circulation. Maxton was perhaps the greatest orator of his day. With a fringe of ink-black hair flopping over a high, pale forehead, set above the angular face of a latter-day saint, he resembled Robespierre, and his words were equally fiery. Over him and his colleagues hung an air of sea-green incorruptibility, mingled with a taste for anarchism, and a distaste for social advancement unusual in the ranks of socialism. Maxton and his merry men were British to the core, thoroughly inoculated by training and experience against the Stalinist virus. Liberty, even libertarianism, was their watchword, and they did not believe it existed in the U.S.S.R. Amongst its members outside the House of Commons, it numbered some promising writers, Fenner Brockway himself, Reginald Reynolds, C. L. R. James, George Padmore, Jennie Lee (Aneurin Bevan's wife), Edward Conze, Jomo Kenyatta, Ethel Mannin and George Orwell. Orwell was then a coming novelist on the Gollancz list, whose early books had brought him a big reputation and a tiny income. It was Brockway's belief that some of these writers would be glad to bring their books to me.

Brockway's proposition excited me. My little firm needed authors, as an army needs banners. But, were these the ones to support, politically or commercially? Certainly the communists would review them without enthusiasm in the literary and political magazines. The I.L.P. writers were not communists, but socialists, and socialists of a peculiar brand, libertarian socialists, anarchists even, whose attitude to the U.S.S.R. was at best ambivalent, at worst plain hostile. They were authors the communists would smear with the label, Trotskyist or Trotskyite, words that in those days were made to sound like a bad smell. Their books might or might not be good books, but if they sold it would be without benefit of communist clergy. If Brockway's proposal was tempting, it was also double-edged. Despite my association with him over a book on the Routledge list a year or two before, he would never, I felt, have approached me, had he been able to place the work of his members and friends with a stronger and better established house.

This was the problem I sat down to discuss with my wife in the latter half of 1936, with the explosions of the Spanish War sounding in my ears. Some of the guns and nearly all the planes had been provided by the U.S.S.R. The Soviet Union was an ally worth having. Should I not ally myself with it?

We do not know precisely how in ancient times the Greeks consulted the Delphic Oracle, whether for instance they asked their important questions direct and straight out—for instance: Is it fated that I murder my mother? or, Would it be prudent to declare war on Sparta next week? Or whether, on the other hand, they wrapped it up a bit, edging crab-wise into the heart of the problem. In consulting my wife, I have always found the latter method more effective. There is nothing Pamela likes less than being pinned down by a direct question, nothing that she enjoys more than what she calls 'a little chat'. This enables her to talk at large on different aspects of the subject, and come up triumphantly with the answer after a long and some-times fatiguing steeplechase over the surrounding country.

On this occasion, as on others, I chose my initial question with care, selecting one that was distant, but not too far distant from what might be described as the nub of the matter. 'Do you consider,' I said, 'that the Spanish Government is wise in accepting military aid from the Soviet Union?'

My wife looked at me in amazement . 'Wise, of course they're wise,' she said. 'Chamberlain and Daladier aren't giving the Spaniards arms, so naturally they must take what they can get from Stalin. Wouldn't you?'

'But doesn't it follow,' I persisted, 'that Spain will fall completely under communist domination when the Franco revolt is suppressed?'

'Certainly not,' my wife replied vigorously, 'the Spaniards will murder the lot after the war, they're not a namby-pamby people like the English.'

Suppressing my urge to defend the English against a charge of namby-pambiness, since I felt certain that they could murder with the best of them under appropriate conditions, I asked whether she did not consider that the English should also collaborate with the communists in resistance to Fascism.

My wife stared at me suspiciously. 'You're not thinking of joining the Communist Party, are you?' she asked coldly, with that maddening facility for reducing a general question to a personal one that ruins every masculine attempt at a thorough-going discussion. 'Because if you are I shall leave you. I'd rather be married to a miser than to an English communist.'

'Many distinguished men have joined the communist Party during the last few years,' I ventured tentatively.

'More fools they,' my wife said bluntly, 'but *you* don't have to go messing about with them. Look at our highbrow friends who've joined, a rotten lot they are, failures and misfits to a man. They underpay their charwomen, while they drivel on about the injustice of the capitalist system. They make me sick. And they're so puritanical, even when they sleep with each other's wives.'

'Adultery is no danger to the U.S.S.R.,' I said, 'but capitalism is. And perhaps capitalism is a menace to us as well, at least Neville Chamberlain's brand of it.'

'Don't talk to me about Chamberlain,' my wife said. 'You know I can't stand the man. It's the upper classes who'll save England, as I've always told you, that is, if it can still be saved, which personally I doubt.'

'England may lose the first battle,' I said, 'but she will certainly win the war, if it comes.'

My wife ignored this platitude. 'What have you really got on your mind?' she asked me quietly.

I explained to her Brockway's proposition and its consequences.

'Obviously,' I said, 'I shall not be popular with the Right Wing. Look at the way they received Langdon-Davies' book on Spain. But, as soon as I start publishing books by the I.L.P. and its friends, I shall be in real trouble. The Labour Party will never forgive me.'

'Why should you worry? What's the Labour Party doing to stop Hitler? They don't even support Chamberlain's rearmament proposals, feeble though they are. As long as I live, I shall never understand why they can't see what's going on under their noses.'

'They can't bring themselves to believe that Hitler means what he says. I can hardly believe it myself.'

'It always takes you a year or two,' my wife remarked, 'to catch up with what I've been telling you all along. And what's so maddening is that, even then, it's usually because some solemn idiot has been talking to you on the same subject.'

Intervening hastily to prevent further discussion of my alleged short-sightedness, I reverted to the earlier question. 'The liberals and the independent socialists have no love for communists,' I said. 'Yet is it wise to attack the communists when they seem to be our only reliable allies?'

'The Soviet Union is quite big enough to stand a little criticism,' my wife said. 'And obviously you need these books for your list. Don't you think yourself it's the right thing for you to do?'

'I'm not sure,' I said. 'The Russian revolution was a kind of earthquake, based on the doctrine of the perfectibility of man. Naturally it was brutal and naturally it became

209

terribly lop-sided. But is capitalism so much better? Take a look at its horrible excesses in Germany and Italy.'

'Feudalism,' my wife remarked, 'is by far the best form of society. I'd have enjoyed being the mistress of a castle and looking after the health and welfare of the serfs with herbs and simples and things.'

'I dare say you would,' I said, 'but you were fortunately born centuries too late for that kind of thing. Communism stands for the equality of man, a noble doctrine—to each according to his needs, from each according to his skill.'

'There's only one kind of equality for man,' my wife said sharply, 'and that is that all of us are born from here.' She patted her stomach, rather high up, I thought, for what she had in mind. 'Of course,' she went on, 'everybody should have a minimum wage, and a big one too if they work hard, that goes without saying.'

Abruptly I brought the conversation back to the matter in hand. 'Do you feel that I should reject the communists' suggestions?' I asked.

'You should never have listened to them,' Pamela said. 'Communism may be good for the Russians, it would be hopeless in this country.'

'And accept Brockway's proposals?' I persisted.

'Of course. I only hope these books of Brockway's friends will be real sellers.'

It was clear that nothing more remained to be said. If only Brailsford had had lunch with my wife instead of with me, communism, I thought, would have lost another luke-warm supporter.

During the next three years over thirty books of the ninety we published were of a Left political flavour. Only three of them were communist—a translation of Ostrovski's novel, *The Making of a Hero*; a translation of Tarlé's

Bonaparte, a fine study of an earlier revolutionary period by a Soviet historian later to be purged; and Ralph Fox's novel, *This Was Their Youth*. Fox was a brave man, the most likeable Party member I ever knew. He died in the fighting round Madrid; many said from bullets not fired by the enemy. With his death, my last intimate personal ties with communism were severed. All the other books on my list were either non-communist or anti-communist.

One of the first authors introduced to me by Brockway was C. L. R. James, and his book, *World Revolution*, became a kind of Bible of Trotskyism. We published it in April 1937. It was dedicated to the Marxist Group. How many members composed this group at the time I don't know, probably less than fifty, for it was a quality of Trotskyist groups to break into two, like the amoeba when reproducing itself, and to continue doing so until the fission process had reduced the group to a mere handful. Trotskyism in fact resembled a corps of guerilla fighters, partisans—and how partisan they were!—harassing the communist enemy, to whom they were linked by a burning and ambivalent emotion.

The Trotskyists, and James foremost among them, believed in the wickedness of capitalism, and were convinced that Nazism was simply capitalism gone rotten. With simple naïveté they put their faith in collective ownership, which wisely they did not define, since it would have brought them up with a bump against an intolerable stumbling-block—the obvious fact that industrial workers had no intention whatever of spending their spare time in high-level management with responsibilities rather than in the familiar pleasures of working-class life. The Trotskyists loved the U.S.S.R. as children love their mother, but they knew that the wicked father, Stalin, had debauched her and produced a miscarriage. So they felt free to criticize

211

the U.S.S.R. for Stalin's crimes, while loving it for the beautiful thing it might have become, if only Lenin and Trotsky had survived in power to create the Utopia that was just round the corner. The Trotskyists naturally advocated the spread of communism throughout the world to replace 'the horrors of capitalist decadence'. So they believed in a world revolution, and loathed Stalin for ousting Trotsky on this central issue.

Stalin himself probably believed in Trotskyism, possibly more vigorously even than Trotsky himself. But, of course, he had the responsibility of running the Soviet Union in its pioneer period. This was a Herculean task inside Russia itself, since it involved turning millions of lazy and drunken peasants into alert and efficient machine-minders. But outside Russia too the problems confronting Stalin were tremendous. Unpopular with almost all the nations of the world, he was threatened by the active hostility and urge to expansion of Germany on his western border, Japan on his eastern. In this predicament, during the period of the Popular Front (1933–9) Stalin and the Third International tried to develop a system of collective security through the League of Nations to protect the U.S.S.R. from its two principal enemies. The pillars of this system were to be the allegedly peace-loving nations, that is, the nations which felt no need to alter the balance of power either in Europe or the Far East. Great Britain, France and the U.S.A. were foremost among the 'peace-loving' nations.

To increase their love of peace, Stalin pretended as far as possible to be a democrat himself and he encouraged the communist parties in the Western world to collaborate with the real democrats in the socialist parties, wherever they existed. In Spain, as soon as the election of 1936 brought the liberals to power, he supported them against

Franco and the Falangists. But to a Trotskyist any partnership between communists and democrats was 'a betrayal
of the Revolution', since a social democrat or labour leader
was 'a tool of capitalism', whether he knew it or not.
No good, they believed, could possibly arise from having
any truck with such wolves in sheep's clothing.

Even in those pre-war days of confusion, when my own
mind was addled by the rancours and persistent slogans of
eloquent but dishonest advocates, I regarded these
Trotskyist theories with a measure of scepticism. But to
James and those like him, they were the truth revealed,
as clear as the propositions of Euclid to those who understand geometry. Hence James made two prophecies. The
first was that the workers of the Soviet Union would revolt
against Stalin when the inevitable capitalist war developed;
the second that the U.S.S.R. could not survive without a
new and revolutionary international. The Trotskyist newspaper, *The Red Flag*, carried proudly under its mast-head,
the words, 'The Organ of the Fourth International.'
Fortunately James' prophecies remained unfulfilled, since
otherwise it can hardly be doubted that Nazi Germany
would have won the war.

Trotskyism, it seems to me now, was a symptom of
despair engendered by the real and frightful atrocities that
were being committed all over the world. Like communism,
it presupposed the breakdown of patriotism (except in
Russia). It was a faith liable to take hold in naturally
religious minds which were unable to accept a belief in God.
It was a political philosophy held by those to whom
capitalism was abhorrent, and who saw the great alternative
developing on crude and brutal lines which they detested.
But one of the merits of the Trotskyist heresy was its
refusal to accept everything as gospel truth which was
advanced by the lying champions of Soviet perfection.

213

The Trotskyists pointed out, with maddening persistence, that the Russian worker was poor, bullied by bureaucrats, the subject of an awesome tyranny, spied upon by a secret police. The state in Russia, they claimed, far from withering away, as Marx had expected, had become more omnipresent than ever. No wonder the communists detested them, and me and my firm for daring to publish such 'objectively fascist' books. For in those days, as now, all that was not for the Soviet Union was against it, and what was against it was, at the very best, 'objectively fascist', and at the worst, 'reptilian'.

Despite the atmosphere of hate and arid dispute in his writings, James himself was one of the most delightful and easy-going personalities I have known, colourful in more senses than one. A dark-skinned West Indian negro from Trinidad, he stood six feet three inches in his socks and was noticeably good-looking. His memory was extraordinary. He could quote, not only passages from the Marxist classics but long extracts from Shakespeare, in a soft lilting English which was a delight to hear. Immensely amiable, he loved the fleshpots of capitalism, fine cooking, fine clothes, fine furniture and beautiful women, without a trace of the guilty remorse to be expected from a seasoned warrior of the class war. He was brave. Night after night he would address meetings in London and the provinces, denouncing the crimes of the blood-thirsty Stalin, until he was hoarse and his wonderful voice a mere croaking in the throat. The communists who heckled him would have torn him limb from limb, had it not been for the ubiquity of the police and their insensitivity to propaganda of whatever hue. If you told him of some new communist argument, he would listen with a smile of infinite tolerance on his dark face, wag the index finger of his right hand solemnly, and announce in an understanding tone—'we know them, we know them'—as of a man who has plumbed human wickedness to its depth and forgiven it, since man even in his wickedness is pitiable.

If politics was his religion and Marx his god, if literature was his passion and Shakespeare his prince among writers, cricket was his beloved activity. He wrote splendid articles on county matches for the *Manchester Guardian* during the summer. Indeed, it was only between April and October that he was in funds. Sometimes he came for the week-end to our cottage near West Hoathly in Sussex and turned out for the local team. He was a demon bowler, and a powerful if erratic batsman. The village loved him, referring to him affectionately as 'the black bastard'. In Sussex politics were forgotten. Instead, I can hear today the opening words of *Twelfth Night*, delivered beautifully from his full sensitive lips: 'If music be the food of love, play on; give me excess of it.' Excess, perhaps, was James' crime, an excess of words whose relevance to the contemporary tragedy was less than he supposed. Later he wrote an excellent book for us about the great Negro leader, Toussaint Louverture, *The Black Jacobins*. He had a copy specially bound in beautiful black morocco for my wife. Had he not been a revolutionary thinker, what a wonderful capitalist he might have made!

World Revolution sold moderately well, if you apply low enough standards of sale to it. So did some of the other books of that period. Cedric Dover's *Half-Caste*, a fair but bitter account of Eurasians and their place in society, went into a second printing. So did Reginald Reynolds' first book, *The White Sahibs in India*, an energetic attack on British imperialism from the standpoint of a Quaker and a friend of Mahatma Gandhi. Indeed, the book was banned by the authorities in India right up till 1940.

But the book did well in England and an edition was sold to the United States, which brought it out of the red.[1]

Other ventures were far less successful. Heinz Liepmann's *Death From The Skies*, for instance, a somewhat alarmist study of the effects of bombing on built-up areas, written under the influence of Douhet's well-known doctrine, sold only 730 copies. The British public had no intention of allowing itself to be terrorized by mere words. George Padmore's *Africa and World Peace* was a flop. So was Mairin Mitchell's *Storm Over Spain*, the only pacifist study I ever read of the Spanish War.

Probably the most significant book we published that second year in the political field was André Gide's *Back from the U.S.S.R.*, an attack far more damaging because far more concentrated than C. L. R. James' on the communist paradise. Infinitely polite, diffident and completely horrifying, the little book—it was only 122 pages—exploded like a hand-grenade in a packed trench. Gide, *Membre de l'Académie Française*, who was to become a Nobel prize-winner ten years later, venerable atheist, and master of the calculated effect, had felt a more than passing sympathy with the U.S.S.R.

He had listened to the fables and fallacies of the French communist intelligentzia, and swallowed them hook, line and sinker. Here was a recruit worth a hundred thousand horny-handed sons of toil, a real feather to stick in their cap. Plans were made, welcomes prepared, red carpets laid down, as the best-known literary panjandrum of France made ready to visit the U.S.S.R. He went, he saw, he returned to distill the poisons of a master craftsman into

---

[1] Reginald Reynolds died at the end of 1958, after writing books on a number of unusual subjects, of which the best known, *Cleanliness and Godliness*, dealt with the history and use of water-closets. For some years, following Sagittarius, he contributed brilliant satirical poems to the *New Statesman*. I never published another book for him, though at one time he was co-author with George Orwell of a collection of British pamphlets.

the Soviet body politic. In his Foreword he wrote: 'It is indeed worth while living, I thought, in order to be present at this rebirth, and worth while giving one's life in order to help it on. In our hearts and minds we resolutely linked the future of culture itself with the glorious destiny of the U.S.S.R.' And later, 'Who shall say what the Soviet Union has been to us? More than a chosen land—an example, a guide. What we have dreamt of, what we have hardly dared to hope . . . was coming into being over there. A land existed where Utopia was in process of becoming reality. Tremendous achievements had already made us exacting. . . .' But reality shattered many of his illusions. He complains of the low standard of manufactured goods. 'The State heeds none of this, for the State has no rival. Quality? Why trouble about it, since there is no competition.' Of conformity of opinion. 'In the U.S.S.R. everybody knows beforehand, once and for all, that on any and every subject there can be only one opinion. . . . Are these really the people who made the revolution? No, they are the people who profit by it.' Of the re-appearance of social strata, 'an aristocracy of respectability.' Of the tyranny, 'the smallest protest, the least criticism, is liable to the severest penalties . . . I doubt whether in any other country in the world, even Hitler's Germany, thought be less free, more bowed down, more fearful, more vassalized.'

'I doubt whether in any other country in the world, even Hitler's Germany, thought be less free.' The statement spread consternation and rage through the communist ranks. Members of the Left Book Club, carefully shielded by their committee from the truth, must have rubbed their eyes in astonishment if they happened to light on these lines of Gide. Blasphemous, treacherous, reptilian, a sin against the Holy Ghost, the futile outpourings of a decaying homosexual, such were the anathemata launched against

Gide's pamphlet. Today, when Kruschev has blown the gaff on Stalin and many of his works, it is hard to conceive the horror Gide's simple words provoked. As for the publisher of such filth, no punishment could be great enough to fit the crime. I was cold-shouldered at parties; little groups of young men could be seen in corners of the room whispering about the progressive publisher who was turning out a black reactionary. Sometimes I even feared that well-drilled mobs would invade the office and beat me up, but in fact not a window was broken. The communists knew their business too well for that. Assault and battery on a London publisher, however unsuccessful and undistinguished, would bring him publicity and perhaps popularity. Better by far to ignore his books where possible, or damn them with faint praise if a review could not be avoided. This policy was followed with scrupulous care. It did nothing to enhance the sales of our books, nothing to swing our balance-sheet from the red to the black.

Back from the U.S.S.R. was secured for the firm by Senhouse, an old friend of Gide's. It was his most important editorial contribution till then. Published at half a crown in an edition of 2,000 copies, it was twice reprinted. Out of the 6,000 copies, we sold 4,509 within the first six months. Yet this book, with its modest circulation, must have done more to change public opinion about the realities of life in the Soviet Union than any other book of its day. There is a great deal more in publishing than the figures of sales set out in the publisher's balance-sheet.

In 1937 we published forty books. There were not to be as many published in one year till the 1950s. Even though the balance-sheet for 1937 has disappeared in one of the many convulsions we have endured, it is easy to guess that the losses were serious. So the financial situation remained as desperate as ever. We were perhaps spending a little less money on advertising, but all too much was locked up in stock, translations and advances to authors. By now the capital of the firm had increased by several thousand pounds as devoted friends and relations of Senhouse and myself aided us to keep afloat. But in many ways my training at Routledge proved to be a handicap. There it was possible to take in one's stride a fat academic book costing £1,000 or over with a slow sale over a long period. Now the addition of a £250 book threatened to become the last straw on the publishing camel's back. But, in a lordly fashion, I ignored such mundane details. I had been taught to publish in the grand manner, and in that manner I continued, as far as I was able, despite the changed circumstances. It was magnificent, but it was hardly wise.

10   From Wigan
to Barcelona

THE PROCESSES of publishing are not only uncertain
and complicated, but slow-moving. A new firm must
inevitably take four or five years to get going. The efforts
to create an organization, however minute and provisional;
the search for authors, books, talent; the early failures of
books neither specially distinguished nor saleable; the over-
advertisement, the occasional success, the financial anxieties,
the constant struggle to make bricks without straw, these
are the invariable experiences of the new publisher. At
least, they were mine. But, at the end of five years at most,
a firm must have displayed unmistakably its abilities and
character, if it is to survive and prosper. I think it's true
to say that by 1938–9 the firm of Secker & Warburg showed
clearly what it stood for.

Needless to say, we made a loss in 1938 (£3,197) but it
was a distinguished loss, if the phrase is permissible. The
list contained some good books, and a few great ones. It was
not by any means the fact that the great books sold well.
But in the long run, the appearance of great books on a
new publisher's list does more for it than the easy but
insignificant seller. Prestige is more important even than

sales, if only the money holds out. There were nine novels and twenty-six general books in the list, thirty-five titles in all. The turnover reached the substantial figure for those days of £11,358, roughly equivalent to £30,000 at today's prices. We were getting into our stride. Frank Swinnerton summed up our publishing attitude in a memorable sentence, when, writing of the small independent firms of the last thirty years, he said: 'They published what they liked, and did their weeping in private.' Today we still publish that way, for to publish what you like is to publish with enthusiasm, and enthusiasm is the life-blood of publishing.

In April we published two really remarkable books— Mann's *Joseph in Egypt* in two volumes, and George Orwell's *Homage to Catalonia*. Neither was successful at first, neither made a profit till many years later. Mann's *Joseph* was imported from the U.S., where it was first published, and bound and jacketed in England. Less than 1,000 were sold in the first year. The copies remaining in 1941 were to be destroyed by German bombs. Once again a masterpiece of the great German writer had failed; the story of Joseph and Potiphar's wife, Mann's magnificent recreation of the Egypt of the Pharaohs, found the English reader apathetic. But the fate of *Homage to Catalonia* was perhaps even more heartbreaking.

It was at the end of 1936, when I had embarked on a policy of anti-fascist publishing which paid no heed to communist susceptibilities, that Brockway sent George Orwell to see me. The case of Orwell was wholly different to that of the other writers I had signed up, for he had already a publisher of his own, well known and prosperous, who had published several of his novels and two important works of non-fiction, *Down and Out in Paris and London* and *The Road to Wigan Pier*.[1] This publisher was Victor Gollancz, founder of the Left Book Club, king-pin of the cultural and political activities of the United Front, a demon of energy, capable, trustworthy, and possessed of so overwhelming a belief in the righteousness of his opinions as to bear a recognizable resemblance to the ancient Hebrew prophets. How did it happen that an author of Orwell's already considerable stature, firmly tied by option to Gollancz, at least for his novels, should have decided to leave the security of an established and efficient firm to come to me? The facts are among the most dramatic of the secret publishing history of the 1930s.

The link between an author and his publisher can be of various kinds. There is the link existing on commercial grounds alone; Author X finds Publisher Y generous in his advance and royalties, honest in his accounting, competent in his production and promotion. He is satisfied with him, and the association may last a lifetime without even the necessity of author and publisher meeting save for an exchange of pleasantries. This kind of relationship is not uncommon; it would normally exist between a fairly well-known author and a rather big concern, whose list is unselective and variable in quality. Such a linkage is perhaps rather commoner in the U.S. than in the British publishing world.

But more frequent, in England at any rate, is a link based on some degree of familiarity between author and publisher. This may vary from a casual acquaintanceship to a deep and enduring friendship with every degree of shading between the two extremes. Many examples could be mentioned, starting with the famous alliance between Byron and John Murray, or in more recent times, Graham

---

[1] *The Road to Wigan Pier* must have been in the press, but not actually published, when I first met Orwell.

Greene and A. S. Frere of Heinemann. It is obvious that in this case the personality of the publisher himself is a matter of over-riding importance, whereas in the previous one it is only the publishing ability of the firm which counts.

But there is another type of link, more interesting and more fundamental than either, a link based on a harmony of attitude between author and publisher. At a simple level, it is for instance the factor which induces a writer of technical books on flying to publish with a house specializing in such books. But, in the field of general literature, the matter is more complicated. In this sphere the publisher's imprint must stand for something recognizable by an author, which will induce him to say of Publisher Z 'he's the man for me'. All major publishing houses have at some time in their evolution stood for some definite kind of books, even if later on, as they grew larger or their directing intelligence retired, they have lapsed into a blur of activity. It was this kind of house, with a sharply defined policy or personality, which I endeavoured to create from the start. It was, I believed, my only chance of establishing a sound new firm. Even today, when the number of titles we publish is two to three times as large as it was in the second half of the 'thirties, the imprint of Secker & Warburg stands, I am certain, for a definite type of book, with a more or less precise quality.

In the period 1933-9, when the political wind blew with ever increasing intensity from the left, though many publishers issued the occasional leftish book, Gollancz, through his energy and his brilliant conception of the Left Book Club, had established a near monopoly in this field. His thoughts moved, at least in those days, on Marxist lines, which enabled him to represent as a publisher the communist and fellow-travelling writers without doing violence to his inner convictions. It was this monopoly that I challenged within six months of my start as an independent publisher. The liberal, socialist and anarchist books which appeared under my imprint, the critical or downright hostile studies of the Soviet Union, provided an invaluable antidote to the dubious nostrums so frequently recommended with a wealth of jargon by the orange-covered volumes of the Left Book Club. George Orwell, the writer whose fulfilment lay a decade ahead, may be regarded from this point of view as a touchstone for testing the relative standards of Gollancz's house and mine.

Orwell had been commissioned by Gollancz in 1936 to make an investigation into the lives of the unemployed in the North of England. Gollancz hoped, no doubt, that this talented writer would produce a book suitable for a L.B.C. choice, that is, a book which viewed the problem of capitalist slump and decay through Marxist spectacles, a work to edify the faithful and to convert the uninitiated. But a startling surprise was in store for him. His chosen champion turned out to be, not a scientific socialist with a doctrine and a dogma, but a humanitarian, not a Marxist but a kind of anarchist, with a hatred of machine civilization amounting almost to mania.

The Road to Wigan Pier, recently reissued by my own firm, was the first wholly political book Orwell wrote, and his first major success, a substantial work of 264 pages, divided into two main parts.[1] The first contains an account of a journey through the industrial North, undertaken by the author 'conscious of an immense weight of guilt that I had got to expiate. . . . I had reduced everything to the simple theory that the oppressed are always right and the oppressors are always wrong: a mistaken theory, but a natural result of being one of the oppressors yourself.'[2]

[1] All quotations from *The Road to Wigan Pier* are from the new 1959 edition published by Secker & Warburg.
[2] *The Road to Wigan Pier*, page 150.

This, of course, was a reference to his years as a policeman in Burma. Orwell expected to discover that the working-classes 'were the symbolic victims of injustice, playing the same part in England as the Burmese played in Burma'. Certainly he took the greatest possible trouble to share the lives of the most unsuccessful, the most submerged, section of the workers, for he wrote mainly about unemployed miners living in the worst slums he could find.

A slum of some kind was for Orwell a place where he could always feel more at home than anywhere else. In this respect, both in his books and his real life outside them, Orwell's adventures follow an extraordinary and significant pattern. In his first novel, *The Clergyman's Daughter* (not yet reprinted) he places much of the action among the hop-pickers of Kent, casual workers doing unskilled labour for trivial wages under shocking conditions. In *Down and Out in Paris and London* (1933) Orwell rooms in the London doss-houses among the misfits of civilization. In his third novel, *Keep the Aspidistra Flying* (1936), his hero is a bookseller's assistant, working for a pittance while struggling unsuccessfully to become a writer. In *Wigan Pier* (1937) it is with unemployed miners in slums that Orwell lives. The pattern is repeated again and again. For Orwell to work with or among even the moderately successful was distasteful, even downright intolerable. And this, it occurs to me, may have been the reason why he chose Secker & Warburg, rather than one of the many firms who would have welcomed him with open arms, when he required a publisher for *Homage to Catalonia*. At least, we were not tainted in 1936 with the smear of success!

The first part of *Wigan Pier* ranks among the best reporting of its day. In a lean unemphatic style, Orwell grimly reveals the horrors of unemployment, the filth of the slums, the vileness of overcrowding, the harshness of the means test and the bureaucrats who administer it. All power, he seems to say, corrupts, but *trivial* power corrupts absolutely. Black beetles, crumbling plaster, mounds of dirty tripe, brimming chamber-pots, monotonous and ill-cooked food, all are described with a kind of joyous detestation, a challenge to the doctrinaire formulas of the politicians and economists and to the complacency of an electorate that allowed such things to exist.

But suddenly and unexpectedly towards the end, cheerfulness breaks in. Orwell the pessimist gives way to a kind of post-Dickensian optimist who has seen the other side of the medal. 'In a working-class home,' he writes on page 117, 'you breathe a warm, decent, deeply human atmosphere. . . . I should say that a manual worker . . . has a better chance of being happy than an "educated" man. His home life seems to fall more naturally into a sane and comely shape.'

Here we have the basic image that was to dominate Orwell's imagination in the years to come. On the one hand, there is the decent human being, whom the privileged exploit, but who remains happier than the educated unless the exploitation is carried too far. The beasts in *Animal Farm* and the proles in *1984* are a development from the workers in *Wigan Pier*. On the other, the exploiters, in the West the capitalists, in the East the political and bureaucratic dictators who literally rule the roost in *Animal Farm* and torture the heretics in *1984*. But from the very beginning of his career as a writer, Orwell has tilted the balance of reality and distorted the picture. Not all workers are decent, nor are all capitalists and communist bureaucrats mere bullying bloodsuckers. Orwell was forced by some inner necessity to distort, and to make this distortion more acceptable to his own mind, he chose with unerring skill the *extreme* cases which made his distortion plausible. Some day an imaginative biographer will reveal the hidden spring which animated this extraordinary creative mechanism.

The first part of *Wigan Pier* was a cinch for the Left Book Club, all that they could ask for and a gift to the Stalinist doctrinaires and fellow-travellers of the day. The second part was a tougher nut to crack. Right at the beginning (page 123) Orwell remarks that 'before you can be sure whether you are genuinely in favour of Socialism, you have got to decide whether things at present are tolerable or not tolerable, and you have got to take up a definite attitude on the terribly difficult issue of class.' The subject of class is indeed taken up in the next fifty pages, and presents itself to Orwell as an absolutely insoluble problem. To him the gap between the middle-class and the working-class is unbridgeable; there is the question of accent, of interest, and believe it or not of smell. 'The lower orders smell,' according to Orwell, in a way that is nauseating to the middle-class, who don't smell or perhaps smell different (lavender water, cigars, tweed?). 'Perhaps,' he concludes, 'a classless society *doesn't* mean a beatific state of affairs . . . ; perhaps it means a bleak world in which all our ideals, our codes, our tastes—our "ideology", in fact, will have no meaning.' Hard words these for members of the L.B.C. to take; harsh doctrine for communists who work for nothing less than a classless society; a difficult decision for the members of the L.B.C. committee, whether to accept this piece of dynamite as a choice.

But the second half of Part Two made their decision doubly difficult. Here we get Orwell's views on Socialism itself, and for full measure on Socialists, in pages which combine deep humanitarian feeling with passages of knockabout satire as amusing as they are unfair. Socialism, Orwell maintains with justice, is bound up with the idea of progress through machine production. Its object is that 'everything now made of leather, wood or stone will be made of rubber, glass and steel; there will be no disorder, no loose ends, no wildernesses, no wild animals, no weeds, no disease, no poverty, no pain . . . the Socialist world is to be above all things an *ordered* world, an *efficient* world. But it is precisely from that vision of the future . . . that sensitive minds recoil.' Since people know that 'in some way or another "progress" is a swindle' and since 'the truth is that many of the qualities we admire in human beings can only function in opposition to some kind of disaster, pain or difficulty', Orwell abominates the socialist vision. 'Above the level of a third- or fourth-grade moron, life has got to be lived largely in terms of effort. For man is not . . . a kind of walking stomach; he has also got a hand, an eye, and a brain.' Mechanize the world, as the socialists demand, and 'whichever way you turn there will be some machine cutting you off from the chance of working—that is, of living.' In these passages and other like them it is easy to see the ideas that were to crystallize in 1948 into his nightmare masterpiece, *1984*.

But if Orwell is damning about the nature of a Socialist world, it is hard to find words to describe his detestation of socialist leaders and preachers. 'The typical Socialist,' he says, 'is either a youthful snob-Bolshevik . . . or, still more typically, a prim little man with a white-collar job, usually a secret teetotaller[1] and often with vegetarian leanings, with a history of Noncomformity behind him and, above all, with a social position which he has no intention of

---

[1] It seems to me difficult to be a *secret* teetotaller, though easy to be a secret drunkard. Orwell himself was an abstemious man, who liked his glass of beer and on a cold night a tot of rum, but his hatred of what he believes to be typical Socialists here carries him wholly away.

forfeiting. In addition to this there is the horrible . . . prevalence of cranks wherever Socialists are gathered together. One sometimes gets the impression that the mere words "Socialism" and "Communism" draw towards them with magnetic force every fruit-juice drinker, nudist, sandal-wearer, sex maniac, Quaker, "Nature cure quack", pacifist and feminist in England.' If this passage throws more light on Orwell's likes and dislikes than on the stalwart leaders of the English working-classes, it at least makes clear that Orwell was no Marxist.

The Road to Wigan Pier must be one of the most contradictory books ever written, a book in favour of socialism, seen as human decency and justice, by one of the most powerful antagonists of socialism, seen as Marxism, our age has produced. After reading it, one might well be expected to run down the road to fill in a membership form for the Conservative Party. Its final words, themselves riddled with contradictions, constitute perhaps the most luke-warm advocacy of a creed ever penned. Orwell, envisaging a world in which, after a revolutionary struggle, a real Socialist state has been achieved, declares: 'And then perhaps this misery of class-prejudice will fade away, and we of the middle-class . . . may sink without further struggles into the working-class where we belong, and probably when we get there it will not be so dreadful as we feared, for, after all, we have nothing to lose but our aitches.' For Orwell, the world of Socialism was in fact a land fit for failures and misfits to live in.

It was indeed brave of the L.B.C. committee to present this lemon in orange clothing to the devout membership. But obviously some explanation must be vouchsafed to forestall the possibility of mass resignations. This was provided by Gollancz in person in his most schoolmasterish manner. In his Foreword, he suggests that Orwell did not believe what he wrote. There is mention of Orwell's coming 'forward as a devil's advocate' to put the case against Socialism, but hardly a reference to the fact that the case is never withdrawn. Gollancz then denies that the views expressed by the author of this or any other L.B.C. choice are shared by the selectors. Since Gollancz, the late H. J. Laski and John Strachey were the selectors, this was undoubtedly true for *Wigan Pier*. Next he contradicts the view that *Wigan Pier* or the other choices 'incorporate the L.B.C. policy'. Indeed, it is suggested that 'the L.B.C. has no "policy": or rather it has no policy other than that of equipping people to fight against war and Fascism'. Perhaps dissatisfied with his statement about a policy which is not a policy, Gollancz attempts in the next sentence to define it further. 'It would not even be true to say that the People's Front is the "policy" of the L.B.C., though all three selectors are *enthusiastically in favour of it*.[1] What we rather feel is that . . . we are creating the mass basis without which a genuine People's Front is impossible. In other words, the People's Front is not the "policy" of the L.B.C., but the very existence of the L.B.C. tends towards a People's Front.'

Beneath this extraordinary agglomeration of words, it is perhaps permissible to deduce that all three members of the L.B.C.'s selection committee were enthusiastic People's Fronters, but that from time to time they were prepared to temper the wind to the shorn lamb, that is, to give their members a full-blooded, readable, non-Marxist book to read, *provided that* their members were warned not to believe what it said.

It was on the ambiguous battlefield of *Wigan Pier* that the outstanding political publisher of the 'thirties and the finest political writer of the 'thirties and 'forties parted

[1] My italics.

company. Though Gollancz was to publish in 1939 Orwell's next novel, *Coming Up For Air*, on which he had an option, he was not prepared to send him to Spain to interpret the Spanish War for L.B.C. members. In this, he was undoubtedly wise from his own point of view. The book he would have received could not have been published in the L.B.C., even if all three members of the Committee had written forewords a mile long. In 1944, when Orwell had completed *Animal Farm*, bound by his contract he offered the book to Gollancz, who rejected it to Orwell's great relief. The foreword to *Wigan Pier* had not increased any admiration Orwell might have felt for his first publisher.[1]

Urged on by Brockway, with whom Orwell was associated in the I.L.P., and enthusiastic, as I have suggested, to entrust his next publication, to a firm as unpopular and insignificant as Secker & Warburg was then, Orwell came to me in December 1936 to discuss a visit to Spain and a book on the Spanish War. When he appeared in my office, I had no inkling of the fact that he came bearing gifts more valuable than rubies. To me he was a brilliant young author without a big success to his name, for *Wigan Pier* had not yet been published. But I welcomed him for his talent and his empirical attitude to the problems of politics, which I shared. Of his first meeting with me I remember little. It was short, business-like, and highly undramatic. 'I want to go to Spain and have a look at the fighting,' he said, 'write a book about it. Good chaps, those Spaniards, can't let them down. Can probably give you the book a month or two after I get back.' Some such

---

[1] *Wigan Pier* sold just under 2,000 copies in hard covers and just over 40,000 copies in the limp cloth binding of the L.B.C. The figures indicate with extraordinary clarity the lack of interest among middle-class readers in the disastrous economic policies of the Conservative Government of that time. Equally obvious is the extent of the indignation among those mobilized by the L.B.C. campaigns, among whom a majority were probably Communists or fellow-travellers.

words as these were the prelude to the signature of a contract which was the most important I signed in my whole career. The advance asked by his agent was £150, and we paid it, though not without difficulty. It was to be fourteen years before it was earned, a few weeks after Orwell's death! I wished Orwell luck, and he left me. When I saw him next some seven months later, he had escaped death by a millimetre and acquired the experience which led him to *Animal Farm, 1984* and a world reputation.

When Orwell went to Spain he was neither pro- nor anti-communist.[1] Certainly he regarded with loathing most of the communists and fellow-travellers he had met around the L.B.C. and the political weeklies, but then he disliked with an almost equal intensity the I.L.P.-ers and followers of Cripps whom also he castigated in *Wigan Pier*. With introductions from Fenner Brockway and H. N. Brailsford, he left with his first wife, Eileen, and met John McNair at his office in Barcelona, where he was in administrative charge of the I.L.P. volunteers in the war against Franco. 'When I came to Spain,' Orwell wrote in *Homage to Catalonia* (pages 47–8),[2] 'and for some time afterwards, I was not only uninterested in the political situation but unaware of it. I knew there was a war on, but I had no notion what kind of a war. If you had asked me why I had joined the militia I should have answered, "To fight against Fascism", and if you had asked me what I was fighting *for*, I should have answered, "Common decency".' It was precisely the answer to be expected from the author of *Wigan Pier*.

It was McNair's view, presumably based on informa-

---

[1] Some of the information in this section derives from a conversation in November 1958 with John McNair, of the I.L.P. All views expressed should nevertheless be attributed to me.
[2] All references are to the uniform edition (1951) of *Homage*.

tion from London, that Orwell had come to Spain to write a book. He therefore offered him a room and facilities and all the material at his disposal in the Barcelona office. But Orwell could not wait to get to the front. He had not left London merely to pursue a safe and familiar routine, but to fight, to wipe out (as he puts it in one of his essays) the guilt he felt at having been born too late to take part in World War I. Here was his chance to let rip his long-frustrated instincts of aggression. The bloated capitalists, the calculating imperialists, the left-wing busy-bodies of dear old England, whom he had attacked so viciously in *Wigan Pier*, were second-rate targets compared to the real and dangerous Fascist enemy. Besides, the former were English, and many of them his friends. He must certainly have been aware that they were not quite as black as he painted them.

When McNair understood what Orwell wanted, he suggested that he join the fighting forces of the C.N.T., the Anarchists, as the most numerous and powerful army deployed against Franco on the Catalan front. But Orwell refused. He joined the P.O.U.M. militia, 'because I happened to arrive in Barcelona with I.L.P. papers, but I did not realize that there were serious differences between the political parties.' This statement we must accept, at least in part, but we may surely assert also that once again Orwell was following, however unconsciously, the deepest need of his nature. Though the bold and unrealistic doctrines of Anarchism must have tempted him sorely to join their army, it was the Anarchists who were in full control in Catalonia, they were in fact basically the government, and Orwell could never bring himself to be a government man. The P.O.U.M. Militia, on the contrary, were few, ill-equipped, poorly thought of and politically muddled (half-anarchist, half-Marxist, with a tinge of

Trotsky-ist bitters for full measure). They were the equivalent of the bug-infested unemployed miners of *Wigan Pier*, of the unsuccessful publishing house he had chosen to patronize. Orwell joined them as a matter of course; it came to him as naturally as breathing.

Orwell arrived in Barcelona in December 1936, and by January 1937 must have been in the trenches. Winter in the high sierras was cold and wet, and he suffered agonies from the hostility of the weather. Of course, no man with Orwell's medical record would have attempted the task he set himself, unless he had been under the direst compulsion. Orwell's compulsion came from within, for in Spain he was a foreigner and an intruder, a volunteer in a crusade. The Civil War was his only because he chose to make it so. It was probably not the first time, as it was certainly not the last, that Orwell put his life in jeopardy at the urging of his *daemon*. On this occasion, as on others to come, the game can be made superficially to seem worth the candle. Yet I cannot but believe that he risked his life unnecessarily, extravagantly, and without good cause, not only in Spain, but during the bombing of London, in the whirlpools round Jura, and in his persistent neglect of elementary medical precautions in the last few years of his life. The urge to die before his time proved in the end too strong for him to resist. Obliteration was finally the sole remedy for his overpowering sense of guilt.

Homage was begun in February in the trenches, written on scraps, the backs of envelopes, toilet paper. The written material was sent to Barcelona to McNair's office, where his wife, working as a volunteer, typed it out section by section. Slowly it grew into a sizeable parcel. McNair kept it in his own room. In London I waited, but little news of Orwell or his book came through to me. What did come through, however, was the report of the rising in

Barcelona, though who rose against whom was a matter of angry discussion. Orwell happened to be on leave in Barcelona during this critical period. 'About midday on 3 May a friend crossing the lounge of the hotel said casually: "There's been some kind of trouble at the Telephone Exchange, I hear." For some reason I paid no attention to it at the time.' So, casually, on page 161 of *Homage*, Orwell introduces his description of the civil war within the civil war, in which the communists seized absolute power from the anarchists and their allies throughout Cataıonia. These events, in which, as usual, Orwell was on the losing side, must have burned themselves into his imagination. They were to animate all the important work he did before his death.

What did Orwell observe during these May days? First, the power of the police. 'The issue was clear enough. On one side the C.N.T. (the anarchist federation), on the other side the police. I have no particular love for the idealized "worker" as he appears in the bourgeois Communist's mind, but when I see an actual flesh-and-blood worker in conflict with his natural enemy, the policeman, I do not have to ask myself which side I am on' (page 132). Second, the deliberate blackening of your enemy by false accusation. 'The affair was represented . . . as a deliberate planned insurrection against the Government, engineered solely by the P.O.U.M. . . . More than this, it was definitely a Fascist plot' (page 171). Third, the arrest, and frequently the murder, of political opponents without trial. 'I had the ineradicable English belief that "they" cannot arrest you unless you have broken the law. It is a most dangerous belief to have during a political pogrom. . . . The arrests . . . were continuing without pause; practically everyone we knew, except those who were still at the front, was in jail by this time' (page 242). Fourth, the falsification of history. Fifth, the disruption of the unity of the working-class by the alleged necessities of communist tactics. 'There is already the beginning of a dangerous split in the world working-class movement. A few more libels against life-long Socialists, a few more frame-ups like the charges against the P.O.U.M., and the split may become irreconcilable' (page 192).

Today it may appear commonplace to detail such obvious facts as these. But in England in the spring of 1937 there were few who had experienced these things at first hand and lived to bear witness to them. There were in fact few in those days who believed what Orwell wrote in *Homage*. It seemed to the naïve too disgusting. To the more intelligent, who had their suspicions of what could be done in the name of political necessity, the communists sang sweet soothing syren songs or lied loudly with brassy voices. *Homage to Catalonia*, when it was published in April 1938, caused barely a ripple on the political pond. It was ignored or hectored into failure.

As a matter of fact, it was fortunate even to reach the hands of printer and publisher. McNair has told me how he hid the manuscript on his window ledge when the police ransacked his flat during the Barcelona rising. A few days later, he was caught with the manuscript in his bag. What is it, they asked him, turning over the pages, since fortunately they could not read English. But McNair had quick wits and a thorough understanding of the political imbroglio in which he was involved. Though they questioned him for two-and-a-half hours, he stuck to his story: 'Comrades, it is a book written by a comrade, a gallant anti-fascist fighter. He is a friend of Harry Pollitt, leader of the Communist Party in England. My comrade is a well-known English author, who writes to tell the English working-class of the brave battle fought by the Spanish comrades

236

on their behalf. He writes to rouse his English comrades from their lethargy, to inspire them to send help, arms, supplies, medical necessities. My comrade stands linked indissolubly with the proletariat of Spain, the workers of the world who must unite. . . . Salud!' The trick worked; the police respectfully returned the dirty typescript to McNair's keeping, and let him go.

The day before Orwell had seen McNair, and told him: 'This is bloody awful . . . these buggers (the police) are shooting our chaps in the back.' But, despite his developing hatred of the communists and what they stood for, Orwell returned a little later to the front. He would fight the Fascists till he dropped or was arrested by his own side. 'Since 1930 the Fascists had won all the victories,' he wrote, 'it was time they got a beating, it hardly mattered from whom. If we could drive Franco and his foreign mercenaries into the sea, it might make an immense improvement in the world situation, even if Spain itself emerged . . . with all its best men in jail.' Here, in this frail novelist's body, was contained a power of resolve to put the waverers to shame. As Orwell was to write later of an Italian soldier who fought with him

> 'But the thing that I saw in your face
> No power can disinherit:
> No bomb that ever burst
> Shatters the crystal spirit.'

The words apply with equal force to the man who wrote them.

A few weeks later, Orwell was wounded. A sniper's bullet passed through his throat within a millimetre of the windpipe. Though the Spanish doctors prophesied that he would lose his voice, they were mistaken. Slowly it came back to him, reedy and high-pitched. But now in

Barcelona, where Orwell returned from the hospital, there was a warrant out for his arrest. The time to disappear had arrived. With his wife, John McNair, and Stafford Cotman, an I.L.P. volunteer like himself, Orwell slipped over the French border on 27 June and returned through Paris to London. The Spanish adventure was over. 'My only souvenirs of Spain were a goatskin water-bottle and one of those tiny iron-lamps in which the Aragon peasants burn olive-oil' (page 245). But here at least Orwell was mistaken, for his souvenirs from Spain included far more, nothing less than the experiences he described in *Homage*, the raw material from which a decade later he was to fashion his two greatest books. As he travelled in the boat-train to London and surveyed from his carriage window the England that was so dear to him, he had a flash of prophecy as he saw the familiar landscape 'all sleeping the deep, deep sleep of England, from which I sometimes fear that we shall never wake till we are jerked out of it by the roar of bombs' (final page). But Orwell himself was wide awake, and remained so till death closed his eyes. It was just as well.

Orwell must have finished *Homage* by the end of 1937, and we published it in April 1938. The printing number was 1,500 copies, the sales in the first six months 683, thereafter its annual sale was less than fifty copies. As I have said, the remaining copies of the first edition stayed in our warehouse until after Orwell's death in 1950, when they sold rapidly. Twelve years after its publication, *Homage to Catalonia* attracted the readers it had been so long without. Franco by then had been in power for a decade. No comment seems quite adequate, but on to my tongue comes the useful French expletive—*Merde!*

11 Drifting to Disaster

'MERDE' is a word applicable to the whole of that dreadful year, 1938. It was the year in which the Sudeten-land was detached from Czechoslovakia and incorporated into the Reich, the year in which England and France were chased round the ring by the reigning world heavy-weight champion, Hitler, and floored for what seemed to be the count in September, the month of the Munich Agreement. But to me in the spring and summer such disasters were too intolerable to contemplate, and ostrich-like I buried my head in the problems of my firm drifting towards insolvency. Between January and the end of May we published fifteen new books, including Mann's *Joseph in Egypt* and Orwell's *Catalonia*. Most of them lost money, not one of them was a pronounced success.

By now the staff had grown a little bigger, we had a packer and a postal clerk, so the overhead expenses were up. With forty new books in 1937 and thirty-five in 1938 it was inevitable. But the biggest change of all in the personnel was the resignation of Martin Secker. Secker can never have been happy since Senhouse and I took over the reins. It was too much to expect that a man who has founded a firm

239

and run it with brilliance for twenty-five years could settle down to work under a new boss. Besides, the leftist books that we published must have shocked him profoundly. Conservative to the core and interested in literature rather than politics, he must have regarded me as a ruthless barbarian bent on destroying the delicate flavour of a list that was, or had been, famous all over the world.

His place as production manager was taken by John Lloyd, a tall, dark-haired, bony-faced young man who was soon to marry the daughter of B. F. Cummings, who wrote, under the pseudonym of W. N. P. Barbellion, one of the most moving revelations in English autobiography, *The Diary of a Disappointed Man*, to which H. G. Wells contributed a preface. Lloyd had thrown up a job in his father's motor business to join me as an apprentice in 1937. He was mad keen to get his hands on books, particularly good-looking ones, since he had a passion for typography, illustration, binding, all the arts of book production. Like myself, though in a far less privileged position, he worked his way up from the bottom, the trade counter, the packing room, invoicing, the ledgers, the royalty accounts. Soon he started learning about the physical processes of printing in the establishment of our jobbing printer, A. S. Atkinson. When Secker left, rather hurriedly, it was natural that I should put the production into Lloyd's hands. Within months he had displayed a talent quite out of the ordinary for the manufacture of books, and ours soon began to display an originality and brilliance markedly different from the traditional refinement of Secker's taste.

But still the gap between the gross profits and the overheads opened wider, and the capital, though it had increased, was barely enough to support a list half the size of ours. Disaster drew nearer week by week. Gloomily I consulted Senhouse about the raising of a substantial new

investment. But he had no consolation for me. Temporarily
at any rate he had run out of backers. Forced against my
will to divert my energies from publishing to financial
matters, I began to consider a further approach to Aunt
Agnes, whom I had left in peace since 1936. My wife
spurred me on. 'I always told you,' she reminded me,
'that you should have asked Aunt Agnes for more money.
You could have got it easily two years ago. Now it will
be much more difficult, because of all this mess.' She waved
her arm in a spacious gesture to indicate that the world
was out of joint, that the British were mainly responsible,
and that I as an Englishman must shoulder my share of
the guilt.

The demanding of money, with or without menaces,
has always appeared a formidable task to me, one to be
undertaken only as a last resort. But now I could see no
way round, and away I went to see my Aunt. As always
she was sympathetic. 'I don't have the time to read many
of your publications,' she told me, 'but everyone says
your list is most distinguished. Only why do you have to
publish so many of those horrid Socialist books and attacking dear Mr. Chamberlain too?' Sheering away from this
dangerous topic, I explained our situation and suggested
that £5,000 would put us on our feet for ever.

'It's a lot of money,' she said, quietly, 'and I'm getting
too old for this kind of thing. I have put all my affairs
into the hands of Siegmund Warburg of the New Trading Co.
You'd better go and see him. I'll write him a letter, asking
him to do his best for you.'

My distant cousin, Siegmund, was then in the early days
of his career as a merchant banker, in which he has since
become so prominent and so feared. Hero, with Lionel
Fraser of Helbert Wagg, in the recent battle for the control
of British Aluminium Ltd. against the massed banking

battalions ranged against them, he took as much trouble over my miserable £5,000 investment as he could have done over the millions involved in the aluminium affair. The £5,000 went in, and with it a new director nominated by Siegmund to advise Senhouse and myself on the handling of our resources. His name was Hans Lothar, and he had been forced by the Nazis to leave his important post on the *Frankfurter Zeitung* for exile in London. Lothar was active on our behalf for about four years. He brought one or two excellent books on to the list, including Hermann Rauschning's *Make and Break With the Nazis* published in September 1941, but by the time he left us it is unlikely that he had rubbed much financial sense into my thick head.

In a recent letter to me John Lloyd has described the way I looked to him then, 'very stern and severe apparently, a good deal of it due to the financial worries of the period. . . . It was always difficult going in to see you, as you sat at the end of that long room with the window almost behind you, so that it was impossible to see your face and get any idea of what you were thinking. You were pretty inscrutable anyway, even when the light was on your face.' Inscrutable! The adjective astonishes me. I would have supposed that anxiety, depression and at times dismay shone out of my face like a beam from a lighthouse. *We were not selling nearly enough books to keep us in business.* It was as simple as that. Trade was shocking, as Hitler bawled his menaces at the world's statesmen. Our list was good; some of the authors highly distinguished; production under Lloyd's direction was first-rate; the advertising, which I laid out myself, was copious and in my own opinion splendidly devised. What then was lacking? Sales know-how! It is this which in most cases is the Achilles' heel of the new and untried publisher. We had one good traveller in London, Roth, who performed miracles in selling dangerously radical books to ultra-conservative booksellers. But outside London and overseas, there were faults to find, faults which I had no means of remedying. And inside the office not one of us had the experience or instincts of a sales manager, that vital executive who drives the travellers on to do their best, supplying them as he does so with a constant stream of accurate and useful information. The fact was, we lacked punch!

In this precarious and even dangerous situation, with the overheads rising, the creditors clamouring for something on account, and with too many titles to finance on too little capital, I spent anxious hours staring out of my window, wondering what to do next. It has always been hard for me to glimpse the obvious, at least in a business sense, and on this occasion also I had to work my way through dense thickets of confusion before I came upon a clearing.

Then at last I found myself muttering the magic words —'what we need is a best-seller'. Since the publication of *Clochemerle* we certainly hadn't had one. The remedy was simple; its execution as difficult as the climbing of Everest. Every general publisher in London was looking for a best-seller, all day and many hours of the night. How could I expect to find this needle in a haystack, when all the best publishing brains in London had picked over the hay, straw by straw? But now my mind was racing over the possibilities. As I saw it, there was just one chance in a thousand of getting a best-seller to publish within the next twelve months, before in fact it was too late. It was from H. G. Wells. If I could induce him to publish with us, we might yet recoup our tottering fortunes. On this desperate venture I embarked without delay.

What induced me to imagine that Wells might entertain

the idea of giving a book to me, or even that he knew who I was? The close friendship existing between Tanya's mother, Baroness Budberg, and the great writer. Gay, vital and tolerant of his faults, Baroness Budberg gave Wells in the last decade of his life a warmth and a comfort that consoled him for growing old. She lunched or dined with him when otherwise he might have been alone. She acted as his hostess. She understood the turmoil of his writer's mind. After all, she had known the great Maxim Gorki in her youth before the Bolsheviks drove her from the family estate. With Tanya and her mother to speak on my behalf, perhaps Wells would consider taking a chance with a new publisher whose spurs were not yet won.

Wells was then approaching seventy. His fame was immense, equally as the greatest English novelist of the first quarter of the twentieth century, and as a radical whose belief in scientific progress had been maintained in many a hard-fought battle with the polite society of the day. Had I really the effrontery, I asked myself, to approach this almost mythical figure? Bracing myself for the effort, I called my secretary into my room. Tanya came in with the half-dozen letters I had dictated to her that morning. I read them carefully, correcting the usual spelling mistakes, and handed them back.

'Sit down, Tanya,' I said.

Tanya sat down.

'Do you think H.G. would do a book for us, if I asked him?' I inquired. 'The financial situation is ominous. Too many good books and too few sellers are ruining us.'

Tanya nodded gravely. It was no news to her. In a small office nothing can be hidden. 'I think you might be able to persuade him,' she remarked, 'he's none too pleased with any of his present publishers; he says they have no appreciation whatever of what he's up to. But he can be an absolute fiend when he wants to. Surely we shall never be able to pay him as large an advance as he's certain to ask?'

'We've got to afford to pay him a big advance,' I said, grimly. 'What's the alternative? We simply can't go on the way we are. Will you speak to him for me?'

'I'll get him to ask you to lunch at 13 Hanover Terrace,' Tanya said.

A week or two later the momentous day arrived. I put on my best suit, stuck a flower in my buttonhole, and set out for Regents Park. The lake gleamed under a brilliant sun. As usual before a great occasion, I was nervous, pessimistic about the possibility of success, but firmly resolved to play such cards as I had in my hand with skill and finesse. After all, I thought, my firm after only two years is already being talked about as one with a future, not yet a star of the first magnitude but definitely a visible twinkle in the sky. I rang the bell, and was shown by a neat parlourmaid into a sitting-room. A minute later the great man joined me. As we shook hands, my mouth felt a trifle dry. 'My dear Warburg,' he said, 'I've heard a lot about you from Tanya. She tells me you're quite a good publisher. Considering what asses most of you fellows are, you should have quite a decent future.' Soon we went in to lunch.

We sat one at each end of a magnificent long table. Period furniture filled the room. Rather unsympathetic pictures hung on the walls, and fine Russian china plates decorated the wall behind the sideboard. H.G. held forth in his peculiar squeaky voice on a variety of subjects, and my mind wandered while I ate the roast beef and roast potatoes put before me. Had the time come to broach the object of my visit or was it wiser to postpone till coffee was served? Suddenly I realized that a question had been thrown at me.

'So you're ambitious enough, young man, to want to publish one of my books,' H.G. said.

Blessing Tanya under my breath for having made the introduction of the subject so simple, 'Yes, Mr. Wells,' I said, 'it would give me very great pleasure to become your publisher.'

'It so happens,' H.G. went on, 'that I'm working at a book now, *The Fate of Homo Sapiens*. It will be finished by the end of the year. I might possibly allow you to make a contract for it.'

'What is its theme?' I inquired cautiously.

H.G. pretended to look annoyed. 'Oho,' he said, 'at first I hear you want to publish one of my books, any book that I'm kind enough to offer you. Now it appears you've changed your tune. You actually have the impertinence to demand what it's about. That's not the way I deal with my publishers. I expect slavish obedience from them. They are, after all, merely men of commerce, honest for the most part, greedy as a matter of course, but wholly unfitted to pick and choose among masterpieces. Either you publish what I write without quibbling or I'll look elsewhere for a man of business.'

'Then you'd better look elsewhere,' I replied as calmly as I could, 'because my firm has no intention of publishing blind even books by so distinguished a writer as yourself. Naturally I can't imagine that we would ever refuse a book of yours, but we must reserve the right to do so.'[1]

H.G. looked at me quizzically. 'I ought to throw you

[1] About 1943, Wells collected under the title *Crux Ansata* some indifferent and wildly partisan essays on the Catholic Church which he detested. When he offered them to me, I declined them with a polite note. Wells was furious, and rang up to call me every name under the sun. After listening to the torrent of abuse, and finding it impossible to get a word in edgeways, I hung up on him. That, I thought, will finish my career as Wells' publisher. But I was mistaken. Two days later, I received a charming letter from him, apologizing for his bad manners and telling me to forget the whole incident. We did in fact continue to publish his more important books till the end of his life. It is, however, typical of Wells that he did not consign *Crux Ansata* to a bottom drawer, but persuaded Penguin Books to publish it. It appeared also in the U.S.

out of my house for your damned impertinence,' he said,
'but I rather like a young man who seems to know his
own mind and isn't mealy-mouthed in expressing it.'
Whereupon he launched into a long description of the work
in hand to which I listened with fascination, interjecting
every now and again an 'of course', a 'yes, certainly', a
'that's very true' to show that I was attending. 'The
world not facing up to need for rapid and fundamental
change . . . put Freud and Darwin together as significant
figures in human enlightenment . . . aviation and radio
communication have abolished distance . . . unity of world
an imperative necessity . . . cornucopia of invention . . .
I've been privileged to attend special deliberations of
British Association . . . apprehension of scientists about
work they are asked to do . . . politicians and would-be
statesmen with no understanding of technology, ecology,
psychology . . . nationalism and its dangers . . . conscience,
experience, cunning, hatred, skulduggery . . . walking into
a trap.' The squeaking, high-pitched, irascible voice went
on and on. It was magnificent, but it was making me sleepy.
Too much beef, four glasses of Burgundy, a hot day, the
excitement, the anxiety were wearing me down. At that
moment, the maid brought in the coffee, and I seized my
opportunity. 'Let me assure you, Mr. Wells,' I said, with
all the emphasis at my disposal, 'my firm and I would be
pleased, would indeed be proud, to become the publishers
of *The Fate of Homo Sapiens*. When will it be ready?
When may I read it?' It had been a near thing, but the
danger was past.

Now, however, a fresh difficulty arose. Wells, stimulated
by his vision of the shape of disasters to come, intended to make me jump through all the hoops his
ingenious anti-publisher mind could set up. 'Not so fast,
young man,' he said, 'I've taken quite a fancy to you,

but there is always one matter I insist on with all my publishers.'

'A big advance,' I blurted out before I could stop myself.

Wells looked hurt. 'Naturally I require a good advance,' he said, 'but that need not worry you. I'm not half as greedy as they say I am. Why should I be? I'm rich, you know. I could show you a fine list of my investments in the next room. What I want from you is a guarantee of really large-scale advertising.'

'Of course we shall advertise your book extensively,' I said, 'we shall be only too delighted to boast of having so distinguished a man of letters on our list. You need have no worry on that score.'

'That's not what I mean at all,' H.G. said, with a diabolical grin on his face, 'I expect my publishers to *bankrupt* themselves on my behalf. Will you do that?'

My heart sank. So this was the way the hard-fought battle was to be lost. So let it be. I would perish with my face turned resolutely to the enemy.

'What a monstrous suggestion,' I said. 'The answer is no! I intend my firm to stay permanently in business.'

There was a stilly silence. I could hear the raucous cries of the gulls flying over the lake outside. Then, it seemed almost without transition, we were talking about women and sex. It must have been Wells who began it, but I made my contribution from time to time. Out of Wells' mouth poured a lively and turbulent flood of reminiscence, intended perhaps to shock, perhaps to impress me. 'Women can hold out till they're forty,' he told me, 'then they begin to go downhill. . . . Some mistresses spend so much money you wish them in hell; others can hardly be induced even to purchase a new hat.' I heard about titled women, tweedy women, womanly women, amazons, bluestockings and milkmaids. I absorbed his views on the beginnings, middles and ends of love-affairs. We discussed the merits of patriarchal and matriarchal societies. But in the end we always returned to the personal, to the problem that Wells presented to himself—why he had such a need of women.

'My friends tell me that I'm tremendously oversexed,' he said, 'it's been a burden to me all my life.'

Sipping my brandy and excited by the paradisical world of Wells' love affairs spread before me, I said sharply, 'No, I don't agree with you there.'

'What on earth do you mean?' he demanded in surprise.

'I mean that you are *not* oversexed. You are undersexed. It is this that forces you to prove to your own satisfaction that your virility remains strong and unimpaired.' Drawing upon vague memories of my analytical sessions with Professor Flugel six years before, I delivered a forceful and unsound lecture on the subject of the libido and its demands. The strongly sexed man, I said, makes love to women rarely, and then only when he is attracted by a unique combination of physical and spiritual loveliness. The undersexed man, on the other hand, needs constant reassurance and will be forced to search for and obtain it with whatever personable woman presents herself at the critical time.

As I developed my nonsensical argument, I could not help wondering whether I had not gone too far. Wells was old enough to be my father, if not my grandfather. Besides, I expected some lucid and destructive retort from his agile mind. What if he asked me whether I drank wine to make sure that I still had a strong head, or read books in order to be certain that my eyesight was still sound? But the riposte never came. Wells was delighted. No one before had ever dared to describe him as undersexed. It tickled his fancy, gave him a new idea of himself for a few hours until he forgot it. After that, there was no trouble at all about the contract. It was fixed up then and there. A fifteen per cent flat royalty, an advance on publication of £250. The money was a fleabite compared to what Wells could easily have obtained elsewhere. We parted cordially. So, strangely, began an association that was to last almost till his death. Secker & Warburg published eight out of his last ten major books. We never had any trouble at all on terms.

It was about this time that my anger with the Stalinists rose to a new peak. Sick of being described as 'a Trotskyist reptile' and 'a crypto-fascist', I decided to hit back. We took a full-page advertisement in the *New Statesman*, and listed in it the various social, economic and political books we had published over the last eighteen months. At the bottom, in letters which I wished could have been printed in fire not ink, the following slogan appeared:

WE MUST ALL FIGHT

FOR LIBERTY AGAINST FASCISM

but we need not all fall in

behind the communist steamroller[1]

The steamroller however continued to roll on with massive deliberation. Slowly but surely it was crushing the strength out of the political half of my list. It was advising those who would listen not to offer their books to so dastardly a character as myself. Given a little more time, it would have destroyed us.

In June we published three books. The final volume of Arnold Zweig's trilogy, *Crowning of a King*, had a small

---

[1] Since all our records were destroyed by a V1 in August 1944, the exact words of this advertisement depend on the hazards of my memory.

success, but as a seller Zweig was no longer important. Freda Utley had written an interesting work, *Japan's Gamble in China,* which about covered its costs. The third book was to have a curious history, an illustration of the fact that in publishing present disaster can sometimes become future success. Jomo Kenyatta in those days was a young African student working on anthropology at the London School of Economics under my old friend Professor Malinowski. It was, however, Brockway who had sent him to me, since Kenyatta was associated with the Independent Labour Party as an expert on African affairs. *Facing Mount Kenya* was only part-written, but what I saw convinced me that, when completed, it would be an original and indeed unique contribution to African studies. No African before Kenyatta had had the ability or the specialized anthropological training to turn out a work in any way comparable with his. Malinowski himself promised to write a preface, a contract was signed, and in due course the book was completed, delivered, and published. It was the first book of its kind to appear on our list, and I was immensely proud of it.

The volume was a substantial one with interesting illustrations. It dealt with the origins and kinship nexus of Kenyatta's tribe, the Gikuyu, and with their economic, educational, religious and sexual systems. Kenyatta dedicated it to 'Moigoi and Wamboi and all the dispossessed youth of Africa; for perpetuation of communion with ancestral spirits through the fight for African Freedom, and in the firm faith that the dead, the living and the unborn will unite to rebuild the destroyed shrines.' In his preface, after thanking his friends, Kenyatta continues: 'I owe thanks also to my enemies, for the stimulating discouragement which has kept up my spirits to persist in the task. Long life and health to them to go on with the

251

good work.' This revolutionary, if revolutionary he was, certainly had a sense of humour. Malinowski's preface was enthusiastic. He wrote, 'Mr. Kenyatta is outspoken and honest to an extent rarely found in students of social science: he recognizes the dangers of his own bias. In fairness to him, we have to recognize the fact that an African who looks at things from the tribal point of view and at the same time from the standpoint of Western civilization, experiences the tragedy of the modern world in an especially acute manner. For, to quote William James, "progress is a terrible thing".' The wise words of Malinowski were underlined by Kenyatta himself (on page 317): 'It is all these different aspects of life together that make up a social culture. And it is the culture which he inherits that gives a man his human dignity. . . . But a culture has no meaning apart from the social organization of life on which it is built. When the European comes to the Gikuyu country and robs the people of their land, he is taking away not only their livelihood, but the material symbol that holds family and tribe together. In doing this he gives one blow which cuts away the foundations from the whole of Gikuyu life. . . . There certainly are some progressive ideas among the Europeans . . . ideas of material prosperity, of medicine and hygiene, and literacy which enable people to take part in world culture. But so far the Europeans who visit Africa have not been conspicuously zealous in imparting these parts of their inheritance to the Africans, and seem to think that the only way to do it is by police discipline and armed force. They speak as if it was somehow beneficial to an African to work for them instead of for himself, and to make sure that he will receive this benefit they do their best to take away his land.'

These strong and menacing words from the Gikuyu chieftain and the learned professor were read by only

517 people, for despite excellent reviews this was the number of copies sold; the book with its warning message was a dismal flop; the advance of £30 was barely earned; the balance of the 1,500 copies printed languished in our warehouse until destroyed by bombs in 1941. Such was the fate of a book which, had its words been heeded, might have averted the frightful Mau Mau Rebellion.

Was Kenyatta guilty in fact of the charges brought against him by the British Government in 1954? I have no idea. To me in 1938 he appeared amiable, intelligent, perhaps a trifle vain. His venom against the British settlers in his country seemed no more than might be expected from a man of his birth, colour and blood. My wife and I are unlikely to forget the evening he came to dinner. When the bell rang and he was shown into our drawing-room, I staggered back in amazement. There stood Kenyatta, tall, massively muscled, a high forehead over a bony face, curly black hair and beard close-cropped. Across his huge chest and over his right shoulder he wore a leopard skin; a long and dangerous looking spear was held in one hand. His appearance was magnificent. Perhaps it was his way of underlining the gulf between black and white, even though they were to eat together; perhaps merely a desire to impress; conceivably he felt that an author should be fully armed in the presence of so dangerous a man as his publisher. My wife showed her usual sangfroid. 'Put your spear in the corner and let me give you a drink,' she said, 'a leopard-skin costume suits you much better than it does the women who wear them up and down Bond Street.'

Soon after the outbreak of the Mau Mau Rebellion, we re-issued *Facing Mount Kenya*, unchanged after sixteen years. For a work of anthropology it made an extraordinary come-back, and the number of copies sold to date is over

8,000. The book has become the Africans' *Mein Kampf*. To Kenyatta out of jail, after serving a seven-year sentence, we owe a very substantial sum in royalties. I hope we may be allowed to pay them to him before long.

With the contract for Wells' *Future of Homo Sapiens* in our agreement book and my aunt's £5,000 injecting new life into the firm, I faced the second half of 1938 with some assurance. Certainly it was to be needed, as the drift to the Munich betrayal intensified. A few days before this disgusting political event took place, warlike preparations began in London, or at least a few amateur trenches were dug in the parks or on open land. A nightmare quality imbued this period for me through the advice kindly telephoned to my wife by a well-known military commentator. 'Get out of London by the week-end,' he told her. 'If war comes and the Germans drop bombs, there's nothing to stop them.' My wife called me at the office without delay.

'Is it true,' she demanded, 'that we are totally unprepared for war?' In military matters my wife tends to treat me as an expert, in marked contradistinction to her normal attitude in more everyday affairs.

'It probably is true,' I replied, 'at any rate they can't spare an A.A. gun to defend Waterloo Bridge, the Palace Theatre or the Secker & Warburg offices. The best they can manage is to set up a machine-gun right across the river from here.'

'Will that be useful?' my wife asked earnestly.

'It could create absolute havoc,' I said, 'among a flock of low-flying pigeons.'

My wife was annoyed. 'It's no laughing matter,' she said, 'when I think of the fearful amount of money we have to pay out in taxes. What have they got to show us

254

for it? Absolutely nothing except this thing for shooting the poor pigeons. The Minister for War should be hung and Chamberlain had up for high treason!'

'It's difficult to manufacture war equipment in a year or so,' I told her, soothingly, 'the armament factories take a long time to get tooled up.'

'Then why on earth,' my wife inquired, 'couldn't they have started earlier? Anybody could have told them that Hitler was a menace. I've been telling you so for years, long before you took any notice of me.'

Since there was perhaps an element of truth in this last thrust, I answered it warily, 'I agree that you warned me about the Nazis long ago. I admit it. A woman's intuition is a marvellous thing, so often coming to the right conclusions for the wrong reasons. But,' I hurried on, anticipating an explosion, 'what I want to know is whether you will take Captain X's advice and get out of town.'

'Certainly not,' my wife said firmly, 'I've far too much to do in London. Besides, I never pay attention to threats, especially from horrible little vulgarians like that man. But please, please come home early this evening. I don't like the idea of bombs falling on me, especially in a top-floor flat like ours.'

'It's safer on the top floor,' I said, hopefully, 'further away from the blast. But I'll come home early just the same, don't worry.'

A day or so later came Chamberlain's flight to Hitler at Berchtesgaden, or maybe it was the second one to Bad Godesberg. For a moment it seemed to me like a good thing, but Pamela's voice broke urgently into my delusion. 'Chamberlain should never go to see Hitler,' she remarked, 'it's conniving or whatever it's called. If they must meet, Hitler should come to London. When you and

I have a row, I don't come to you to fix it up. Naturally you come to me.'

'Naturally,' I said. She could hardly have made the international situation clearer.

The Munich crisis was bad for trade. There was too much to read in the newspapers, too much to listen to on the radio. Early in September we published a most important book, Lewis Mumford's *The Culture of Cities*. This was the second volume of the tetralogy which was to occupy twenty years of his life and firmly establish him as one of the great humanists of our time.

How did it happen that Mumford offered his new book to me rather than to Routledge who had successfully published *Technics and Civilization*? It was many years before I found out. In New York Mumford went to his publisher Brace for advice, and the question was discussed in detail. Should he stay with the substantial and well-organized firm with which I had been associated or should he take a chance with me, the new imprint? I shall always feel grateful for Mumford's decision and Brace's advice to him. They were among the first to bet on the new man, the young adventurer. No doubt, too, they approved the stand I was attempting in the political field against the fascists and the communists. Perhaps at a distance of 3,000 miles they were unaware of the perilous seas on which I was sailing. But the book came to me first of all . . . and very nearly we rejected it!

A small firm cannot afford the big investment in a single venture that its established rivals can accept without thinking. *Cities* was a large book that would eat up a substantial slice of our meagre capital. Like *Technics* before it, it might well be a slow seller. Enthusiastic as I was after reading it, in the face of Senhouse's doubts I decided we must have a reader's report. We sent it to Raymond Mortimer. Anxiously I awaited word from this distinguished writer, but when it came it did not satisfy me. The report was not plainly hostile, but it was lukewarm and particularly pessimistic about the sales possibilities. Senhouse was gloomy, but I was more determined than ever to see the book on our list. I gave Senhouse a lecture.

'Readers,' I told him, 'like all other experts, must be ignored on occasion. A commander-in-chief listens to the advice of his staff officers, but in the last resort he must make his own mind up. It is his responsibility alone, and his privilege.'

'In that case,' Senhouse remarked, reasonably enough, 'why bother to send the book to Mortimer.'

'For this reason,' I said, 'if Mortimer had been enthusiastic and agreed with me wholeheartedly, we could have gone big on the book. But, since he's lukewarm, we shall have to proceed cautiously.'

Casuistical or not, this has always been my attitude to reader's reports. Only the publisher can decide what to publish and what to discard. The reader's advice is only a guide and sometimes a warning. Unless it converts me to its view, I ignore it. The practice has led me to many of my greatest triumphs, and to a disaster or two.

We published *Culture of Cities* at 21*s.*, an expensive book indeed in those days, equivalent to 50*s.* or more at the present time. We bought 1,000 copies from Harcourt Brace. The advance sale was around 150! The booksellers were as pessimistic as Mortimer about the possibilities. The press however was favourable, and slowly the orders began to come in. The book, at first throttled by anxiety over the Czechoslovakian tragedy, survived. In July 1939 we ordered another 250 copies from Harcourt Brace. This, I now felt certain, was a book that would last. But even I, in my optimism, did not foresee what was to happen. The book jogged along, making friends, until the first 1,250 copies were gone. But in December 1940, with a touch of publishing genius, we published a cheaper edition of 2,625 copies. This lasted a couple of years, by which time much of London and of other great towns in England had been destroyed, and citizens became passionately interested in what should be done when their cities were rebuilt after victory. The prestige of Mumford's book rose higher and higher. It was reprinted again early in 1943, again in 1944 and in 1945. In February 1948 we printed yet another 5,000 copies and sold over half by the end of that year. To date the sales amount to over 17,000 copies, a tremendous record for a work of such fine general scholarship. *The Culture of Cities* is probably too well known to describe. A completely new edition is being prepared by Mumford, and I hope we shall publish it next year or the year after. It has always seemed to me the most human of humanist studies, the work of a man with an infinitely flexible mind.

Mumford must be described as a socialist or a socializer; Thomas Mann spoke from the conservative side. In the same month as *Cities*, we published at half a crown his little book *The Coming Victory of Democracy*. Its essence seemed to me hewn from the same solid rock as Mumford quarried. 'The reform I have in mind,' wrote Mann on page 58, 'must be a social reform. Only in this way can democracy take the wind out of the sails of fascism and also of bolshevism. . . . Moreover it must aim at spiritual as well as economic freedom. In both directions the times of Manchesterism and of passive liberalism are gone forever. Freedom has been driven out of liberalism, driven out by deepest anguish. . . . Freedom must discover its virility.' *The Coming Victory of Democracy* was published by a tragic irony one day before the final Munich betrayal of

30 September. Even the prophetic eye of Mann could not have foreseen that freedom would have to go down to the depths before its regeneration in 1945, seven long years later.

Mann and Mumford, Wells and Orwell, one German, one American, two Englishmen, those four great humanists of the mid-century, agreed absolutely on the principle of the supremacy of man the individual in conflict with the forces attempting to enslave him. Individualism cannot die so long as it has such eloquent adherents. It was perhaps the measure of my success, the proof that my firm stood staunchly by the eternal values of the West in a time of degeneracy and corruption, that this company of giants should publish with us, all of them within three years of our coming into existence. The limping list of a hard-up publisher contained them all, a tragi-comedy that was not without significance and that all four of them would have appreciated.

Early in 1938 a young writer came to London from Palestine with the plan of a book. T. R. Fyvel was his name, a Jew from a respected family in the Sudetenland. He offered a synopsis of the book to Victor Gollancz who rejected it, then came to me, attracted by the thought of appearing on the same list of André Gide. We commissioned the work which appeared in October under the title of *No Ease in Zion*.

It was a study of Zionism, a brand of nationalism unique in representing a revival among a community which had almost vanished and whose members had ceased to regard themselves as belonging to it. In a series of brilliant chapters, Fyvel traced the history of Zionism from the time of Herzl and earlier to its incarnation, partial though it then was, in Palestine of the 'thirties. Holding an even balance between the claims of Jews, Arabs and British, whose mistakes he criticized with sad and good-natured ferocity, Fyvel pointed out that the problem of the European Jews could not be solved apart from the other problems posed by the aggression of Hitler and Mussolini. 'Not only peace, but intellectual sanity, has become indivisible,' he concluded. The work, which was a substantial one, had only a modest success, but it established its author firmly as a highly perceptive political writer, and brought him into touch with a group of non-communist leftists who were desperately attempting to retain their 'intellectual sanity' in a sloganized world. Among them was George Orwell, from whom he was to extract in 1940 the only positive statement of his views Orwell ever committed to paper, *The Lion and the Unicorn*, the first of a series designed to blueprint the post-war world. Even so un-partisan a book as *No Ease* aroused a storm of criticism among the Zionists, desperate for the survival of the threatened Jews of Europe, but the storm was nothing compared to the tempest which arose over our publication of L. MacNeill Weir's bitter study, *The Tragedy of Ramsay MacDonald*, a month later.

Weir had been parliamentary private secretary to MacDonald in the late 1920's up to the time of the crisis which led to the 'National' Government of 1931. He had been his fervent admirer and devoted aide through the months of his precarious premiership since 1929. But Weir could not accept the zigzag in policy which led MacDonald to forsake his own party and team up with the conservatives and liberals. For him, as for the vast majority of labour supporters, it was a gross betrayal. 'It is evident now,' Weir wrote in his introduction, 'that MacDonald never really accepted the Socialist faith of a classless world, based on unselfish service. It can be seen that he never

could have at heart believed in the principles of Brotherhood and self-denial, which are the bases of Socialism.

> "Just for a handful of silver he left us,
> Just for a ribbon to stick in his coat".'

When Scotsman turns against Scotsman, a disciple
against his master, the sparks can be expected to fly, and
fly they did both before and after the publication of this
study in alleged treachery. At first, an attempt was made
by those concerned to persuade the author not to publish.
He was told that the book was against the public interest
as it damaged the government's prestige. Soon persuasion
turned to coercion. He was threatened that he would be
prosecuted under the Official Secrets Act. Since no 'secrets'
were revealed, this line also failed to shift Weir from his
purpose. The final effort was based on the law of libel,
that bane of authors, editors and book publishers. Minor
characters in the narrative, and some major ones, were
approached and urged to threaten the publisher with legal
proceedings. Letters were written and had their effect.
The original publisher abandoned his contract. Others to
whom it was offered refused it. Finally, in desperation
perhaps, the author offered it to me.

I read it, as may be imagined, with intense interest.
Obviously biased though it was, it seemed to me basically
true. But dared I publish it? A babble of voices was raised.
At a time of crisis, every patriot must support the government of the day. You should not attack a dead man.
The work is in execrable taste. Libel, defamation, official
secrecy, every manner of argument was thrown at me.
But, with Senhouse, I stood firm. We signed a contract
with the author. Manufacturing began. Before long a letter
arrived from a firm of solicitors, representing the MacDonald
family. It threatened proceedings not merely for civil but

261

for criminal libel! I sent the book to our own legal advisers. They told me to go ahead. A date was set, and the book appeared. Naturally the reviews were mixed, but many of them were favourable. The book had a large advance and a large sale, over 4,000 copies at the then high price of 15s. in the first six months. Nobody took legal action. The bubble, which had frightened at least half a dozen publishers out of their wits, had burst harmlessly. It was yet another example of the importance of keeping your head. Like the child in the fairy-tale, I had seen and insisted that 'the emperor has no clothes'. The reward was substantial.

So we entered into the last year of peace, but with a smaller list. It turned out that we were to publish only nineteen titles in this feverish year. The first book appeared in February; it was an interesting but melancholy work by José Martin Blázquez, a regular officer in the Spanish Army who had sided with the anti-Franco forces. *I Helped to Build an Army* described his efforts to impart knowledge and instil discipline into the troops of the government. The author had escaped, to Mexico I think, after the Franco victory and looked back with disgust on the wrecking of his hopes and his life. It was no surprise to me that the book was a failure.

In March Mumford published with us a challenging small book, designed to rally those in America who had a firm belief in democracy to stand up and fight for their beliefs. Bitterly critical of the policy of appeasement, it yet made clear that there were healthy forces in Europe who needed the support of the U.S. in their struggle against apathy and nihilism. 'The fact is,' he wrote, 'that the political system cannot be effectively democratic until a similar diffusion of power and responsibility takes place

in the economic system. People who spend their hours
accepting decisions made for them elsewhere, and then
spend the rest of their waking day under the spell of
advertisers, salesmen and radio announcers . . . cannot
effectively control their political life.' The words seem
entirely appropriate today. Naturally the book was a
relative flop.

In March Hitler marched into Prague and announced
the annexation of Memel. The sands in Europe were running
out fast. Silently the British Communist Party sharpened
its knives and made a final effort to enlist deluded non-
members, such as myself, into their ranks. I received an
invitation to dinner at the house of John Langdon-Davies
on Clapham Common.

In his love for Spain and in detestation of the slow
strangulation of the anti-fascists by Franco's armies, he
had moved nearer to the communist line than was perhaps
permissible. Now it was his pleasure to bring me together
with Palme Dutt, top theoretician of King Street, the C.P.
headquarters, in a final effort to remove the anti-communist
'prejudices' from which I was known to suffer and from
which the Party hoped to rescue me even at this late hour.
I was flattered. If Palme Dutt had been chosen as the
instrument of my conversion, I must, I felt, be a more
important element in the anti-communist front than I had
hitherto supposed.

Dinner was delicious. Langdon-Davies, an excellent
cook, had prepared Spanish food of unimpeachable
authenticity. We drank an excellent Spanish white wine.
Conversation was general, and all would have been
harmonious, had not my wife suddenly recalled that Dutt
had recently published a book on India. It had inevitably
been a study of India and British imperialism from the
narrowest Marxist point of view and naturally enough it

had been a choice of the L.B.C. 'What part of India were you born in?' my wife asked Dutt in honeyed tones.

'I was born in England,' he replied.

'But you have spent a long time in India?' my wife inquired.

'I have never been there,' he replied, 'I hope to visit India soon.'

My wife feigned surprise. There was a pregnant silence, until our host changed the subject.

After dinner we listened to Spanish music on gramophone records. I felt pleasantly relaxed, but I was only too well aware that the real business of the evening had yet to come. Soon enough the moment arrived. 'You want a talk with Dutt,' Langdon-Davies said. 'Dutt wants a talk with me,' I should have replied, but did not. Perhaps it didn't matter, but my wife pointed out my lapse to me after we had got home. Soon I was closeted alone with my would-be seducer in the study, and we had a long, long talk. What was said I can no longer remember. Nothing can be duller than the dialectical debates of yesteryear. But the conclusion of our talk I recall with an exactitude that time will never dim.

'What do you think, Mr. Dutt, of the possibility of an alliance between Nazi-Germany and the Soviet Union?' I asked him. This was already a matter for debate in leftist circles in London. Like a bombshell came his reply, 'I do not regard it as diplomatically impossible.' It was the first time that I had heard from so authoritative a source of the surprises ahead. At least for the honesty of Dutt's answer I have always been grateful.

By July there was yet another financial crisis at the office. The first half of 1939 had been disastrous. Only seven new books had appeared, and not one of them had been really successful. Aunt Agnes' £5,000 had gone with the wind. It seemed to be a race between bankruptcy and war, with the odds on the former. But at this point Senhouse stepped into the arena, with a statement whose unruffled calm I have always admired. 'Don't worry, Fred,' he remarked, 'of course, I can raise another £5,000 without any difficulty at all.'

'Where on earth will you get it from?', I inquired. But the oracle had spoken. The mysteries were not to be revealed.

It was many weeks later before the money came in, and during those weeks a financial storm of unparalleled force drove me almost to madness. One day, in a frenzy, I demanded the resignation of Senhouse for not keeping his promise about the investment. I demanded the resignation of Lothar. Had there been other directors whose resignation I could have demanded, I would have done so. No one resigned. In dribs and drabs Senhouse's money came in. It was almost, but not quite, too late. In the end the storm died down, but I had been shaken. Perhaps it was this that led me to the sacking of Tanya Benckendorff in August.

Poor Tanya! The firm owed her far more than the pitiful salary we had been paying her. Kind, stoical and still an indifferent speller, she had been a tower of strength, warding off from me a lunatic fringe of authors bent on reading their manuscripts aloud, persuading some fiery Trotskyist or hard-up anarchist to leave without applying for another £5 on account, examining some tatty manuscript and advising the author that it was not yet ready for submission, distilling a gentle feminine influence over an otherwise masculine office. But, alas, the morning came when I told her to go. Exasperated beyond bounds at her inability to produce allegedly important documents

265

entrusted to her care, I said good-bye to her. She never reproached me. Indeed, she got married a few months later, which consoled me for my harshness. Today we are still good friends, and at last I am able to offer her my apology in public.

John Lloyd left too, but for a different reason. For many months he had been training in the reserve force for R.A.F. officers. Now they called him up to a distinguished career as a fighter pilot. In 1941 he was to win the Air Flying Cross.

The trade department too had disappeared. Pattisson and Lothar had persuaded me to abandon it and join the Book Centre, a mechanized organization for the invoicing and distribution of books created by Sir Isaac Pitman & Sons for their own use. Secker & Warburg was the first outside publisher to join, and it saw us through the difficulties of the war years as we could never have done for ourselves.

Only Senhouse and Pattisson remained now of the little band who had been so busy on the firm's behalf since we had started, and Pattisson was to join an armoured regiment in 1941. All was changing, shifting, collapsing as the shadow of war drew near.

But on 3 August we published two new books, the last to appear on our list in peace time. The first was a novel called *Everything Will Be Better Tomorrow*. With the war just one month ahead, the title had an odd ring to it. The book failed, with less than 1,000 copies sold. Its author's chance was to come over a decade later. Her name was Anne-Marie Selinko. Her next novel was *Désirée*. It sold 338,000 copies! But the publishers were Heinemann!

Next came the long-awaited work of H. G. Wells, *The Fate of Homo Sapiens*, in which Senhouse and I had invested so many of our hopes and so high a proportion of our cash. Would it sell, or had the magic of that mighty

name ebbed away for the new generation? We were doubtful. Only 3,000 copies were printed of the first edition.

Wells' programme followed a pattern I came to know
well. About a month before publication, when stock of his
book had reached our office from the binders, he would
make an appointment to visit us. The desk in my room was
cleared, and fifty copies of the new work placed upon it.
At the appointed hour the great man would arrive,
cheerful and smiling, to be greeted by the directors and
any other members of the staff able to crowd themselves
into the act. Calmly confident, he would seat himself in
my chair, take out his pen, write in the top copy on the
pile beside him a short or not so short dedicatory note in
his neat spidery hand, lay the book, opened at the flyleaf,
aside, and go on to the next. It took almost two hours
to complete the chore, with intervals for conversation in
between. These copies went out to a wide range of personal
friends, among whom the percentage of women was very
high indeed. Wells was grateful to his women friends, after
his fashion. Out of the eight we published for him, my
wife has six inscribed copies given to her. Here are his
notes in them.

> August 1939 *The Fate of Homo Sapiens*
> To Pamela de Bayou bless her from H.G.
> (I've tried to make it cheerful; but there it is.)

> January 1940 *New World Order*
> To Madame Pamela de Bayou with the warmest
> possible good wishes for the New Year and the
> most profound homage from H. G. Wells.

> December 1941 *You Can't Be Too Careful*, a novel
> To Pamela de Bayou. I've sent her this time with
> all the best wishes of H. G. Wells. Xmas 1941.

February 1942 *The Outlook for Homo Sapiens*
To Pamela de Bayou from the Reluctant Hen
from H.G.

July 1942 *Phoenix*
To Pamela de Bayou, the Fortunate Wife of the
Publisher of the World Revolution from H. G.
Wells.

May 1944 **'42** *to* **'44**: a Contemporary Memoir Upon
Human Behaviour during the Crisis Of The
World Revolution.
To Mrs. Warburg from H. G. Wells, May 16,
'44 with all the best wishes in the world H.G.

For reasons now obscure to me, no inscribed copies were
given, or at least none survive, of the two other Wells'
titles we published, *All Aboard for Ararat* (1940) a charming
parable on the theme of Noah, and *Babes in the Darkling
Wood* (1940) a novel hardly to be ranked among his most
successful. There is no explanation of the phrase 'The
Reluctant Hen', but it can hardly be doubted that my
wife had bestowed this appellation on the great writer in
some moment of criticism, and that H.G. had cottoned
joyfully on to it.

The Fate of Homo Sapiens sold well, in spite of being
engulfed by World War II so soon after publication. Probably
readers hoped that the prophet Wells would inform them
of the shape of things to come. But he can hardly be said
to have satisfied this desire. Wells' prophecies were long-
term ones, covering hundreds or even thousands of years.
A short six-year war counted for but a flash in the scale
of geological or biological time dear to his heart. We had
to reprint *Homo Sapiens* before publication, a further 2,000
copies. Another 3,000 were printed in November, and 3,000

more in the following January. In all over 13,000 copies were sold, and it contributed substantially to the reduction of the annual loss to which we had become so unpleasantly innured. In 1940 it was almost halved. So at last after a twelvemonth I reaped the harvest of the seed sown that warm summer's day in Hanover Terrace, Regent's Park. Wells had much to do with the success of Secker & Warburg during the war years, which he spent in London spitting defiance at the bombs. He was the first of the big authors with a prolific output to come to me. Difficult as he was said to be, he and I at any rate never had a quarrel. To me he was venerable and in his final years as pitiable as Lear. To him I was the young 'open conspirator' who would spread his seminal ideas over the widest possible field. It was a cordial partnership.

Three weeks after the appearance of Wells' book, the fate of homo sapiens was settled for six frightful years in Berlin. Chamberlain had sent William Strang to Moscow in a final desperate effort to negotiate a defensive alliance between Britain, France and Russia. The effort failed. It was too little and too late. Already the Nazi-Soviet Pact of 23 August was in the bag. The pictures in the papers of an awkward-looking Molotov shaking hands with a beaming Ribbentrop made me feel frightened.

But my fright was a simple and straightforward affair compared to the illness in store for the communists and fellow-travellers. To me the pact was simply a disaster likely to lead to war, death, and the extinction of European glory, but to the communist left it was all this and hell beside. The omnipotent god of their world, the divine and far-seeing Stalin, had made a pact with the devil himself, Hitler. It was a blasphemy, whose effects on them were devastating. In droves they went to bed with political arthritis, a disease into which medical research might do well to inquire. It was a painful ailment, and weeks afterwards many were still walking round with a severe limp. To me, after the insults to which they had subjected me, it was a compensation and a balm. It helped, however slightly, to take my mind off the frightful spot we were all in. Beneath the complex of my emotions, I detected also a dawning realization that there was a kind of insane logic about what was going on; the sheep were at last being sorted out from the goats; the two great totalitarian powers had joined forces. Wheedle as they might, the con men of the C.P. had lost their most seductive argument; things could never be the same again. Dialectics were done for quite a time. The era of political publishing was over. I breathed a deep sigh of relief. The bombs, when they came, might injure our bodies; but our minds were freed at last from the insidious Stalinist poisons. The air seemed cleaner.

At the end of September we issued a massive book of 704 pages by Boris Souvarine, simply entitled *Stalin*. The author was an ex-member of the Communist International, and had studied the workings and the devious thought-process of the master, Stalin, with loving care or perhaps more accurately, with careful hate. The translation, by C. L. R. James, had been in preparation for many months, and the delay was fortunate. By the time the book appeared, within a month of the Nazi-Soviet Pact, the public was agog to read it. Thoroughly documented, written with a fine narrative sweep, imbued with a firsthand knowledge of its subject, it was and probably remains the best book available on Stalin's life and policy up to 1936. It is unfortunately out of print. Thousands who would have greeted it with howls of abuse only two short months before now accepted it as gospel truth and a revelation of previously hidden iniquity. I can't help feeling that Kruschev himself would have found it useful a year or two back, when he made his famous exposure of Stalin at the 20th Congress.

Its advance sale was modest, a mere 348 copies. But it had sold over 1,700 by the end of 1939 and over 2,000 by June 1940. We made a satisfactory deal with an American publisher for the rights in the U.S. and the book was manufactured in Australia where it also had a good sale. There can be little doubt that it sold three times as well as it would have done if James had been prompt with his delivery of the translation, an illustration of the importance of timing in publishing. Our profits were substantial, despite the heavy production costs.

Souvarine, now living in Paris, was labelled as a Trotskyist, but he was no more one than I was. Here are the final words of his book, written in the second half of 1937:

'The force of things and the behaviour of men have contradicted all Lenin's optimistic forecasts, his hopes of a superior democracy as much as his semi-libertarian ideas. . . . Nothing in the individual theses of Trotsky has stood the test any better. . . . Lenin died too soon to write the epilogue to the miscarriage of Bolshevism. Trotsky has not availed himself of the leisure afforded by exile to make a true and conscientious examination. . . . Democratic socialism in its various forms, in the name of legitimate defence against fascism, is almost everywhere allowing itself to be led, circumvented and compromised by dictatorial communism. The death agony of socialist hope in the world thus opens up an immeasurable ideo-logical crisis. It will be the part of the epigones of a power-less generation to make out the balance-sheet of national Bolshevism, of international communism and of traditional

271

socialism, and to draw from it some useful lessons. And this should logically lead them to examine what is still alive and what is dead in the parent doctrine, Marxism.'

These are noble words, coming from a man who spent many of his early years as an active communist. Twenty years later, as I write, they come over to me with perhaps an even greater urgency than when they were just written. 'The death agony of socialist hope thus opens up an immeasurable ideological crisis.' The crisis remains with us today; the doctrine of socialism still exists, tattered though it may be; but where is the hope? Where is the fervour that inspired the socialist reformers up till 1939, where the political doctrine imbued with a belief in the splendour of man's capacities? Could even Orwell, had he lived, have passed beyond the agony of *Animal Farm* and the despair of *1984* to a moral and political conception fitted for the world in which we live now? We do not know. But there is one thing we should know by now, and I learned it the hard way in the 1930's. It was the ghastly effects of plausible propaganda on certain types of intellectuals. This propaganda nearly succeeded twenty years ago. 'Democratic socialism is almost everywhere allowing itself to be led, circumvented and compromised by dictatorial communism', as Souvarine wrote. It could so easily happen again, and if it does books will be communism's most dangerous weapons. The power of the pen and the printed word is strong, which is why the trade of publishing is among the most absorbing a man can practise.

On 3 September my wife and I sat down at 11 a.m. to listen to the long-awaited broadcast of Neville Chamberlain. Immediately afterwards, the air-raid sirens screamed. 'That,' said Pamela, 'is the most *real* sound I've heard for years.' She stood up and looked out of the window at the

marriage were past, and I was out in the open. From being wealthy I had descended to being rather hard up. There are many things that money cannot buy, but among those it can, must be counted the power to buy you out of all material difficulties. This power I had lost. When my St. John's Wood house began to subside in 1934, I had the money to prop it up again, but there was not much left when the bill was paid. When I needed cash to back myself as a publisher, I hadn't got it. So I was forced to beg from my aunt. Begging is not a bad character-builder.

To the loss of parents, a wife, children, and money must be added the loss of my job, and with it my security. Routledge may have been a dull firm, but it was a safe one. I had expected to be there all my life, with my hair greying slowly at the temples while I directed its dignified operations. But a dust-up with the Board, and I was out on my ear, adrift in a jobless world. Not everyone, it appeared, was disposed to love and admire me, not my first wife certainly, not my co-managing director at Routledge, not the distinguished publishers whose firms I had wished to enter. I was clearly not a universally popular figure. Perhaps I had not taken the trouble to make myself liked, perhaps I was not likeable.

So at last I had been forced to think for myself, to stop being the passive personality to whom things happen, the man who gave free advice out of the depths of his inexperience, the individual who was reluctant to ask a favour in case it was refused, the one incapable of making his presence felt. Bit by bit, the stiff upper lip of the traditional upper-class Englishman was beginning to wobble. I was learning to lose my temper, to laugh, to weep, and to want. I was learning aggression, how to fight for what I wanted. I was becoming, but slowly, dynamic. Emotional asceticism was being abandoned. I was less objective, more unfair. I had faults which had to be hidden, disreputable motives which had to be concealed except from myself. Impurity was creeping in. I was almost human at last. If maturity is a mountain to be climbed, I was half-way up or nearly so. But, my goodness, how late I had left it, how nearly too late!

What had wrenched open the shell of the oyster? Who had inserted the knife? It is not difficult to name the oyster-opener. It was, of course, my second wife. In this book I have painted a portrait of her which she claims is grossly unfair. 'You have made me appear,' she says, 'wayward, aggressive, childish, angry, extravagant, insulting, talkative and generally dislikeable. You have not shown my tender and loving side, the subtlety of my behaviour, the delicacy of my intuitions.' It may be so. It may be that my picture is out of focus though on the target. Of this it is difficult for me to judge, especially since my vanity as a writer is being attacked. But of one thing I am fairly certain. Had my portrait of Pamela been *wholly* misleading, she would have torn up and burnt the pages on which I had laboriously written it. Had I rewritten them against her wishes and locked them away in a safe place for my publisher, she would have left me and not returned until I had yielded. For to her compromise in a vital matter smacks of dishonesty, and never has my wife been dishonest with me. How many times have I longed in vain for her to be so!

Though I had matured emotionally to some extent by the outbreak of war, I had not attained any superlative level of competence as a publisher. Secker & Warburg was not then a success, at least in terms of the market-place.

In 1939 we made our biggest loss of all, £3,766. In 1940 we were to lose another £2,159. Nothing seemed able to halt our Gadarene rush to bankruptcy. We had published Mann and Mumford, Wells and Orwell, Zweig and Caldwell and Gide. We had romped away with *Clochemerle*. It seemed all in vain. Of me it might well have been said in an adaptation of Tacitus' famous epigram on Galba—'he might have been thought expert as a publisher, had only he never published.'

What was wrong with my firm in those days? It is easy enough to say the times were out of joint, that trade was bad, that publishing houses with more capital than mine at their disposal were failing every few months. Easy and absolutely true, but not, I fear, the whole truth. The whole truth is less palatable, but I may as well face it while the mood of confession is on me. The fact was that I was a fool in handling money and incompetent in dealing with sales.

The control of finance seemed to me then a difficult and distasteful job. Let Senhouse do it. But the unfortunate Senhouse, as he had told me right at the beginning, was no better at handling money than I was, though he had certainly raised a larger part of the capital than I. To lean on a shaky prop is to fall and bloody your nose, and certainly I fell and got up, fell and got up again, time after time. It was undignified, and perhaps it was unnecessary. Often, of course, I consulted our accountants. They were good accountants, but their words were dreadfully monotonous. 'You must increase the turnover and reduce the overheads,' they told me, year after year. As if I didn't know! But how could I manage to achieve either of these desirable aims? I wasn't sure, so I left the sales to Pattisson who did his best, but he had an awful lot of other things to do besides. The fact is that, in a really small publishing business, such as we were then, you must combine in yourself, if you are to survive, a multiplicity of talents rarely if ever found in one person. Some of them I had; otherwise we would have collapsed in our first or second years. Some of them I had yet to acquire.

What talents does a fully-fledged publisher need, and which of them did I possess in 1939? Like a cricket team, a fully-fledged publishing house—which we became only a few years after World War II was over—needs specialists and all-rounders. There must be executives in the firm who have a good financial brain, administrative skill, know-how about advertising and sales promotion, the ability to manufacture books economically, editorial judgement. Not one of these qualities taken by itself will keep a publishing house solvent for longer than a year or two. That is where the all-rounder is indispensable, to integrate these and other activities into the finely tempered instrument that a publishing house is. It is the all-rounder in publishing who makes the best captain. As an all-rounder in 1939 I was not altogether negligible. I knew a lot about nearly every aspect of the business; my thirteen years at Routledge had not been wasted.

But a captain, or a managing director, needs more than knowledge. He requires courage, the power to make decisions and stick to them (at least when they are correct), judgement, energy, the will to work, and an ability to inspire his executives. Modesty forbids me to assess myself on these vital matters; the history and record of my firm is a more accurate measuring-rod than any I could employ here. In 1939 we published nineteen books which produced a turnover of £11,555; twenty years later, as I write, we are publishing between eighty and ninety books a year, with a turnover twenty times as large.

There is an old publishing adage that a small firm either grows or goes bankrupt, and it is true. So we have grown from the tiny toddler, whose first tottering steps I have described in this book, to the well-muscled adult whose activities will be the theme of a second volume. In growing have we lost the daring and exuberance of our early years? Does that middle-age spread impede our energy? Has our individuality been lost? Or was the child the true father of the man?

In a humdrum world of growing uniformity these are important questions, especially important because the trade of general publishing deals with the highest achievements of man's creativity. And the publisher himself is a creator of an unusual and special type. This aspect of publishing has been beautifully expressed by Thomas Mann in a tribute in 1940 to his American publisher, Alfred Knopf. He wrote: 'The publisher is not a soloist of spiritual exertion, but the conductor of the orchestra. Whereas the author, in his public loneliness, with only himself to rely on, hemmed in of necessity by his ego, struggles to do his best, the publisher selects from the common effort whatever his instinct and his feeling for the necessary considers as just and beneficial. He takes it over, impresses the stamp of his enterprise upon it, and hurls it in its collective variety into the battle of life, where it must contend with the powers of obstinacy, ignorance and death. . . . What a glorious occupation, this mixture of business sense and strategic friendship with the spirit! What a noble way to gain a livelihood! I called it easy, but this was a blunder. I am well aware that in these days the life of a publisher is far from easy. But happy I may certainly call it, in spite of all its difficulties. It must be happy, free from the torture and frailty which all individual creation involves—and yet with an opportunity to serve the spirit.'

I'll settle for that as a definition, and abide by it. This is the standard I have nailed to my mast. I will publish, and continue to publish 'whatever my feeling for the necessary considers as just and beneficial.' For this is the pride of my craft and the secret of my happiness.

Index

Index